Colonialism and Development in the Contemporary World

Colonialism and Development in the Contemporary World

edited by Chris Dixon and Michael J. Heffernan

MANSELL

First published in 1991 by Mansell Publishing Limited
A Cassell Imprint

Villiers House, 41/47 Strand, London WC2N 5JE, England
387 Park Avenue South, New York, NY 10016–8810, USA

British Library Cataloguing in Publication Data

Colonialism and development in the contemporary world.
   1. Developing countries. Economic development. Effects of imperialism
   I. Dixon, C.J. (Christopher John) *1944–* II. Heffernan, Michael J.
330.91724

   ISBN 0–7201–2072–1

Library of Congress Cataloging-in-Publication Data

Colonialism and development in the contemporary world / edited by
  Chris Dixon and Michael J. Heffernan.
     p.   cm.
  Includes bibliographical references and index.
  ISBN 0–7201–2072–1
   1. Europe–Colonies–Africa–History. 2. Europe–Colonies–Asia–
History. 3. Colonies–Africa–History. 4. Colonies–Asia–
History. I. Dixon, C.J. (Chris J.) II. Heffernan, Michael J.,
1942– .
JV236.C65 1991
325'.34'09–dc20   90–19398
                                       CIP

Printed and bound in Great Britain by Biddles Ltd, Guildford and King's Lynn

Contents

Contributors

Robert Aldrich   Senior Lecturer in Economic History, University of Sydney, Australia

John Connell   Senior Lecturer in Geography, University of Sydney, Australia

Stuart Corbridge   Lecturer in Geography, University of Cambridge, UK

Jonathan Crush   Associate Professor of Geography, Queen's University, Kingston, Canada

Chris Dixon   Professor of Geography, City of London Polytechnic, UK

Jenny Elliott   Lecturer in Geography, Staffordshire Polytechnic, UK

W.T.S. Gould   Senior Lecturer in Geography, University of Liverpool, UK

Michael J. Heffernan   Lecturer in Geography, University of Technology, Loughborough, UK

Michael J.G. Parnwell   Lecturer, Centre for South-East Asian Studies, University of Hull, UK

David Simon   Lecturer in Development Geography, Royal Holloway and Bedford New College, University of London, UK

Peter M. Slowe   Lecturer in Geography, West Sussex Institute of Higher Education, UK

Keith Sutton   Senior Lecturer in Geography, University of
                          Manchester, UK

Peter J. Taylor   Professor of Geography,
                          University of Newcastle upon Tyne, UK

Introduction

Chris Dixon and Michael J. Heffernan

This book has its origin in the papers presented at a joint meeting of the Historical Geography and Developing Areas research groups of the Institute of British Geographers held at Coventry Polytechnic in January 1989. It takes as its general theme the geographical impact of European colonial domination on the non-European world from the nineteenth century to the present day. This is, of course, a huge and complex topic and the chapters that follow can only hint at the issues involved.

In 1914, at the peak of European colonial domination, the Western powers (including Russia and the United States) controlled, in one form or another, over 72 million square kilometres of land outside Europe and the non-colonial Americas, embracing more than 560 million people. The British Empire – with over 33 million square kilometres and nearly 390 million people – was easily the largest realm. Although the Russian 'Empire' in Asia covered over 16 million square kilometres, the most important rival to Britain was France, whose African and Asian possessions accounted for around 10.5 million square kilometres and more than 46 million people. The Dutch, German, Belgian, Portuguese and Italian colonies each accounted for between 1.5 and 3 million square kilometres and represented a total population of over 73 million people (Ansprenger, 1989, p. 305). The existence of these vast empires has left a deep and all-pervading legacy on both colonised and coloniser alike. Yet, the sheer scale of these territories makes it very difficult to generalise about the impact of the colonial experience. The nature of colonialism varied enormously within and between these huge empires in response to the different and changing systems of colonial management developed by the colonisers and as a result of the differing human and environmental circumstances in the colonised territories.

This complexity has led some observers to question the value of general, theoretical discussion of colonialism or imperialism. Ronald Hyam (1976), for example, has argued that the nature of the colonial experience can only be conveyed through detailed empirical studies of particular colonial and imperial circumstances and, to an extent, this volume seeks to provide a series of richly textured local studies of the sort advocated by Hyam; each chapter tells its own particular story and develops its own perspective on the general theme. Yet, to eschew all generalisation is to invite confusion and it is necessary in such a volume to put forward a few basic statements and definitions by way of introduction.

The general context is set by Peter Taylor's opening chapter, which examines key issues in the debate about the nature of imperialism. In the context of the studies presented here, imperialism is seen as an integral component of global capitalism. Imperialism was identified by Hobson (1902), Lenin (1917) and Bukharin (1917) as representing a particular 'final' stage in the development of capitalism, characterised by the emergence of monopoly capitalism at the national level, the dominance of finance capital, the export of capital and capitalist relations of production, and the division of the world between a small group of metropolitan powers. However, this view of imperialism has been the subject of considerable debate, both amongst and between Marxists and non-Marxists (Brewer, 1980; Kemp, 1967).

Taylor argues that imperialism is a structural relationship of the capitalist world economy and has existed, and will continue to exist, as long as this global system persists. According to this view, imperialism is depicted as having developed in two major cycles: the first rising in the sixteenth century and declining in the early nineteenth, and the second rising in the late nineteenth century and waning in the mid-twentieth century. In both cycles, the decline in formal imperialism was replaced by informal structures as territory was decolonised. Indeed, many writers describe the informal imperialism of the late twentieth century as neo-colonialism. The whole question of formal and informal imperialism has been an area of particular debate (Gallagher and Robinson, 1953; Robinson and Gallagher, 1981; Lewis, 1976).

The term 'colonialism' is used in this volume to indicate the imposition of some form of 'direct' political and economic control by a metropolitan power (this includes the so-called 'indirect' form of colonial rule that was the dominant model of British colonialism). In some cases foreign occupation was accompanied by the settlement of significant colonist populations from the metropolitan power. The establishment of formal colonial structures is therefore only one peculiar and comparatively short-lived element of the imperialist global system.

The initial wave of colonial development, confined largely to the Americas, was based on the rise of mercantile capital. In Africa, and more especially Asia, the existence of powerful and often technologically sophisticated states largely precluded the imposition of control by European states until they had undergone the rapid industrialisation of the eighteenth and nineteenth centuries. Indeed, the rise of industrial capital provided both the means and the imperative for the establishment of colonial structures. Colonisation was intensified as industrialisation spread and accelerated. This process finally came to completion with the internationalisation of individual and finance capital in the last decades of the nineteenth century and the early years of the twentieth century. It was accompanied by a new and more extensive wave of European colonialism that continued after the virtual completion of an imperial global economy by *c.* 1900. This final phase of European colonialism continued and intensified during the early years of the twentieth century as the dominant colonial states began to influence more directly and intimately the social, economic and political life of their colonial possessions. The granting of various forms of independence by Britain to the white-settler dominion territories after 1918 represented the first disengagement from the formal mechanisms of colonialism. This decolonisation accelerated rapidly after 1945 as the leading colonial powers, Britain and France, emerged shell-shocked and bankrupt from the Second World War. Despite the political and moral difficulties, the bloodshed and the heartache, European decolonisation is now nearing completion (Ansprenger, 1989; Betts, 1985; Chamberlain, 1985; Grimal, 1978; Holland, 1985).

Yet the ending of formal colonialism should not be seen as the ending of imperialism. In their various ways, all the chapters in this volume indicate that the granting of formal independence has rarely been accompanied by a dismantling of the deeper structures of imperialism that perpetuate the social and economic divisions within and between nations. This is the theme developed by David Simon, in his discussion of colonialism, decolonisation and neo-colonisation in southern Africa. Simon examines the contemporary structures within the overall context of sub-imperialism. This refers to a situation where a country or group of countries occupies an intermediate position between the metropolitan centres of the world economy and the periphery. Such a situation is also frequently referred to as the semi-periphery. The neo-colonial domination of southern Africa by South Africa is also taken up by Jonathan Crush in a more specific case study of the migrant-labour process. Jenny Elliott develops an analogous argument in her detailed account of the politics of environmental degradation and soil conservation in Rhodesia/Zimbabwe. She indicates that, despite the best efforts of different government agencies in independent Zimbabwe, colonial mentalities and Western tech-nocratic solutions to environmental problems continue to influence, and perhaps to mislead, official environmental strategies. Similarly, as W. T. S. Gould shows in his chapter on religious missions and migration in colonial Kenya, even the activities of explicitly anti-Western and anti-colonial organi-sations have tended, despite their express wishes, to perpetuate the patterns of population mobility and socio-economic dislocation that were generated under direct colonial rule. The lessons of this era have yet to be learnt; post-independence educational schemes, though designed to foster balanced regional economic development, in practice accelerate rural–urban migration and increase regional economic divisions within the country.

Peter Slowe, in a general examination of Guinea, indicates how the experience of French colonial rule transformed, and continues to influence, the economic and political structure of the independent state. The French theme is continued by Michael Heffernan and Keith Sutton, who focus on the transformation of Algeria's rural settlement pattern during the 132 years of French colonial domination. They demonstrate that the process of colonial agrarian transformation, motivated by a potent mixture of political, military and economic objectives, has continued with few modifications into the post-colonial era.

Stuart Corbridge examines the experience of tribal communities of Jharkhand in north-east India, and charts their struggle to control their own territory and environment, from the pre-colonial period through to independence. Paying particular attention to forestry, Corbridge demonstrates how control over the exploitation of forest resources in the region has been a powerful tool used to extend the authority of both the colonial and the post-colonial state within tribal society.

In the penultimate chapter John Connell and Robert Aldrich examine the strategic political, economic and military importance of the 'last colonies' and analyse the reasons why these few remaining outposts of formal colonialism survive.

Finally, Chris Dixon and Michael Parnwell deal with Thailand, one of the few areas of the world that retained its independence throughout the era of European colonialism. The authors argue that, despite this nominal independence, Thailand was drawn into a colonial relationship with the major metropolitan powers in general and Britain in particular. Indeed, Thailand came to exhibit patterns of economic activity, spatial inequality and international trade remarkably similar to those of the colonial territories of South-East Asia.

Editing volumes of essays is rarely an easy task, but it has been made a great deal less burdensome by the assistance and technical support given willingly by a number of institutions and individuals. The editors would like to thank, in particular, Cheryl McEwan, of the Geography Department at Loughborough, for her help with the index and Erica Milwain, of the same department, for producing the maps at relatively short notice. Thanks must also be extended to both the Developing Areas Research Group and the Historical Geography Research Group of the Institute of British Geographers for their enthusiastic support. Finally, Penny Beck and Peter Harrison, formerly and currently of Mansell Publishing, deserve much credit for their good-humoured patience.

References

Ansprenger, F. (1989) *The Dissolution of the Colonial Empires*, London: Routledge.

Betts, R. F. (1985) *Uncertain Dimensions: Western Overseas Empires in the Twentieth Century*, Oxford: Oxford University Press.

Brewer, A. (1980) *Marxist Theories of Imperialism: A Critical Survey*, London: Routledge & Kegan Paul.

Bukharin, N. (1917) *Imperialism and the World Economy*, London: Merlin Press, 1972.

Chamberlain, M. E. (1985) *Decolonisation*, Oxford: Blackwell.

Gallagher, J., and Robinson, R. (1953) 'The imperialism of free trade', *Economic History Review*, 4 (1), pp. 1–15.

Grimal, H. (1978) *Decolonisation: The British, French, Dutch and Belgian Empires*, London: Routledge & Kegan Paul.

Hobson, J. A. (1902) *Imperialism: A Study*, London: Allen & Unwin.

Holland, R. F. (1985) *European Decolonisation, 1918–1981*, London: Macmillan.

Hyam, R. (1976) *Britain's Imperial Century, 1815–1914: A Study of Empire and Expansion*, London: Batsford.

Kemp, T. (1967) *Theories of Imperialism*, London: Dobson.

Lenin, V. I. (1917) *Imperialism, the Highest Stage of Capitalism*, Moscow: Progress, 1966.

Lewis, W. R. (1976) *Imperialism: The Robinson and Gallagher Controversy*, New York: New Viewpoint.

Robinson, R., and Gallagher, J. (with Denny, A.) (1981) *Africa and the Victorians: The Official Mind of Imperialism*, London: Macmillan.

CHAPTER 1

The Legacy of Imperialism

Peter J. Taylor

People who write about imperialism have always to start by defining the term. The word is controversial. This very fact makes it interesting. It is controversial first of all because it is used commonly as a term of political abuse. This was not always so. At the turn of the century several countries experienced what may be termed 'imperialism general elections' when expansionary foreign policy platforms were hugely popular among the electorate. Within a relatively short time, however, imperialism took on its derogatory connotation. In such circumstances imperialists had to redefine their objects. In the first half of this century the British Empire, for instance, began to be transmuted into the British Commonwealth, a terminology with egalitarian overtones. This enabled one famous imperial apologist to argue in 1940 that 'Imperialism is not a word for scholars' (Hancock, 1940; Cohen, 1973, p. 9; Etherington, 1984, p. 220). But the rest of the world seemed less concerned for British imperial sensitivities. Imperialism lived on as a word as well as a practice.

But how should we treat this word? Imperialism, perhaps more than any other term describing social practices, confirms that we can never produce 'objective' definitions in social science. As Cohen has pointed out, agreeing on a definition of imperialism 'is tantamount to accepting a particular line of argument' (Cohen, 1973, p. 12). In discussions of imperialism, theory most explicitly comes before definition. This is helpful. It means that we can identify two basic definitional types that correspond to the fundamental political oppositions in the world. There are narrow definitions which emphasise political processes in the past which supporters of *status quo* political positions favour. Radical theorists and politicians, on the other hand, have favoured broad definitions that emphasise the economic processes of their particular contemporary period. I am going to employ the latter type of definition although, as we shall see, not based on conventional radical theory.

Imperialism is a structural relation of the capitalist world-economy. It is a relation of dominance whereby institutions in one zone of the world economy – agents of imperialism – control the destiny of the people of another zone – the victims of imperialism. This core/periphery hierarchical spatial model is never absolute, of course. The power differentials across zones are never such that agents of imperialism can ever totally control the periphery. And of course the territorial division is itself more subtle than the simple core/periphery model expresses. Internal colonialism in the core and collaborationist agents of imperialism in the periphery are just the two most explicit violations of a neat spatial division. Imperialism is complex. At the very minimum such various phenomena as informal spheres of influence, formal political governance and colonial settlement must be identified. Nevertheless imperialism as a spatially defined dominance relation does constitute a set of distinctive social practices that provide a framework for analysing the capitalist world-economy. Thus defined and despite all the controversy, imperialism is most certainly not a chaotic conception.

Given this definition, the legacy of imperialism is easy to specify: one world. It is the dominance relation that has operated to expand the capitalist world-economy from its European-Atlantic cradle to become global in scope by about 1900. But it was not any world that was generated: the legacy was a highly unequal system. Imperialism continued to sustain the core/periphery world it helped to create. In this general essay about the legacy of imperialism, I will highlight some key features that readers may look out for in the more specific essays that follow.

The legacy of imperialism will be described in terms of four main levels of analysis. First, I rehearse the structural debate on the nature of imperialism, and argue that it is a necessary and integral component of the modern world-system. Structures are the result of processes and in the second part of the chapter I describe the two major processes of imperialism – incorporation and spatial reproduction. Since it is the latter process that continues today I concentrate on reproduction of the unequal spatial hierarchy that is the world-system. Processes can operate only as mechanisms carried out by agents – people and the institutions through which they operate. The third part of the chapter is concerned with the 'institutional vortex' behind reproduction, and is a preliminary statement about how households, classes, peoples and states interact to keep the inequalities in order. But these mechanisms can be disrupted. In the final section I consider the political movements that exist to change the system and reduce or eliminate the inequalities. This structure–processes–mechanisms–movements sequence of discussion is then brought to a conclusion with an interpretation of the legacy of imperialism in the light of this argument.

Structures: Suppositions and History

Of all the debates between Marxists and their critics the one concerning imperialism has probably been the least fruitful. Marxist analyses of the monopoly tendencies in capitalism and imperial rivalries in the context of the international crisis that culminated in the First World War were converted by later historians into the 'economic theory of empires' which could be easily 'disproved' by, for instance, careful study of the motives behind the 'scramble for Africa'. This pseudo-debate between dead revolutionaries and live historians produced a classic 'straw man' theory (Etherington, 1984, pp. 3–4). By carefully selecting Marxist writings and presenting them out of context, the historians 'used a theory originally devised to explain global politics *after 1900* to explain colonial annexations *before 1900*' (Etherington, 1984, p. 192; italics in original). This simple exercise in 'proving Lenin wrong' became one of the most important contributions of Western historians to the Cold War.

There is an intriguing irony resulting from this pseudo-debate. By framing their studies in the light of the early Marxist theories of imperialism, Western historians have diffused these ideas and given them a longevity they might not otherwise have enjoyed. The result has been that we have all – Marxists and their critics alike – been trapped in what Wallerstein calls the Hobson–Lenin paradigm (Wallerstein, 1980). The existence of this paradigm can be identified most easily by an author's temporal definition of imperialism as an 'age' or a 'stage'. In this section I chart one particular escape route from the Hobson–Lenin trap. From the definition of imperialism above, it will be apparent that I treat the phenomenon as far too pervasive to be so temporally restricted. I argue that imperialism is part of the structure of the capitalist world economy and hence has existed and will continue to exist as long as this world-system exists.

Structural imperative

Imperialism is not part of Marx's model of capitalism in *Das Kapital*. Marx describes a system of pure competitive capitalism that operates with minimum state support and no external complications. This abstraction has been criticised by Chase-Dunn (1989, p. 22) for distorting 'the essential processes of capitalist development'. Using insights from Wallerstein's world-systems analysis, Chase-Dunn (1989, p. 23) sets out additions to Marx's model 'to reformulate a new theory of the essential kernel of capitalism'. For our purposes, two of Chase-Dunn's additions are directly relevant. First, military–political practices of states are integral to capitalist development. Chase-Dunn reaches this conclusion by arguing that the kernel of capitalism should relate to the fundamental competitive processes of the system which includes a logic of interstate competition as well as the logic of world market competition. Second, uneven development, a core/periphery hierarchy, is not merely an outcome of capitalism but is 'a permanent, necessary and reproduced feature of the capitalist mode of production' (Chase-Dunn, 1989, p. 42).

The implications of these additions to understanding imperialism are profound. The two spatial determinants of imperialism, an interstate system and a core/periphery hierarchy, are brought to the very centre stage of capitalist development. The conclusion Chase-Dunn derives from this is that imperialism is necessary for the existence of capitalism; imperialism is a structural feature of the capitalist world-economy.

This world-systems conclusion derives ultimately from the observation of the failure of capitalism to generate expected economic development levels throughout most of the periphery. Early world-systems interpretations posited an alternative 'distorted' capitalism in the periphery which was unable to replicate the economic successes of capitalism in the core (Amin, 1974). This description of Frank's (1967) contrast between development in the core and the 'development of under development' in the periphery was disputed by

Warren (1980) who argued for a uniform capitalism that was in fact developing all parts of the world albeit on different time-scales. What Chase-Dunn has achieved is to unify Amin's two capitalisms into a single system while retaining core/periphery differentiation. In the process, imperialism as a historical liberator in Warren's orthodox Marxist interpretation is transformed into a structural oppressor at the heart of global material inequalities.

This interpretation is, of course, highly controversial. Geographers who have written on spatial uneven development have, on the whole, not incorporated either the interstate system or the core/periphery hierarchy in the kernel of the capitalist process. Harvey's (1982) 'spatial fix', for instance, is just that, a fix. It is a strategy available for capitalists for surviving or exploiting the endemic crises of capitalism. But it is not a necessary feature of the system because it allows for 'the possible existence of a world in which the core/periphery hierarchy has disappeared and yet capitalism remains the dominant mode of production' (Chase-Dunn, 1989, p. 221). In short, imperialism is a contingent rather than a structural relation. The basic text on uneven development by a Marxist geographer confirms this position. Smith (1984, p. 141) explains global uneven development by 'inherited patterns of capital accumulation', a contingent blockage to development which may, however unlikely, be cleared away in the future.

The differences in expectations between Warren and Smith are quite revealing. Warren believes that current 'Third World industrialisation' is a precursor of a relatively uniform capitalist world. Smith argues that 'empirically' 'a general and sustained industrialisation seems unlikely' (p. 158). From a world-systems perspective Smith's prediction is a sound one but is not backed up by theory. Chase-Dunn's additions to Marx's kernel of capitalism provide us with a theoretical argument that places uneven development, the core/periphery hierarchy and therefore imperialism as integral to capitalist development. The reason for Smith's 'empirical' opinion is, of course, that historically capitalism has *only* existed within a framework of uneven development and the core/periphery hierarchy. As Chase-Dunn (1989, p. 28) says, the system 'was imperialistic from the beginning' in the 'long sixteenth century'. Given this situation and therefore the 'impossibility' of empirically refuting the world systems position, the choice between structural imperative and mere contingent relation reduces to a pragmatic consideration of the benefits in adopting either position.

The rest of this chapter explores the world-systems interpretation of imperialism as a structural feature of capitalism and in the process I hope justifies my particular choice of position.

Historical imperialism

Our 'if capitalism, then imperialism' formula directs us first of all to look at the concrete expressions of imperialism in the capitalist world economy. This 'historical' imperialism is illustrated through alternative forms of dominance relations. The fact that imperialism is a necessary relation does not mean that it is constant in the sense of being unchangeable. Imperialism has existed in a bewildering array of types ranging from military plunder reminiscent of the expansion of pre-capitalist systems to the sophisticated investment strategies of contemporary global corporations. However, using just the two categories, formal and informal imperialism, general patterns have been identi- fied in world-systems analysis which are becoming generally accepted as a basis for discussing such dominance relations. The basic approach replaces the orthodox interpretation of stage theories of imperialism with system-wide cyclical models (Wallerstein, 1980). These models are explicitly economic *and* political in nature. Only their rudimentary characteristics will be described here (Chase-Dunn, 1989; Goldstein, 1988).

The imperialism facet of capitalist development has proceeded as follows (Bergesen and Schoenberg, 1980; Taylor, 1989). There have been two major cycles of formal imperialism, one rising in the sixteenth century and declining in the early nineteenth century and a second rising in the late nineteenth century to largely disappear in the second half of the twentieth century. These two cycles are to a large extent geographically distinct, encompassing the 'new' (Americas) and 'old' (Africa/Asia) worlds respectively. The two declines in formal imperialism are each associated with the occurrence of a hegemonic power in the interstate system – Britain and the liberation of the Americas, the USA and the liberation of Africa and Asia. But this liberation is only a political release from the domination of one imperial state, the general economic domination of core over periphery continues as informal imperi- alism. The classic example remains Britain's 'informal empire' in Latin America in the nineteenth century. In the twentieth century informal imperialism, often referred to as 'neo-colonialism', has continued after decolonisation, often led by the ex-colonial power's corporations or by US corporations. The earlier and only other hegemonic power, Holland in the seventeenth century, had had its informal empire in eastern Europe which was restructured to serve an expanding west European core via Baltic trade.

This changing mixture of formal and informal imperialism is associated with the changing nature of the interstate system, therefore. In this interpre- tation the 'age' or 'stage' of imperialism of the orthodox debate relates to the inter-core rivalry emanating from the decline of British hegemony. Of course, the pattern is not always as neat as the models predict. As has often been pointed out, British hegemony did not mean any lessening of British control of the most important of all formal colonies, India. Nevertheless a general pattern of imperialisms is easily discernible through the existence of the capitalist world-economy as described above.

The contemporary legacy of all this for the periphery is as follows. Latin America has experienced about 300 years of formal imperialism followed by about 150 years of informal imperialism. Africa and Asia have generally experienced less than a century of formal imperialism and just a few decades of informal imperialism. In their opposite ways India and China are very large exceptions to this general statement. No matter, it is clear that imperialism has been experienced in all parts of the world beyond the core providing the opportunity to transform what was to be found there. We are now in a position to begin to consider what those tranformations, the social legacy of imperialism, really are.

Processes: Incorporation and Reproduction

Structures are constituted of processes. Every structure is the result of two general processes, that which creates it and that which then maintains it. In the case of imperialism these are the original process of incorporation into the capitalist world-economy and then the reproduction of the core/periphery hierarchy which was thus constructed.

Expanding the system: incorporation

In a system like the capitalist world-economy with its logic of ceaseless capital accumulation geographical expansion would seem to be inevitable. But it was by no means a continuous process. Expansion, by either formal or informal imperialism, came in a 'few major jumps' related to the internal cyclical nature of the world economy. According to Hopkins and Wallerstein (1987, p. 776) expansion was a means of compensating for the periodic accumulation problems of the system. But expansion was always difficult to achieve and occurred only as much as was necessary at any one time; hence its discontinuous nature.

The purpose of geographical expansion was to incorporate new territory into the division of labour that defines the world-economy. Hopkins and Wallerstein (1987) describe this 'distinctive process' of incorporation in some detail. Unlike the conquest and plunder of other geographical expansions, incorporation into the capitalist world economy involves a basic reforming of the affected territory. There is a reorientation of production towards the world market. This involves the spread of the law of value so that production decisions are made in the context of a price-setting market. This means the destruction of previous 'moral economies' with their dominant non-capitalist practices (Watts, 1983). To enable this restructuring to take place the political order of the territory has also to be overhauled. This can take many forms from restructuring existing politics (the 'modernisation strategies' of political elites in China, Turkey and Japan, for example) to creating completely new polities as colonies and with various forms of 'indirect rule' in between. In every case the territory becomes a part of the interstate system.

The end result of this process after two or three generations of transition is a new peripheral zone incorporated into the capitalist world-economy. Despite the vast variety of pre-capitalist territories that have been incorporated, Hopkins and Wallerstein (1987, p. 779) suggest that the incorporation process is so powerful that equivalent outcomes can be observed. All new peripheries are divided into three sections: a production zone for the world market; a food-producing zone for the production zone which is no longer self-sufficient in food; and a labour zone which provides the additional workers required for the creation of the first two zones. One very useful indicator of the completion of the incorporation process is the regular movement of labour across these zones. When these migrations are regularised then we have entered the phase of reproduction of the system.

Maintaining the system: reproduction

It is when the framework of social organisation is routinely reproduced through the regular day-to-day activities of people and institutions that we know a structure has been constructed. In these circumstances maintaining the particular framework seems inevitable and even 'natural'. This is the measure of the achievement of the incorporation process.

Reproduction of social systems can be studied in many ways. The most common approach is to deal with economic, political and cultural imperialisms separately. Such analyses will obviously be liable to partial treatments that miss the overall process of reproducing the imperialist structure. Here I will concentrate on the basic institutions through which reproduction is carried on. There are, of course, a myriad of institutions involved in the day-to-day maintenance of the system. Wallerstein (1984) identifies four institutions which between them cover all aspects of reproduction: households, classes, 'peoples' (ethnic groups, nations, etc.) and states.

Households are the 'atoms' of the system. They are defined as small groups of people who share a budget through a pooling of incomes. There is a wide variety of types of households depending on their members' membership of the other institutions. Classes are the economic strata of the system and are classically divided between direct producers and the controllers of capital. In addition, of course, there is a large intermediate stratum which has had an important stabilising influence on the social polarisation. 'Peoples' are an indistinct form of institution ranging from nations with their own states to ethnic groups within states. They are distinctive in giving their members particular cultural identities. Finally the states are where formal power lies, where the laws covering the other institutions are made and enacted. States order the system.

Although each institution may have important precursors in pre-capitalist systems, all four are unique to the capitalist world-economy in the forms defined above. They are all necessary for the reproduction of that system. Another definition of incorporation, therefore, is the construction of households, 'peoples', classes and states to maintain the capitalist world-economy. The interrelations and interdependencies between these institutions are what Wallerstein (1984) terms the 'institutional vortex' that underwrites the whole system. It is through these institutions, therefore, that the particular legacies of imperialism to be found in the periphery today are generated. We are now, finally, in a position to begin to enumerate the more important of these legacies.

Mechanisms: The Institutional Vortex

The general processes described in the last section operate through specific mechanisms to achieve their functions. For incorporation, for instance, mechanisms of 'opening up' old empires or conquering weaker polities are among the means of achieving the capitalist ends. For reproduction we will develop our discussion of the four basic institutions and show how each under-writes fundamental mechanisms that maintain the periphery.

Households: reproducing labour

Peripheries do not just emerge; they have to be constructed. Applying a world-systems approach to the problems of construction leads to two distinctive emphases in analysis. First, the question of labour-force construction is brought to centre stage at the expense of traditional concerns for military coercion. While it is true that resistance to imperialism will take both political and economic forms, the ultimate test of peripheralisation is the integration of the production processes of a territory into the capitalist world-economy. For this interdependence to be created a labour force must be constituted that produces for the world market: hence Wallerstein and Martin's (1979, p. 140) conclusion that 'In order for peripheralisation to proceed, the key element is the availability of labour.'

The second emphasis derived from the world-systems approach is that this labour should be analysed through the particular lens of the household. As we have seen, households are considered to be the basic 'atoms' of the system, the units through which day-to-day reproduction occurs. In discussions of labour forces in the periphery the focus is often limited to the *individual* male labourer at the expense of the household of which he is a member (Wallerstein and Martin, 1979, p. 142). In our analysis the household is fundamental to any understanding of labour-force construction.

To produce and reproduce a periphery two conditions have to be met. A supply of labour has to be ensured and that labour must be secured at a cheap rate. The first condition is more difficult to achieve than at first may be thought. A territory incorporated into the world-economy will already be populated with people working to reproduce their pre-capitalist economy. But they will not be immediately available for capitalist production. The problem is that it is not just work that is required but a new form of labour in a new mode of production. Under capitalism work is longer, harder and less rewarding so that 'willingness to work' can never be taken for granted in a new periphery (Wallerstein and Martin, 1979, p. 140). Hence the need for policies to destroy the reproductive capacity of the pre-capitalist communities. Aliena-tion of land, specially calibrated taxation and various forms of coercion all undermine the subsistence capacity of the traditional labour processes. As people are forced into wage labour the process of proletarianisation begins and a labour force suitable for capitalist production is created.

The proletarianisation is limited, however. And this is where the household enters the analysis. Under capitalism a completely new type of household is created defined in terms of its income pooling. What is created in the periphery is 'part-lifetime wage labour' in semi-proletarian households. Typically wages from labour are an income source from just some members of the household at a particular period of their life cycle (for example, young male migrants). In this situation much of the reproduction costs of the household, and therefore of the labour, fall on other members of the household outside the labour market. Hence the 'part-time proletarians' can be paid 'below subsistence wages' (Wallerstein and Martin, 1979, p. 141). In effect semi-proletarian households subsidise the production of the periphery for the world market.

All households in the world-economy vary in terms of their dependence on wage labour for reproduction. A key difference between core and periphery is the degree of proletarianisation in this regard. The semi-proletarian household in the periphery encompasses a vital mechanism for reproducing the imperialist dominance relation.

Classes: reproducing capital

The overriding logic of the world-economy is ceaseless capital accumulation. The purpose of capital is to beget more capital. This is achieved by bringing together labour power with the means of production to create commodites. Under capitalism this presupposes a class system which opposes labour or proletarians to capitalists. This classic Marxist formulation is broadly accepted in world-systems analysis as the form that economic stratification within the system takes. Once again, however, there are two particular emphases that a world-systems approach brings to the analysis. First, on the question of class structure, 'the rise of the middle classes' and especially their geography is brought to the fore in a revision of the original polarisation thesis. Second, and related to the first, the global range of the class structure is rediscovered.

Since the mode of production is global in scale and economic strata or classes are defined in terms of function within the mode of production, it follows that classes are global in scope. This relates to the old distinction of classes *of themselves* and classes *for themselves*. Objectively the former are system-wide by definition but subjective classes are fragmented usually into 'national classes' (Wallerstein, 1984). At the global scale we can identify three main classes. There are the controllers of capital (classical capitalist 'owners', but also state officials and corporation executives), the direct producers (classical wage labour but also other workers who contribute to commodity production chains) and in between the 'cadres' of the system who organise, educate, manage, police, plan, heal, supervise, counsel and control the direct producers in their relations with the controller of capital. As capital has evolved into larger and more complex organisations, so this 'middle class' has grown to keep the system operating. It is as necessary to reproduction as the other two classes.

Saying that classes are global in nature does not mean that class relations are everywhere uniform. Quite on the contrary, class relations vary by place, first contingently in terms of particular histories of places and second struc-turally in terms of the uneven development that is the core/periphery hierarchy. In terms of the latter the key contrast is in terms of the balance of the three classes. In the periphery controllers of capital may be core-based with no reciprocal spatial arrangement. But most important of all there is a dearth of the cadre class in the periphery. Class structures in peripheral zones are immensely polarised in comparison to the core structures. This in turn produces relative social and political instability, which is one of the most obvious contrasts between the contemporary core and the periphery.

It is this difference between the balance of classes that has encouraged some writers to identify two alternative forms of capitalism in the two zones of the world-economy (Amin, 1987). In this analysis there is one capitalism which is expressed differently across the world-economy. All classes are constituted of the particular struggles of their locality and, in addition, they exhibit properties derived from their location in the world-economy. The legacy of class structure for the periphery is a small and very affluent 'controllers of capital' class, much of it external; a relatively small cadre class, mostly servicing the controllers, and coercing the direct producers; and a very large class of direct producers. It is, in effect, the inverse of the labour-aristocracy thesis for the core. Since we have argued that these relations are structural it follows that reproducing capital is to reproduce the core/periphery hierarchy.

'Peoples': reproducing consent

'Peoples' are the most complicated of the four institutions. They represent status groups within the world-economy defined by cultural attributes variously known as races, nations and ethnic groups. They are 'solidarity groupings' through which individuals and their households express their basic identities. Although they claim long-term historical lineages, the various 'peoples' are all products of the capitalist world-economy. They are constructed *within* this sytem just as much as households and classes. Wallerstein (1984, p. 20) describes them thus: 'The peoples are not haphazardly defined, but neither are they simple and unfixed derivations from an historical past.' Of the many possible cultural groupings, only a minority become a people. They are 'historical' to the degree that they give their people back their tradition which was lost in the destruction of their moral economies but it is repackaged to fit particular contemporary political needs. Peoples are the result of general political strategies that exploit personal cultural identities.

We can begin to unravel the complexities of this institution by relating different types of peoples to geographical scale. At the global scale peoples are 'races' and relate to various theories that justify imperialism as a white core (Anglo-Saxons, Caucasians, Europeans and/or Christians) and non-white periphery ('orientals', 'natives' and/or heathens). At the state scale, peoples are 'nations' that have a right to political self-determination; that is, their own state. Peoples within states who are not part of the nation are ethnic groups or literally 'minorities' who may aspire to nationhood through creation of their own state. Nations legitimate the existence of the interstate system, the balkanisation of political power, whereas ethnic groups are implicated in culturally based labour hierarchies within most countries.

Nations and would-be nations are the most ambiguous of 'peoples'. In terms of world economy politics they may be either progressive or conservative: '"Nationalism" is a mechanism both of imperium/integration and of resistance/liberation' (Wallerstein, 1984, p. 20). Led by national liberation movements, peoples have confronted and destroyed formal imperialism and recreated the world political map. But peoples are not only the tool of anti-imperialists. Imperialists actively created peoples in their policies of divide and rule throughout their empires. The clashes during decolonisation between 'young' nationalists (Western-educated 'modernisers') and 'traditional' ethnic leaders (former colonial collaborators) are some of the clearest illustrations of alternative uses of peoples.

The legacy of peoples is equally ambiguous. By emphasising the politics–culture link this institution provides plenty of ammunition for political strife. In the periphery especially, where political boundaries were imposed, minorities are omnipresent, nations-in-waiting as it were. On the other hand, peoples are the major means by which individuals and households are socially integrated into the capitalist world-economy. These solidarity groupings based upon identities ultimately generate consent as they reproduce their cultures within the confines of the world-economy. Although national resistance and liberation have been important at particular times and places, the continuous day-to-day reproduction of peoples means 'people know their place', which is a key reproduction of consent.

States: reproducing order

The final crucial institutional creation within the capitalist world-economy are the states. States are territorially defined and mutually recognise one another's sovereignty over their agreed territories. With their power so defined, states make the laws that regulate the social relations of the other three institutions. In addition they control flows of capital, labour and commodities across their boundaries. In short, states reproduce order within clearly defined spaces. Hence, the British were able to describe their nineteenth-century imposition of imperialism through the periphery as the extension of 'Pax Britannica'.

With the reconstruction of traditional politics and the decolonisation of empires, the periphery now has its quota of sovereign states within the inter-state system. The sovereign equality of these new states is symbolised by their membership of the United Nations and the equal voting rights (one state, one vote) in the General Assembly. But, of course, this sovereignty of the peripheral state is a charade, a myth perpetuated as part of informal imperialism. The most important international body for most peripheral states is not the UN General Assembly but the International Monetary Fund. This symbolises the dependence of periphery states on the core.

The question arises as to how we should conceptualise such states. Their most typical feature has come to be military involvement, either direct or indirect, in government. For some theorists, this suggests an authoritarian institution similar to the 'Bonapartist' solution to mid-nineteenth-century European political instability (Alavi, 1979). But such historical analogies are fraught with danger, not least because they ignore the world-system position. The legacy of imperialism is various forms of authoritarian states to be sure, but the coercive order that is achieved covers a very wide spectrum. At one end are the various 'national security states' epitomised by the Latin American political experience of the 1970s where order is maintained by a relatively sophisticated coercive state apparatus. At the other extreme are what are almost 'fictitious states' run by 'warlords' or armed groups with the 'state apparatus' reduced to a matter of personal power. Sandbrook (1985, p. 35) suggests that the African states of Chad, Uganda, Equatorial Guinea and Zaire fit into this category. Even in less authoritarian periphery states such as India, elective office is primarily viewed as a resource for personal aggrandisement (Taylor, 1986a, 1989). Hence order, where it is achieved, is invariably bought at a very heavy price.

States provide the ultimate mechanism for keeping the periphery in order through use of the internal state apparatus responding to internal class needs and external pressures such as those of the IMF.

Movements: Change and Mobilisation

Despite our discussion of general processes and specific mechanisms we must not leave the impression that the capitalist world-economy operates like a well-oiled machine. For both supporters and opponents the system operates in many contradictory ways to provide an endless supply of dilemmas confronting individuals and institutions (Taylor, 1986b). The structures themselves are always ambiguous in their potentials. Structures are constraining on agents, to be sure, but they are also enabling. The capitalist world-economy is reproduced as a structure but it is also as a structure that it will eventually be transformed. From discussions in our previous sections, therefore, it follows that even imperialism is both constraining and enabling.

Social change is not simply created, it is always contested and therefore fought over. In the nineteenth century this was reflected in the emergence of broadly based anti-systemic movements mobilising populations behind socialist and nationalist banners. Using the institutions of either class or peoples these movements identified the state as the 'enabling' Achilles heel of the capitalist and imperialist world. The political strategy bequeathed to our century, therefore, was to win state power. At this level of strategy the anti-systemic movements have been remarkably successful – socialists have shared state power in the 'West' as social democrats, captured state power in the 'East' as communists, and nationalists of various hues have swept all before them in decolonising the 'South' (Wallerstein, 1988). The overall result has been to change the parameters of the interstate system but without seriously restricting the reproduction of the capitalist world-economy. Hence, the crisis of the anti-systemic movements in the late twentieth century.

This crisis of resistance is to be found throughout the world but is particularly clear in the periphery. Even the most radical of nationalist revolutions in the Third World, as Amin (1987) argues, have produced conventional 'bourgeois' state structures with little or no forward momentum towards social change. Those periphery states that have designated themselves Marxist–Leninist are no more successful, of course. During the recent African famines it took an immense amount of political faith to interpret the state boundary between Ethiopia and Sudan as representing an 'iron curtain' between two different worlds, for instance. The pessimism that pervades anti-systemic movements at the end of the twentieth century seems to be well justified in the periphery as elsewhere.

But there is also cause for optimism. The capitalist world-economy is full of contradictions and surprises; politics in this context is typified more by Dunkirks than Waterloos. And the opportunity for recreating viable anti-systemic movements is likely to occur in the near future. The continuing decline of US hegemony, further rivalry in the core and an upturn in the world economy as a new Kondratieff wave is built may between them provide a unique window of opportunity for anti-systemic activity especially in the periphery. But it will not necessarily signal a revival of the 'old social movements' that have their origins in the nineteenth century. The crisis of the movements itself has an important 'positive consequence' as Wallerstein (1988, p. 591) sees it: 'The question that has been opened, or rather re-opened, is whether the *primary* path to the social transformation of the world is via the acquisition of state power by the movements separately in each state'. As the structural basis of uneven development is understood, then 'national economic development' is seen as a viable political strategy for just a favoured few. What the alternatives are has yet to be defined. If class or people mobilisations to gain state power are relegated as a priority other concerns must come to the fore. Wisner (1988) introduces one interesting route forward under his concept of a 'strong' basic-needs approach emphasising relatively independent household reproduction within local communities. This may be a necessary condition for transformation but its localism makes it politically vulnerable so that it cannot be a sufficient condition. Mobilisation of classes and peoples to such ends will still be necessary in order to sustain the anti-imperialism. But all this must remain uncertain. All we can be relatively sure of is that if a viable non-state politics does emerge it will most likely be in the periphery where the states themselves are far less entrenched.

Conclusion: Conditions and Contradictions

The legacy of imperialism is, therefore, the expansion and reproduction of a capitalist world-economy. This is our basic conclusion and stated thus baldly it appears superficially similar to Warren's (1980) argument that imperialism is 'the pioneer of capitalism'. But this is not so, since his capitalism is a narrow national version which is innately 'progressive' wherever it takes hold. Our capitalism is now global and exhibits very different characteristics in different regions and zones. The legacy of imperialism in the 'Third World' is, contrary to Warren's thesis, anything but progressive but rather reflects the core/periphery hierarchical structure. Here, the processes and mechanisms of the imperialist dominance relation have created a bewildering array of different responses to being at the bottom of the hierarchy. Civil wars, famines, religious revivals, military coups, gigantic cities and rampant diseases are just some of the conditions currently inflicted on the peoples of the periphery.

Since 'modernising elites' in the periphery have failed to keep Warren's

18

promise of capitalist development some commentators see these regions 'going backwards'. Traditional ideas and leaders are making a comeback as their erstwhile opponents, the modernisers, inevitably succumb to structural imperatives. But it is wrong to see this contest of elites as a modern versus traditional conflict. Both sides are integral parts of one *modern* world system. Khomeini was no more taking Iran 'back to the Middle Ages' than was his arch-foe the Shah. Similarly in South Africa the Inkatha movement, for all its 'traditional' trimmings, is just as 'modern' as the African National Congress. Such conflicts and the host of contradictions that accompany them are part of what it means to be living in the periphery of the capitalist world economy. Those contradictions are as much a legacy of imperialism as are the conditions from which they emerge.

References

Alavi, H. (1979) 'The state in post-colonial societies', in H. Goulbourne (ed.) *Politics and State in the Third World*, London: Macmillan.

Amin, S. (1974) *Accumulation on a World Scale*, New York: Monthly Review Press.

Amin, S. (1987) 'Democracy and national strategy in the periphery', *Third World Quarterly*, 9, pp. 1129–56.

Bergesen, A., and Schoenberg, R. (1980) 'Long waves of colonial expansion and contraction, 1415–1969', in A. Bergesen (ed.) *Studies of the Modern World-System*, New York: Academic Press.

Chase-Dunn, C. (1989) *Global Formation. Structures of the World-Economy*, Oxford: Blackwell.

Cohen, B.J. (1973) *The Question of Imperialism: The Political Economy of Dominance and Dependence*, London: Macmillan.

Etherington, N. (1984) *Theories of Imperialism: War, Conquest and Capital*, Beckenham: Croom Helm.

Frank, A.G. (1967) 'Sociology of underdevelopment and the underdevelopment of sociology', *Catalyst*, 3, pp. 20–73.

Goldstein, J.S. (1988) *Long Cycles: Prosperity and War in the Modern Age*, New Haven, Conn.: Yale University Press.

Hancock, W.K. (1940) *Survey of British Commonwealth Affairs*, Oxford: Oxford University Press.

Harvey, D. (1982) *The Limits to Capital*, Oxford: Blackwell.

Hopkins, T.K., and Wallerstein, I. (1987) 'Capitalism and the incorporation of new zones into the world-economy', *Review*, 10, pp. 763–79.

Sandbrook, R. (1985) *The Politics of Africa's Economic Stagnation*, Cambridge: Cambridge University Press.

Smith, N. (1984) *Uneven Development*, Oxford: Blackwell.

Taylor, P. J. (1986a) 'An exploration into world-systems analysis of political parties', *Political Geography Quarterly*, 5 (supplement), pp. 5–20.

Taylor, P. J. (1986b) 'Chaotic conceptions, antinomies, dilemmas and dialectics: who's afraid of the capitalist world-economy?' *Political Geography Quarterly*, 5, pp. 87–93.

Taylor, P. J. (1989) *Political Geography: World-Economy, Nation-State and Locality*, 2nd edn, London: Longman.

Wallerstein, I. (1980) 'Imperialism and development', in A. Bergesen (ed.) *Studies of the Modern World-System*, New York: Academic Press.

Wallerstein, I. (1984) *Politics of the World-Economy*, Cambridge: Cambridge University Press.

Wallerstein, I. (1988) 'Typology of crises in the world-system', *Review*, 11, pp. 581–98.

Wallerstein, I., and Martin, W. G. (1979) 'Peripheralization of southern Africa, II: Changes in household structure and labor-force formation', *Review*, 3, pp. 193–210.

Warren, B. (1980) *Imperialism: Pioneer of Capitalism*, London: New Left Books.

Watts, M. (1983) 'Hazards and crises: a political economy of drought and famine in northern Nigeria', *Antipode*, 15(1), pp. 24–34.

Wisner, B. (1988) *Power and Need in Africa. Basic Human Needs and Development Policies*, London: Earthscan.

CHAPTER 2

The Ties That Bind:
Decolonisation and Neo-Colonialism in Southern Africa

David Simon

Introduction

Few regions of the Third World have remained so consistently in the international spotlight as southern Africa (Figure 2.1). As the process of decolonisation from Europe has moved southwards across the continent over the last three and a half decades, conflict with, and within, the white-ruled states in the region has intensified. Apartheid South Africa, in particular, has consistently seen itself as a bastion of the 'free world' in the struggle against the spread of 'international communism'. It sought not only to suppress domestic black nationalist aspirations but also to assist the Portuguese in Angola and Mozambique and the illegal Smith regime in Rhodesia to resist the forces of national liberation.

South Africa's actions may have delayed the achievement of independence by these countries, but were ultimately unsuccessful. Portugal's African empire disintegrated in 1974–5, following the coup which toppled the Salazar–Caetano dictatorship in Lisbon and installed a progressive, military-led government. The colonial authorities ultimately hauled down their flag and fled, handing power to avowedly Marxist–Leninist movements, FRELIMO in Mozambique and the Luanda-centred MPLA in Angola. Attempts to stitch together a coalition government embracing the MPLA and its more pro-capitalist rivals, the FNLA and UNITA, had failed. Statehood for both Angola and Mozambique has been precarious, largely as a result of debilitating guerrilla insurgencies mounted with South African and Western support by UNITA and RENAMO respectively. In April 1980, Zimbabwe emerged as the youngest state in the region after sustained guerrilla campaigns, economic sanctions and political pressure had finally brought Ian Smith to the negotiating table at London's Lancaster House.

Since the beginning of the 1980s, therefore, attention has been focused squarely on South Africa itself and its *de facto* colony, Namibia (formerly South West Africa). Following a struggle second in duration only to that of black people in South Africa itself, Namibians finally won internationally recognised independence on 21 March 1990.

In terms of international law, the process of decolonisation in the subcontinent is therefore now complete, since South Africa has been a sovereign state

2:1 Political geography of Southern Africa. *Source: Simon (1989b)*

since 1910 and a republic outside the Commonwealth since 1961. However, that country is unique in that sovereignty was granted to a white minority regime which, moreover, has systematically oppressed the black majority through the institutionalisation of legislative apartheid. In substance, therefore, South Africa is still awaiting liberation. That objective suddenly seems rather less remote now, in view of initiatives taken under F. W. de Klerk's presidency, especially the release of most political prisoners, the unbanning of the ANC, PAC and other progressive organisations, and the relaxation of some facets of the state of emergency.

The purpose of this chapter is not to speculate on the nature or time-scale of that process, however, but to address some fundamental problems of structural and political inequality in the region. All are historically rooted, and are certain to persist in recognisable form, if not precise detail, for the foreseeable future, irrespective of who rules South Africa. That country has dominated the regional political economy (Figure 2.1) since early colonial days, and virtually all the other states in the subcontinent have continued to feel the weight of Pretoria's iron fist in numerous ways, many inimical to their own efforts to promote development and self-reliance. Some recent and current dimensions of these dominance–dependence relationships are illustrated here by means of a schema which differentiates the degree of South African control. It is important to note, however, that the dramatic changes currently sweeping the region render speculation on future developments hazardous and could alter the situation significantly in a very short time.

Sub-Imperialism and the Case of South Africa

To contend that South Africa dominates the whole of southern Africa is to do no more than state a truism which masks an exceedingly complex web of sometimes· rapidly changing politico-economic relationships. Some of these are relatively easy to document, others covert and extremely difficult. In order to help us understand the particular regional dynamics and the role of South Africa, an analytical schema is constructed which utilises the theory of sub-imperialism and the related concepts of colonialism, neo-colonialism and internal colonialism.

Sub-imperialism refers to a situation where countries occupy an intermediate position between the metropolitan centres and the periphery in the international politico-economic system. Although falling within the sphere of interest of one or more imperial powers, they themselves dominate their weaker regional neighbours in a similar manner. While clearly less powerful in absolute and global terms than the core states of the world economy, sub-imperial states may nowadays have a more intense impact on their own region because of geographical contiguity or proximity. Within the neo-Marxist world systems theory of Immanuel Wallerstein, such intermediate states are conceived of as comprising the semi-periphery.

Definitions of sub-imperialism vary. Some, such as that in the dependency tradition put forward by Samir Amin (1975), are essentially static and uncomplicated. He regards the essence of sub-imperialism as being the export of raw materials to, and import of capital and sophisticated technology from, the metropolitan cores on the one hand, and the export of basic manufactures to, and import of raw materials from, adjacent peripheral countries on the other. Rather more useful are some aspects of Marini's (1972) work on Brazil's position and role within Latin America. He suggests three characteristics of sub-imperialism:

(i) the export of both durable and non-durable manufactures at the expense of domestic consumption, this increasingly capital-intensive production being achieved largely through the import of advanced technologies from the USA and other metropolitan centres;
(ii) increased state expenditure through infrastructural provision, direct state involvement in strategic sectors of the economy and modernisation of the armed forces, thus increasing the market for capital goods, and promoting import substitution;
(iii) the creation of a consumer society through the exploitation of the poor and unemployed classes, enabling the transfer of wealth to the middle and upper classes. This, however, is an unstable condition, because of the dynamics of class struggle and the eventual need to

expand consumer markets through incorporation of additional classes in order to avoid stagnation and ensure continued capital accumulation.

Furthermore, notwithstanding his rather idealistic conclusions with respect to the scope for revolutionary action, Marini's schema embodies explicit linkages between internal and external forces, especially the crucial role of foreign capital and a bellicose authoritarian state. He sees sub-imperialism as the form taken by dependent capitalism on reaching the stage of monopoly and domestic finance capital. It seems to me, however, that this definition is still too economistic, in that it implies that domestic capital formation and accumulation, and attendant class struggles, are the sole cause or rationale for sub-imperial action. While there is obviously a high degree of interdependence between economic and political interests – the essence of political economy – a distinction is necessary.

Consequently, an essential characteristic of sub-imperialism is having *both* the economic *and* the political/military power to dominate the surrounding periphery with a significant degree of autonomy. The extent and nature of such autonomy is likely to grow over time, but not necessarily consistently, given the sub-imperial country's intermediate and perhaps ambiguous position between global core and regional periphery, with all which that implies for tension and volatility in the attendant relationships. Another point worth noting is that the economic characteristics outlined above explain why sub-imperial states generally also fall into the class of newly industrialising countries (NICs).

Although differing in detail, these elements can be distinguished in relation to South Africa, which can therefore be taken to represent a notable example of semi-peripheral sub-imperialism. The objective of this chapter is not to attempt a detailed justification of this assertion as such (Davies and O'Meara, 1984; Kibble and Bush, 1986; Leys and Tostensen, 1982), but rather to examine some contemporary forms of the country's diverse regional relationships in this light. It should be pointed out, however, that recent foreign disinvestment from South Africa as a result of international pressure for sanctions against apartheid has led to a significant increase in the degree of domestic control of the economy. While its overall impact is as yet indeterminate, one consequence of this curiously unforeseen development is increased flexibility and autonomy to act within the world economy. Secondly, South Africa's transition from exporting essentially primary commodities to the core countries of the global economy, to the export of an increasing proportion of manufactured goods has been retarded by the international sanctions campaign. The search for regional markets and for closer co-operation with other outcast states such as Israel, Taiwan and the Latin American dictatorships has therefore assumed greater priority. These considerations probably enhance the validity of the concept of sub-imperialism in the South African case.

Namibia: An Intense and Persistent Form of Colonialism

Conceptual issues and background

Namibia was commonly referred to as Africa's last colony (Green, Kiljunen and Kiljunen, 1981). This label was technically incorrect, since Spain continues to occupy the two enclave colonies of Ceuta and Melilla on Morocco's Mediterranean coast. Morocco is also still attempting to occupy the former Spanish Sahara in the face of determined resistance by the local population, who have declared independence as the Sahrawi Arab Democratic Republic. Furthermore, Eritreans maintain, with some justification in international law, that their country is still colonised by Ethiopia and they are consequently fighting to regain their former independence. Nevertheless, Namibia remained the last colonial territory in sub-Saharan Africa, having been occupied and subjugated initially by imperial Germany and, after the First World War, by neighbouring South Africa.

Since both these powers explicitly used Namibia as a settlement colony and instituted official programmes to encourage settler migration, use of the term colony seems appropriate. The South African state, however, hotly denied this status, having consistently sought to portray its occupation as complying with the original League of Nations C-class Mandate under which South Africa assumed legal control over the territory at Britain's request in 1919. In fact, the terms of the Mandate did permit the territory's administration as an integral part of South Africa, subject to conditions that the material and moral wellbeing and social advancement of the local inhabitants be promoted to the utmost and that laws be modified to suit local conditions where necessary. Essentially, this could be said to amount to a licence for colonialism in all but name (Dugard, 1973; Katjavivi, 1988; Mbuende, 1986; Wellington, 1967).

The dominant thrust of South African policy in Namibia was to obtain its incorporation as a fifth province of the Union. When attempts to achieve this *de jure* status failed on account of growing international distaste for South Africa's racist policies, the goal was pursued unilaterally, achieving a very high degree of *de facto* success. German legislation was replaced by South African statutes, and the panoply of segregation policies, followed after 1948 by apartheid, were implemented. Repression and deliberate underdevelopment of the majority black population were every bit as systematic as in South Africa. Bantustans based on earlier native reserves were established, while whites were accorded South African citizenship and elected representatives to Parliament in Cape Town, where they bolstered the National Party majority.

Frustrated black aspirations led ultimately to the establishment, in the late 1950s and early 1960s, of several political parties seeking liberation. The South West Africa People's Organisation (SWAPO) soon eclipsed its main rival, the South West African National Union (SWANU), and resorted to armed struggle in August 1966 in the face of continued repression and denial of peaceful demands.

Economic expansion and exploitation

Although the conditions for capitalist accumulation were established from an early date, the extent of South African economic involvement was, with a few notable exceptions, generally limited during the Great Depression and the Second World War. White settlement and economic penetration accelerated during the postwar boom. New investment has subsequently fluctuated in accordance with cyclical conditions and political perceptions.

Underpinning South Africa's desire for incorporation was an appreciation of Namibia's considerable mineral wealth, especially diamonds and copper, which the Germans had already successfully begun exploiting. After 1919, South Africa's largest mining conglomerate, Anglo–American–De Beers, moved swiftly to secure the diamond claims, thereby ensuring its domestic monopoly position and greatly enhancing its international importance. The conglomerate's Namibian subsidiary, Consolidated Diamond Mines (CDM), owns or controls all the country's diamond production (Innes, 1980, pp. 538–97). Copper and other base-metal mining is controlled by the Tsumeb Corporation (TCL), which bought out the original German interests in 1947. The US transnationals Newmont and AMAX were majority shareholders in TCL until 1982, when Goldfields of South Africa (a subsidiary of Britain's Consolidated Gold Fields) acquired a 42 per cent stake. The balance is held by several British and South African mining houses. Uranium has recently come to form the third pillar of Namibia's mineral industry. Rössing Uranium Ltd, which is controlled by Britain's Rio Tinto Zinc (RTZ) but has a minority government shareholding, commenced production from the world's largest uranium mine in 1976 in defiance of United Nations Decree No. 1, which prohibited the exploitation of Namibia's mineral resources under South Africa's illegal occupation. The illegality refers to the UN's termination of the Mandate in 1966, a move regarded as invalid by South Africa, but upheld by the International Court of Justice in 1971 after two previous hearings had found in South Africa's favour.

All in all, capitalist relations of production in the mining sector are highly exploitative and oligopolistic. The sector is dominated by only three large corporations which together account for approximately 85 per cent of capital invested in mining (Mbuende, 1986, pp. 110–19). Multiple cross-shareholdings symbolise their mutual interest, while common policies with respect to employment conditions, labour relations and negotiations with the state are formulated through the Chamber of Mines. Exploitation of labour and illegitimate practices such as transfer pricing (confirmed by an official investigation into the diamond industry in the mid-1980s) have contributed to the vast profits earned for South African and Western parent corporations. Moreover, mining has consistently been the single most important sector of the economy in recent times, contributing 28.1 per cent to Namibia's GDP in 1988 (SWA/Namibia, 1989).

Strategic considerations and the struggle for decolonisation

South Africa also long regarded Namibia as having great strategic value. Until the collapse of Portugal's colonial empire, it formed a key link in the 'white South' of Africa, where the demands and armed struggles of nationalist liberation movements were still actively being resisted. After 1975, continued occupation of Namibia enabled South Africa to mount destabilization against socialist Angola, both through direct military intervention and through support for UNITA, on the pretext of combating SWAPO guerrilla insurgency into Namibia. The South African military gained much battle experience and developed new technology in an exercise legitimised to South Africans and the West as resistance to the 'communist onslaught' on the region. Although South Africa's desert border with southern Namibia is far easier to police than the Namibia–Angola border, the physical buffer was deemed useful, at least while attempts were made to foist an acceptable neo-colonial arrangement on Namibia. P. W. Botha also felt compelled, for reasons of domestic politics, to avoid alienating reactionary white voters by 'surrendering' to international pressure to withdraw.

These issues explain much of South Africa's determination to retain control over Namibia. While the West has been prepared to countenance majority rule, its ultimate concern has been that Namibia should remain within the realm of international capitalism (Mbuende, 1986). The considerable overlap of interests provided the South African state with sufficient incentive and support (albeit largely tacit apart from the Reagan administration in the USA) to delay independence until 1990, even though the ultimate inevitability of this outcome had been accepted ever since Portugal relinquished its colonies in 1975.

Namibia's right to freedom was formally recognized by Pretoria during the negotiations leading up to United Nations Security Council Resolutions 432 and 435 in 1978, which established the mechanisms for securing a transition to internationally recognised independence. During the decade of prevarication before signature, in December 1988, of the accords to implement Res. 435, some significant reforms were effected inside Namibia. These removed overt apartheid from most spheres except health and education, but did not affect the underlying political economy (Simon and Moorsom, 1987) and were ultimately inadequate to win sufficient anti-SWAPO support in the 1989 Constituent Assembly elections. Fortunately, SWAPO has led Namibia to independence at a time when the prospects for transition to a post-apartheid era in South Africa, and therefore for greater regional stability and progress, appear unprecedented. However, even under such circumstances, Namibia's economic dependence on South Africa will not evaporate overnight, and one of the new government's prime objectives is to ensure that colonialism is not simply replaced by neo-colonialism.

Internal Colonialism: South Africa's Bantustans

Conceptual issues and background

As the term suggests, internal colonialism is the domestic equivalent of international colonialism, existing between different regions or groups within the same territory. Although the concept can be traced back to the classical Marxist writings of Lenin and Gramsci, its modern usage emerged within the realms of the dependency paradigm (Hechter, 1975) and has apparently waned again recently with the eclipse of that approach. It has been applied to a wide variety of contexts, generating debate as to the concept's precision and ultimate utility (Rogerson, 1980). Many of the definitions used in the literature link internal colonialism specifically to the colonial or post-colonial eras, cultural domination, or exploitation of a dependent majority group. These definitions suffer from non-uniqueness, by failing, for example, to distinguish internal colonialism adequately from neo-colonialism. Following Walton (1975), I would argue that in order for the concept of internal colonialism to have utility, it is essential to examine the underlying process rather than limiting analysis to the features of particular groups. More especially, internal colonialism should be seen as an inextricable part of the expansion of capitalist relations, in which accumulation by particular classes and in particular regions proceeds by the domination and exploitation of others within the same territory. Moreover, the existence of such relations is not restricted to overtly capitalist states; they can and do exist just as readily under a variety of forms of state capitalism and state socialism.

Neo-Marxists and structural Marxists disagree on the precise nature of, and degree of dominance attained by, capitalist relations of production in colonial and internal colonial situations. This debate has created a related controversy as to the appropriate and most effective policy to adopt to overcome internal colonialism. Much of the literature is, however, economistic and deterministic, tied to the overthrow of capitalism by socialism. As stated above, though, some forms of 'socialism' may themselves develop or perpetuate internal colonialism. Besides, the notion of socialism defeating capitalism seems rather quaint at the beginning of the 1990s. Does this mean that there can be no hope for reducing or ending internal colonialism in the foreseeable future? To adopt that view would surely be to hold a very static notion of capitalism, for there is *no* inherent reason why the persistence of internal colonialism should remain in the interests of continued capital accumulation *ad infinitum*. At a certain point, maintenance of rates of profit, and ultimately the continued stability of the system, are likely to require the progressive incorporation of hitherto exploited groups and/or regions (Corbridge, 1986).

South Africa's own bantustans illustrate the phenomenon of internal colonialism and its changing requirements particularly well (Wolpe, 1975). They were formally established by the 1913 Native Land Act as 'scheduled Native areas' covering a mere 7.3 per cent of the country's land. The 1936 Native Trust and Land Act provided for the addition of 'released' areas to the reserves, but even so, approximately 80 per cent of South Africa's population

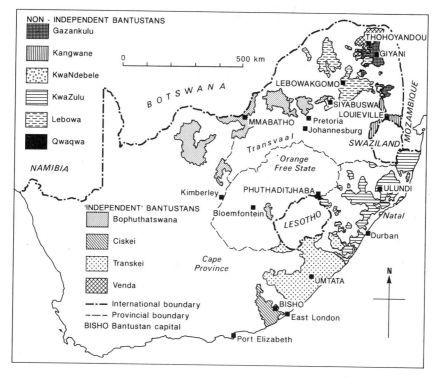

2:2 South Africa's bantustans.

was thus allocated less than 13 per cent of the total land area. These grossly inequitable measures provided the basis for territorial apartheid and had the twin objectives of making adequate agricultural land available for white settlers and forcing Africans onto the labour market and into the cash economy by undermining their peasant subsistence base.

The bantustans were systematised by the National Party government after 1948 to form a cornerstone of grand apartheid. During the 1950s, customary chiefs were given official status and authority as paid state officials, in an effort to undermine the increasingly westernized and urban-based progressive leadership of the African National Congress and other opposition organisations. African representation in Parliament was ended, and the consolidation of the fragmented reserves into eight, and later ten, units began (Figure 2.2). However, on grounds of financial and political costs, only some of the recommendations of the influential 1955 Tomlinson Commission were implemented. The proposals were aimed at development of the reserves by reducing their dependence on migrant labour, by increasing commercial agriculture and by providing industrial employment (Lemon, 1987).

The ultimate objective was to make all Africans 'citizens' of one of these tiny pseudo-states, which would then be granted 'independence', thus ensuring white majority rule within South Africa. Between 1976 and 1981, four (Transkei, Bophuthatswana, Venda, Ciskei) attained this status, recognised only by South Africa, which also continues to underwrite them financially, politically, militarily and in terms of skilled personnel. The remainder have refused to surrender their claim to a share of the country's wealth.

The functionality of superexploitation to capitalist accumulation

There has been extensive debate on the role of the bantustans in South Africa's economic development. The classic liberal explanation for this and other facets of the grand apartheid design was that the state was pursuing an irrational ideology of racial superiority and exclusivity. By extension, the remedy was – and in many influential circles probably still is – seen simply as lying in the abrogation of this ideology. As a result of the radical critique, it became widely accepted that conscious underdevelopment of the bantustans was predicated at least as much on the imperative of securing cheap labour for the white economy as on political ideology (Wolpe, 1972; Legassick, 1974, 1975).

Several mechanisms for coercing and incorporating African labour have been implemented over time, from the original hut and poll taxes payable only in cash to the reserve and then bantustan policy which enabled the institutionalisation of migrant contract labour. By confining Africans to small areas of comparatively marginal agricultural potential, inadequate to provide all their subsistence needs, and by preventing any meaningful development in these reserves, people were forced to sell their labour in the modern economy beyond. Moreover, the fact that migrants *de jure* retained their insertion into the peasant economy, being unable to bring their families with them and having to return annually to their rural abode as a condition of renewal of their contracts, was used to rationalise the payment of poverty wages. Employers argued that they provided accommodation and food, and that the wages were not used to support an entire family, being a monetary supplement to subsistence income. The harsh employment conditions and abysmal standards of accommodation were generally explained away on racist grounds.

Over time, the bantustans have suffered progressively greater impoverishment and environmental degradation, principally as a result of official neglect, the forced relocation there of some 2–3 million people from various part of 'white South Africa' (Platzky and Walker, 1985), and the debilitating long-term effects of migrant labour on household production. A high proportion of households in this vast and increasingly heterogeneous worker–peasant class have, in fact, come to depend for survival on remittances in both cash and kind from their migrant members.

In other words, this extreme form of exploitation, or superexploitation as it is sometimes labelled, has been functional to rapid capital accumulation in the modern, almost exclusively white-owned economy. This has enabled whites to enjoy an average standard of living comparable to that of North Americans and has made South African exports internationally competitive. The conscious and systematic nature of the process can therefore be regarded as a classic example of internal colonialism.

30

In developmental or spatial policy terms, symbolic evidence of this status is provided by the exclusion of the bantustans from South African regional development policy until the 1980s. As stated earlier, many of the proposals of the government's own Tomlinson Commission, which would possibly have enabled less externally dependent development, were not implemented. For example, instead of locating new manufacturing plants within the bantustans, as proposed by the Commission, the state tailored its industrial decentralisation programme to comply with the apartheid imperative and the maintenance of extreme dependence. So-called 'border industries' were located just outside the bantustans and some bantustan boundaries were redrawn to include many large peri-urban African townships, most importantly those outside East London and Durban. In this way, Africans could still be forced to live within the bantustans while continuing to labour for South Africa's industrial growth rather than that of the bantustans (Lemon, 1982; Lincoln, 1982; Taylor, 1982).

South African decentralisation or regional policy has been severely criticised both on account of its ideological underpinnings and because of its great cost and ineffectiveness (Rogerson, 1981, 1982a, b; Wellings and Black, 1986a, b). The state eventually undertook a major restructuring of the policy in 1982, incorporating the bantustans within the scope of the new provisions for the first time. This signal change of direction occurred partly because of the failure of earlier efforts together with continuing metropolitan growth and congestion, but also for reasons associated with the reformist direction taken by the government under P. W. Botha.

Redefinition of the role of the bantustans

During the 1980s, the state took its first hesitant steps away from the rigid prescriptions of grand apartheid, by removing some of the most conspicuous but least fundamental segregative provisions (so-called 'petty apartheid') and by seeking to incorporate the Asian and so-called 'coloured' minorities into the tricameral parliamentary system. Africans were still excluded from this 'new dispensation', although futile efforts were made to buy off those with permanent urban residence rights by upgrading and seeking to confer legitimacy on the subservient local authorities in segregated urban townships. Migrant workers and others without residence rights were still regarded as outsiders, required to exercise their rights in 'their' respective bantustans. This was emphasised by the tightening up of influx control measures and the rate at which Africans without the requisite documentation were arrested and 'deported' to their designated bantustan (West, 1982; Giliomee and Schlemmer, 1985).

In 1985 came the astonishing admission by the government that its grand apartheid plans had failed. No further bantustans were to be forced to accept so-called 'independence', and negotiations would commence to restore South African citizenship to those people who had been deprived of it in the four which were already 'independent'. In reality, relatively few have qualified on account of the numerous conditions imposed. This move was followed in July 1986 by the abolition of the pass laws and their replacement by a supposedly non-racial policy of 'orderly urbanization' (Lemon, 1987; Wellings, 1986a). This has undoubtedly helped many Africans, although the criteria for urban residence rights were actually tightened. Moreover, the state still possesses and uses other powers to restrict the rate and scale of migration to urban areas.

As argued elsewhere, these moves should not be seen as an attempt to abolish apartheid in the short term, but to modernise it by retaining as much as possible of the *status quo* beneath a veneer of change (Simon, 1989a). Some of the changes will have important longer term consequences, but essentially they represent a response to important political and economic imperatives. On the one hand, they represent an attempt to buy time for the regime in the wake of Soweto and subsequent uprisings against the apartheid system, and increasing pressure for international sanctions. On the other, they became necessary as a result of important structural changes in the increasingly sophisticated economy. The consequent shortage of skilled white labour had necessitated the widening of recruitment to other urban inhabitants, especially so-called 'coloureds' and Asians, whose upward economic mobility precipitated strong demands for political incorporation.

The significance of the reconstituted regional policy is that, in defining eight functional regions which include the bantustans, the state officially recognised that the economic interdependence of all South Africa's territory is fundamental and irrevocable. Moreover, the bantustans were more than mere labour reserves and would need to be developed as an integral part of the space economy. The intention was now to focus on the most viable growth points, irrespective of their location. In fact, only 35 of the 114 development and deconcentration points identified are in bantustans. The incentives available in particular cases are determined according to the perceived 'development needs'. Provision of astonishing sweeteners, including labour subsidies of up to 100 per cent in some cases, and state repression of trade union organisation have led to very rapid take-up. Some 188,000 jobs were established over the period 1982–4, but workers generally suffered appalling conditions and exploitation (Wellings and Black, 1986a, b; Cobbett and Nakedi, 1988; Lemon, 1987; Wellings, 1986a).

This overview has sketched the main features and phases of a systematic and long entrenched process of internal colonialism. The intensity of domination and exploitation has not been constant, and developments during the 1980s illustrate well the earlier contention that the respective interests of capital (especially monopoly capital) and the state are likely to change over time. Although these interests frequently coincide, there is no inherent reason why this should always be so. Having become more sophisticated and having effectively 'outgrown' the limits of South Africa's white population, continued capital accumulation has of late required the incorporation of groups (particularly racially defined classes) and regions (including the bantustans) previously excluded. Whether and over what period the bantustans will ultimately lose their status as internal colonies can be mere speculation, but in the last two years or so South Africa's client dictators in Transkei, Venda and Ciskei have been overthrown by more progressive elements in the military. This time the South African army did not intervene to restore the ousted presidents, as it had following the earlier attempted coup in Bophuthatswana. The new leaders are forging links with the ANC and mass democratic movements inside South Africa, raising the prospect that the 'independent' bantustans will be reincorporated politically as well as economically as integral parts of a post-apartheid South Africa.

Sub-Imperialism and Neo-Colonialism: A Regional Problem

Background

I suggested at the outset that the end of overt colonialism and even the advent of majority rule in South Africa would not in themselves change the political economy of southern Africa, although some of the conditions for change might be fulfilled. The region has long been characterised by extremes of wealth and poverty, by systematic underdevelopment and exploitation through land theft and institutionalised migrant labour, by overt and covert South African destabilisation as part of its 'total strategy'. The struggle to overturn this legacy will be long and hard, notwithstanding the great potential which exists, because of the embedded nature of predominantly capitalist interests.

There have indeed been changes in regional relationships, precipitated both by the changing requirements of South African capital accumulation and continued sub-imperial control, and by an explicit strategy on the part of other states in the region to pursue more equitable development strategies and to reduce their dependence on South Africa. Nevertheless, South Africa has still largely been able to set the tone and dictate terms to its neighbours.

The contemporary regional political economy was delineated during the colonial era, since when its fundamental structure has changed relatively little. The peripheral states can therefore be said to be held in sub-imperial and/or neo-colonial relationships by South Africa. Neo-colonialism is the persistence, after the granting of formal political independence, of colonial-type politico-economic relations. As Nkrumah (1965, pp. ix–xv) put it so eloquently:

In place of colonialism as the main instrument of imperialism, we have today neocolonialism. The essence of neocolonialism is that the state which is subject to it is, in theory, independent and has all the trappings of international sovereignty. In reality, its economic system and thus its political policy is directed from outside . . . the rulers of neocolonial states derive their authority to govern not from the will of the people, but from the support which they obtain from their neocolonial masters . . . Neocolonialism is also the worst form of imperialism. For those who practise it, it means power without responsibility and for those who suffer from it, it means exploitation without redress.

The precise nature and intensity of neo-colonial relations vary over both time and space. At one extreme are Botswana, Lesotho and Swaziland (the so-called BLS countries), three of South Africa's immediate neighbours with small populations, which are heavily reliant on South Africa for their economic and, in many respects, their political survival. Certainly Lesotho and Swaziland, tiny enclaves entirely or largely surrounded by South Africa, represent classic neo-colonial states. At the other extreme is Angola, a large, populous and potentially wealthy state which has negligible ties with South Africa and yet has been a direct victim of the latter's sub-imperial strategy since 1975. Moreover, although the subject of this discussion, South Africa is far from being the only source of neo-colonial-type relations. Most states in the region retain strong links with their former colonial masters.

Underdevelopment and destabilisation

The countries of southern Africa have sought diverse paths to development since attaining their independence. Some have achieved notable successes in broadening access to education and health services and in raising average nutritional levels. Few, however, have been able to sustain increased material standards of living; in some, most conspicuously Angola and Mozambique, there have been marked declines for reasons explored below. Malawi and Zimbabwe have enjoyed significant periods of growth in their modern economic sectors but even they have been unable to avoid calling in the IMF's receivers. Botswana stands alone as a consistent growth economy with regular budgetary surpluses. However, despite limited progress in some cases, there has been no radical redistribution of productive assets and income, even in those countries where it is supposedly a key official objective.

Although one should not seek to exonerate government policy in these states, which all too often has been rigid, excessively authoritarian and inappropriate, several formidable structural problems are common to virtually all the countries of the region, including South Africa. Some of the most fundamental, such as the impact of settler commercial agriculture and land policies, widespread rural (and increasingly urban) poverty, exaggerated regional inequalities, limited infrastructure and poor national integration, were inherited at independence.

Others, while to a significant degree rooted in these long-standing structural inequities, are more recent and reflect politico-economic conflicts within the region. Essentially these revolve around the struggle for decolonisation and black majority rule, the related conflict between capitalist and socialist ideologies and modes of production, and differential power relations. Three problems warrant mention here.

(i) South African destabilisation, aimed at ensuring continued sub-imperial domination of the region and preventing the success of socialist development in neighbouring states, has exacted a horrendous toll in lives and material destruction. Generally accepted estimates put the cost of damage and lost production, together with additional defence expenditure necessitated by military aggression from South Africa and rebel movements supported by it, at US$10 billion for the years 1980–4 alone. This is higher than the value of all foreign aid and loans to SADCC members over the same period. The figure for 1985–6 amounted to a staggering additional US$15 billion (Cammack, 1988; Hanlon, 1986a, b; Hardy, 1987; Jourdan, 1986).

(ii) As a result of these internal and international conflicts, large numbers of people have been displaced within their own country or forced to flee as refugees to neighbouring states. For obvious reasons, flows are subject to rapid fluctuation, even where the causes are of long standing as in South Africa and Namibia. Resolution of specific conflicts, such as implementation of the independence processes in Zimbabwe and Namibia, has led to major repatriation exercises involving some 250,000 and 43,000 refugees respectively. Conversely, intensification of the Mozambican war has caused several hundred thousand people to seek refuge in South Africa, Malawi and Zimbabwe since the mid-1980s. Accurate record keeping for the region as a whole is thus difficult, but the figure has remained one of the highest in the continent, where altogether more than 4 million people are registered as refugees (Cammack, 1988; Hart and Rogerson, 1982).

(iii) Although Africa's external indebtedness is far smaller than that of Latin America or Asia, it is rising steadily, particularly if seen relative to the size of national economies. Structural adjustment policies have been widely implemented across sub-Saharan Africa, often causing even greater suffering for the poor in the short term, although the obsession with financial and economic stringency is at last being moderated by some concern with social spheres (Onimode, 1988, 1989; Save the Children Fund and Overseas Development Institute, 1988). At the end of 1985, the total debt burden (including arrears) of the SADCC region stood at US$16.5 billion. Mozambique, Tanzania and Zambia had the highest debt service ratios, each in excess of 80 per cent and thus unsustainable. Whereas their debt is primarily bilateral, that of Malawi and Zimbabwe is mainly multilateral (SADCC, 1986).

Neo-colonial dependence: the case of Lesotho and Swaziland

Lesotho and Swaziland exemplify the most extreme forms of neo-colonial dependence within the region, embracing most spheres of economic and political life. Indicative of their invidious position is their simultaneous membership of both the Southern African Customs Union (SACU) and the Common Monetary Area (CMA) centred on South Africa, as well as SADCC. South African capital has long been almost totally dominant, especially in mining, commerce and manufacturing, hotels and tourism – the last of these earning them the appellation of being South Africa's 'pleasure periphery' (Crush and Wellings, 1983).

Lesotho

South Africa is the enclave state of Lesotho's principal trading partner and conduit for virtually all its other exports and imports, the only exception being a tiny proportion of airfreight (Kingdom of Lesotho, 1984). Labour migration to South Africa provides employment for *c.* 125,000–130,000 Mosotho men and forms the country's principal economic activity, producing foreign exchange and revenue and contributing over 50 per cent of GNP. Vulnerability to changing South African labour demand is consequently extremely high (Cobbe, 1986; Taylor, 1982). Given the severity of chronic rural problems, the government has attempted to promote domestic non-agricultural employment, but its industrial development strategy has suffered from increasingly disadvantageous competition with South Africa's 'independent' bantustans in terms of the labour subsidies and other incentives offered to foreign investors (Wellings, 1985, 1986b, c).

Lesotho's dependence on aid increased during the 1970s and 1980s, to the point where over 90 per cent of domestic investment is financed from this source. As in Swaziland, efforts to promote skill acquisition through technical assistance are undermined by frequent emigration of skilled personnel to South Africa, where wages and prospects are superior (Cobbe, 1990). The dramatic rise in aid, including food, reflects the country's status as a 'least developed country', entitling it to particularly favourable concessions, and successful appeals to the international community on the basis of being a 'hostage to apartheid' (Kingdom of Lesotho, 1984; Wellings, 1982, 1986b, c).

The country's extreme vulnerability to political interference by South Africa was shown dramatically by the latter's imposition of a total economic blockade in December 1985, in retaliation for the increasingly antagonistic attitude of Prime Minister Leabua Jonathan. This quickly precipitated the overthrow of the regime by General Justin Lekhanya, who is rather more favourably disposed towards South Africa. Lesotho was also forced to sign a Nkomati-type accord, denying sanctuary to ANC activists from South Africa.

Swaziland

Swaziland shares many problems with Lesotho, although its border with Mozambique, across which a railway line links it with Maputo harbour, does provide a partial alternative to the main routes through South Africa. However, serious insecurity in southern Mozambique in recent years has reduced the extent to which this alternative can be used.

Swaziland is also to some extent a labour reservoir for South Africa akin to the bantustans but, with only 20,000–30,000 migrants, it is far less dependent on this source of employment and income. Besides, far more economic development is possible in Swaziland. That said, the economy is very externally oriented and under virtually total South African control. Before independence, South Africa provided 70 per cent of foreign investment, although British capital dominated agro-industry and the banking sector.

Although Britain still controls banking and, through the Commonwealth Development Corporation, also sugar cultivation, South African control of agro-industry has increased markedly. The Anglo-American Corporation now controls 90 per cent of citrus production and the bulk of the pulp and paper industry, while another South African firm controls citrus and pineapple canning (Levin, 1986).

The politically conservative ruling monarchy has remained generally well disposed towards South Africa. A secret Nkomati-type pact was signed in 1982, precipitating the expulsion of ANC activists, while South African security forces have operated inside Swaziland for a number of years (Daniel and Vilane, 1986).

Angola and Mozambique: the debilitating impact of destabilisation

Angola and Mozambique inherited arguably the most underdeveloped colonial economies and the least degree of territorial integration in the region. Development had been almost entirely geared to the benefit of Portugal and some 500,000 settlers, virtually all of whom fled at independence, leaving the new states bereft of skilled labour. Nationalisation of abandoned factories and *latifundiae*, while clearly in line with the MPLA and FRELIMO's Marxist policies aimed at achieving socialist transformations, became necessary simply in an attempt to maintain output levels in the short term. The impact on Mozambique was exacerbated by the return to its southern provinces of some 40,000–50,000 former migrants to South Africa and the concomitant loss by the state of its principal source of foreign exchange revenue (Simon, 1989b). In Angola, state revenues have been buoyed to a significant extent by the uninterrupted export of oil from Cabinda.

Domestic policies in Angola and Mozambique have generally failed either to achieve the desired transformations or to raise production. Instead, socialism has been gradually 'rolled back', with increasing encouragement given to peasant and private production, and renewed promotion of foreign investment (Torp, 1989; Roesch, 1988; Somerville, 1986; Young, 1988). This is partly a consequence of the extremely destructive conflicts that have crippled both countries since shortly after independence, rendering virtually all development efforts futile. The destruction wrought has been magnified by the particular combination of internal conflicts, largely funded and supported by South Africa, and direct South African military action. President Machel was pressurised by force of circumstance into signing the Nkomati Accord with President Botha of South Africa in 1984. This committed South Africa to ending support for RENAMO in exchange for Mozambique's expulsion of ANC cadres and a prohibition on the use of Mozambican territory to launch armed raids on South Africa (Goodison and Levin, 1984). South Africa ignored its side of the bargain, instead stepping up its assistance to RENAMO, thereby bringing the country to crisis point. Only since the recent reaffirmation of the Nkomati Accord between the new presidents, Chissano and de Klerk, has there been a real prospect of full implementation of the terms of the treaty.

On the pretext of preventing infiltration into Namibia by SWAPO guerrillas, South African forces occupied extensive stretches of southern Angola for periods ranging from a few days to several years during the late 1970s and 1980s. In reality, they were training and assisting UNITA forces in their campaign to overthrow the MPLA government. The destruction of infrastructure and productive facilities in large parts of the country has been heavy, rural development initiatives have been severely disrupted, and large numbers of people have been killed and displaced (Hanlon, 1986a, b; Somerville, 1986).

Mozambique alone had suffered damage and associated costs exceeding US$5 billion by 1987. Over 100,000 people had been killed, some 10 per cent of the population rendered homeless or displaced, and half a million refugees forced to flee to neighbouring states, including South Africa. Over 100,000 people died during the famine of 1984–5, while approximately 4 million, or a third of the country's population, are again under threat. The famines are almost entirely attributable to the effects of war. South African forces have carried out a few limited lightning strikes, supposedly at ANC targets, but have not occupied Mozambican territory as they have Angolan. Most of the destruction has been due to the often barbaric depredations of RENAMO insurgents, supplied and supported mainly by South Africa since 1980 (Cammack, 1988; Hanlon, 1986a, b; Minter, 1989; Torp, 1989). There is now a growing understanding of the socio-political roots of RENAMO; however savage their raids, they are Mozambicans and cannot altogether be dismissed as mere 'armed bandits' (Minter, 1989; Clarence Smith, 1989).

South Africa's overall regional dominance

Several other dimensions of South Africa's regional economic dominance warrant mention in the present context. Perhaps none has been historically more symbolic than the supply of up to 400,000 migrant labourers to the mines and factories of the Witwatersrand from several surrounding countries. Malawi, Mozambique and Lesotho, in particular, had become labour reservoirs akin to the bantustans, being heavily reliant on this export and the workers' wage remittances. South Africa derived additional benefits from the use of these sources: foreign migrants were generally recruited at even lower rates of pay than domestic workers and were more likely to remain docile, while the sending countries rather than South Africa bore the social costs. Inevitably, these countries faced tremendous structural problems in having to reabsorb several hundred thousand returnees when South Africa began systematically to reduce its reliance on foreign workers in the mid-1970s (Simon, 1989b).

Secondly, South African capital continues to exercise powerful interests in the economies of neighbouring states, even where the latter are ideologically hostile to apartheid and have adopted measures to reduce trade and dependence. The most conspicuous and strategically important example is once again the role of the Anglo-American Corporation and its local subsidiaries in the minerals sector. Exploitation of diamonds in Lesotho and Botswana takes place under joint venture arrangements with the respective governments, while Anglo's technical and managerial expertise remains essential for copper mining in Zambia, despite that country's nationalisation of 51 per cent of the mining industry in 1969 and the termination of Anglo's management contract in 1974 (Daniel, 1979). Copper revenues have long provided some 90–95 per cent of Zambia's export earnings.

In Zimbabwe, the region's most sophisticated economy after South Africa, Anglo's subsidiary controls roughly 45 per cent of the mining sector. British

Table 2.1 **SADCC Members' Trade with South Africa (%)**

	Imports	Exports
Angola[3]	0	0
Botswana[1]	75	6
Lesotho[2]	85	0
Malawi[2]	29	7
Mozambique[1]	14	0
Swaziland[2]	90	20
Tanzania[3]	0	0
Zambia[1]	12	0
Zimbabwe[3]	21	8

Notes: 1–1985, 2–1986, 3–1987. Source: Hanlon (1989).

firms, principally Lonrho, RTZ and Turner & Newall, control a further 30 per cent, while other foreign companies, especially Union Carbide of the USA, have a 10 per cent stake. Domestic control therefore amounts to no more than about 15 per cent. More generally, as a result of the increasingly close co-operation which developed after Ian Smith's white minority regime illegally and unilaterally declared independence in 1965, South African interests control between 25 and 33 per cent of publicly-quoted companies in Zimbabwe (Lines, 1988).

A third element of South African control is the heavy reliance of all southern African states, apart from Angola and Tanzania, on trade with, and freight transit through, South Africa (Table 2.1). There has been little change in the overall data trends over recent years, apart from Zimbabwe's trade with South Africa, which has declined gradually. The level of such interaction has fluctuated in accordance with overall economic conditions and the availability of alternative rail routes and port facilities, but South Africa has been able to exert powerful direct and indirect leverage to maintain its indispensability. This classic sub-imperial behaviour has had several elements: military and economic destabilisation of states seeking alternative paths to development; destruction, often via UNITA or RENAMO, of transport routes through neighbouring states; and attempts to promote international co-operation and development on its own terms. The flagship for the latter strategy was intended to be the Constellation of Southern African States (CONSAS), launched as a response to SADCC, although it has signally failed to attract any members apart from South Africa and its so-called 'independent' bantustans (Uys, 1988).

Against the background of growing South African aggression and a sharp awareness of the problems facing development efforts in the region, SADCC was formed in 1979/80 to promote co-operation among its nine members, namely Angola, Botswana, Lesotho, Malawi, Mozambique, Swaziland, Tanzania, Zambia and Zimbabwe. Shortly after independence in 1990, Namibia became the tenth member. SADCC's objectives are to reduce individual and collective dependence on South Africa, to promote greater collective self-reliance, and to mobilise both internal and external resources for development of the region in a way which individual members could not achieve. The organisation has avoided many of the errors of similar regional groupings, sharing out responsibilities and contributions relatively equitably, and proceeding by consensus and according to agreed procedures. Despite formidable obstacles, it has established a commendable track record of raising funds abroad and implementing its programme. The principal focus over SADCC's first decade of existence has inevitably been rehabilitation and development in transport and communications as the key means of reducing dependence on South Africa. Some US$2 billion has already been secured for this sector and states such as Zambia had succeeded in re-directing significant proportions of their transit traffic by the end of the 1980s (Anglin, 1983; Farai, 1988; Hanlon, 1990; Hardy, 1987; Hill, 1983; Leys and Tostensen, 1982; Moshoeshoe, 1987; Mwase, 1986; SADCC, 1985, 1986, 1989).

More generally, however, there are many obstacles to achieving greater intra-SADCC trade, which has not increased markedly since the organisation's formation and which stood at a mere 4.3 per cent of all SADCC members' exports and 4.6 per cent of their imports in 1987 (Hanlon, 1990). The obstacles include inadequate infrastructure and connectivity between members not sharing a line of rail or major highway; inadequate complementarity of production structures and exports; foreign exchange shortages; high SACU tariff barriers between the BLS states and other SADCC members; and the lack of regionally oriented commercial, institutional and entrepreneurial capacity in many member states. Several smaller and more peripheral members are also concerned lest Zimbabwe's economy become increasingly dominant. Moreover, while SADCC's rationale will not be undermined by the demise of apartheid in South Africa, relations with the regional power will undoubtedly change and positive interaction increase. Already, South African capital is showing renewed interest in trade and investment (Willers, 1988). An end to destabilisation will in itself provide a major direct and indirect boost to regional development initiatives, but the extent to which South African dominance of the region can be reduced must be questionable.

Conclusion

I have argued that various forms of dominance–dependence relations, characterised as forms of sub-imperialism embracing colonialism, internal colonialism and neo-colonialism, persist in southern Africa despite the now complete process of formal decolonization. This analytical schema also assists in the understanding of the complexities of the contemporary regional situation. South Africa has shown itself both able and willing to act with a high degree of autonomy, often in defiance of international opinion. Some of the preconditions for this were set out above, but the country's pariah status has undoubtedly been an important factor.

Continued capital accumulation and white minority rule in South Africa have hitherto required the elaboration of a multifaceted strategy of regional domination. This has taken specific local forms according to the nature of domestic class and racial conflict on the one hand and perceived external challenges to its hegemony on the other. The latter also arises out of particular political and class relations within the respective SADCC member states.

The underlying regional political economy is, for the most part, highly integrated with, and focused on, South Africa. SADCC's track record to date has been more favourable than many observers would have predicted in 1980, yet the ultimate objectives of greater mutual economic integration and reduced dependence on South Africa remain very much long-term goals rather than realistic short-term targets. Namibia's independence will probably assist this process, but the young country will remain very much within South Africa's influence for the foreseeable future. The emergence of a post-apartheid order in South Africa will do much to promote development and co-operation within the region, but this, too, is unlikely to reduce that country's dominant position. On the contrary, it could quite conceivably increase South Africa's economic dominance.

References

Amin, S. (1975) 'Towards a new structural crisis of the capitalist system?', in C. Widstrand (ed.) *Multinational Firms in Africa*, Uppsala: Scandinavian Institute of African Studies.

Anglin, D. (1983) 'Economic liberation and regional co-operation in southern Africa: SADCC and PTA', *International Organization*, 37 (4), pp. 681–711.

Cammack, D. (1988) 'Mozambique: the "human face" of destabilisation', *Review of African Political Economy*, 40, pp. 65–75.

Clarence Smith, W.G. (1989) 'The roots of the Mozambican counter-revolution', *Southern African Review of Books*, April/May, pp. 7–10.

Cobbe, J. (1986) 'Consequences for Lesotho of changing South African labour demand', *African Affairs*, 85 (338), pp. 23–48.

Cobbe, J. (1990) 'Possible negative side effects of aid to South Africa's neighbours', *African Affairs*, 89 (354), pp. 85–96.

Cobbett, W., and Nakedi, B. (1988) 'Behind the "curtain" at Botshabelo: redefining the urban labour market in South Africa', *Review of African Political Economy*, 40, pp. 32–46.

Corbridge, S. (1986) *Capitalist World Development*, London: Macmillan.

Crush, J., and Wellings, P. (1983) 'The southern African pleasure periphery, 1966–83', *Journal of Modern African Studies*, 21 (4), pp. 673–98.

Daniel, J., and Vilane, J. (1986) 'The crisis of political legitimacy in Swaziland', *Review of African Political Economy*, 35, pp. 54–67.

Daniel, P. (1979) *Africanisation, Nationalisation and Inequality: Mining Labour and the Copperbelt in Zambian Development*, Cambridge: Cambridge University Press.

Davies, R., and O'Meara, D. (1984) 'The state of analysis of the southern

African region: issues raised by South African strategy', *Review of African Political Economy*, pp. 64–76.

Dugard, J. (1973) *The South West Africa/Namibia Dispute; Documents and Scholarly Writings on the Controversy between South Africa and the United Nations*, Berkeley: University of California Press.

Farai, I. (1988) 'SADCC meeting draws fresh donor support', *African Business*, 115, pp. 10–11.

Giliomee, H., and Schlemmer, L. (eds) (1985) *Up Against the Fences; Poverty, Passes and Privilege in South Africa*, Cape Town: David Philip.

Goodison, P., and Levin, R. (1984) 'The Nkomati Accord: the illusion of peace in southern Africa', Liverpool: Dept of Political Theory and Institutions, University of Liverpool.

Green, R.H., Kiljunen, M.-L., and Kiljunen, K. (eds) (1981) *Namibia: The Last Colony*, London: Longman.

Hanlon, J. (1986a) *Beggar Your Neighbour*, London: James Currey.

Hanlon, J. (1986b) *Apartheid's Second Front*, Harmondsworth: Penguin.

Hanlon, J. (1989) *SADCC and Sanctions*, Brussels: International Coalition for Development Action.

Hanlon, J. (1990) *SADCC*, London: Economist Intelligence Unit.

Hardy, C. (1987) 'The prospects for growth and structural change in southern Africa', *Development Dialogue*, 2, pp. 33–58.

Hart, T., and Rogerson, C.M. (1982) 'The geography of international refugee movements in southern Africa', *South African Geographical Journal*, 64 (2), pp. 125–37.

Hechter, M. (1975) *Internal Colonialism: The Celtic Fringe in British National Development*, London: Routledge & Kegan Paul.

Hill, C. (1983) 'Regional co-operation in southern Africa', *African Affairs*, 82 (327), pp. 215–39.

Innes, D. (1980) 'Monopoly capital and imperialism in Southern Africa: the role of the Anglo-American Group', Ph.D. thesis, University of Sussex.

Jourdan, P. (1986) 'The effects of South African destabilization on mining in the states of the SADCC', *Raw Materials Report*, 5 (1), pp. 42–53.

Katjavivi, P.H. (1988) *A History of Resistance in Namibia*, London: James Currey.

Kibble, S., and Bush, R. (1986) 'Reform of apartheid and continued destabilisation in southern Africa', *Journal of Modern African Studies*, 24 (2), pp. 203–27.

Kingdom of Lesotho (1984) *Annual Statistical Bulletin*, Maseru: Bureau of Statistics.

Legassick, M. (1974) 'South Africa: capital accumulation and violence', *Economy and Society*, 3 (3), pp. 253–91.

Legassick, M. (1975) 'South Africa: forced labour, industrialization and racial differentiation', in R. Harris (ed.) *The Political Economy of Africa*, Cambridge: Schenkman, pp. 229–70.

Lemon, A. (1982) 'Migrant labour and frontier commuters: reorganizing South Africa's black labour supply', in D.M. Smith (ed.) *Living under Apartheid: Aspects of Urbanization and Social Change in South Africa*, London: Allen & Unwin, pp. 64–89.

Lemon, A. (1987) *Apartheid in Transition*, Aldershot: Gower.

Levin, R. (1986) 'Uneven development in Swaziland: Tibiyo, sugar production and rural development strategy', *Geoforum*, 17 (2), pp. 239–50.

Leys, C., and Tostensen, A. (1982) 'Regional co-operation in southern Africa: the Southern African Development Co-ordination Conference', *Review of African Political Economy*, 23, pp. 52–71.

Lincoln, D. (1982) 'State, capital and the reserve consolidation issue in South Africa', *Tijdschrift voor Economische en Sociale Geografie*, 73 (4), pp. 229–36.

Lines, T. (1988) 'Investment sanctions and Zimbabwe: breaking the rod', *Third World Quarterly*, 10 (3), pp. 1,182–216.

Marini, R.M. (1972) 'Brazilian sub-imperialism', *Monthly Review*, 23 (9), pp. 14–24.

Mbuende, K. (1986) *Namibia, the Broken Shield: Anatomy of Imperialism and Revolution*, Malmö: Liber.

Minter, W. (1989) 'The Mozambican National Resistance as described by ex-participants', *Development Dialogue*, 1, pp. 89–132.

Moshoeshoe II, King (1987) 'Another development for SADCC countries: a clarion call!', *Development Dialogue*, 1987 (1), pp. 77–87.

Mwase, N. (1986) 'Regional co-operation and socialist transformation in southern Africa: prospects and problems', *Journal of African Studies*, 13 (1), pp. 17–24.

Nkrumah, K. (1965) *Neocolonialism; The Last Stage of Imperialism*, London: Nelson.

Onimode, B. (1988) *A Political Economy of Africa's Crisis*, London: Zed.

Onimode, B. (ed.) (1989) *The IMF, the World Bank and the African Debt*, 2 vols, London: Zed.

Platzky, L., and Walker, C. (eds) (1985) *The Surplus People: Forced Removals in South Africa*, Johannesburg: Ravan.

Roesch, O. (1988) 'Rural Mozambique since the Frelimo Party Fourth Congress: the situation in Baixo Limpopo', *Review of African Political Economy*, 41, pp. 73–91.

Rogerson, C.M. (1980) 'Internal colonialism, transnationalisation and spatial inequality', *South African Geographical Journal*, 62 (2), pp. 103–20.

Rogerson, C.M. (1981) 'Industrialisation in the shadows of apartheid: a world-systems analysis', in F.E.I. Hamilton and G.R. Linge (eds) *Spatial Analysis, Industry and the Industrial System*, Chichester: Wiley.

Rogerson, C.M. (1982a) 'Patterns of indigenous and foreign control of South African manufacturing', *South African Geographer*, 10 (2), pp. 123–34.

Rogerson, C.M. (1982b) 'Apartheid, decentralisation and spatial industrial change', in D.M. Smith (ed.) *Living under Apartheid*, London: Allen & Unwin, pp. 47–63.

Save the Children Fund and Overseas Development Institute (1988) *Prospects for Africa*, London: Hodder & Stoughton.

Simon, D. (1989a) 'Crisis and change in South Africa: implications for the apartheid city', *Transactions of the Institute of British Geographers*, 14 (2), pp. 189–206.

Simon, D. (1989b) 'Rural–urban interaction and development in southern Africa: the implications of reduced labour migration', in R. Potter and T. Unwin (eds) *The Geography of Urban–Rural Interaction in Developing Countries*, London: Routledge, 141–68.

Simon, D., and Moorsom, R. (1987) 'Namibia's political economy: a contemporary perspective', in G.H.K. Tötemeyer, V. Kandetu and W. Werner (eds) *Namibia in Review*, Windhoek: Council of Churches in Namibia, pp. 82–101.

Somerville, K. (1986) *Angola*, London: Frances Pinter.

Southern African Development Co-ordination Conference (1985) *Macro-Economic Survey 1986*, Gaborone: SADCC Secretariat.

Southern African Development Co-ordination Conference (1986) *Annual Progress Report 1985–1986*, Luanda: SADCC.

Southern African Development Co-ordination Conference (1989) *Transport and Communications*, Luanda: SADCC.

SWA/Namibia (1989) *Statistical/Economic Review, 1989*, Windhoek: Department of Finance.

Taylor, J. (1982) 'Changing patterns of labour supply to the South African gold mines', *Tijdschrift voor Economische en Sociale Geografie*, 73 (4), pp. 213–20.

Torp, J.E. (1989) 'Mozambique', in J.E. Torp, L.M. Denny and D.I. Ray, *Mozambique, São Tome and Principe: Politics, Economy and Society*, London: Frances Pinter, pp. 1–117.

Uys, S. (1988) 'The short and unhappy life of CONSAS', *South Africa International*, 18 (4), pp. 243–8.

Walton, J. (1975) 'Internal colonialism; problems of definition and measurement', in W.A. Cornelius and F.M. Trueblood (eds) *Urbanization and Inequality: The Political Economy of Urban and Rural Development in Latin America*, Beverly Hills: Sage, pp. 29–50.

Wellings, P. (1982) 'Aid to the southern African periphery: the case of Lesotho', *Applied Geography*, 2 (4), pp. 267–90.

Wellings, P. (1985) 'Lagging behind the bantustans: South African corporate investment in Lesotho', *Journal of Contemporary African Studies*, 4 (1/2), pp. 139–77.

Wellings, P. (1986a) 'Geography and development studies in southern Africa: a progressive prospectus', *Geoforum*, 17 (2), pp. 119–31.

Wellings, P. (1986b) 'Lesotho: crisis and development in the rural sector', *Geoforum*, 17 (2), pp. 217–37.

Wellings, P. (1986c) 'Modern sector development and South African investment: a viable strategy for Lesotho?', *Journal of African Studies*, 13 (1), pp. 4–16.

Wellings, P., and Black, A. (1986a) 'Industrial decentralisation under apartheid: the relocation of industry to the South African periphery', *World Development*, 14 (1), pp. 1–38.

Wellings, P., and Black, A. (1986b) 'Industrial decentralisation in South Africa: tool of apartheid or spontaneous restructuring?', *GeoJournal*, 12 (2), pp. 137–49.

Wellington, J.H. (1967) *South West Africa and Its Human Issues*, Oxford: Oxford University Press.

West, M. (1982) 'From pass courts to deportation: changing patterns of influx control in Cape Town', *African Affairs*, 81, pp. 463–77.

Willers, D. (1988) 'South African business and SADCC: a few observations', *South Africa International*, 18 (4), pp. 249–56.

Wolpe, H. (1972) 'Capitalism and cheap labour power in South Africa: from segregation to apartheid', *Economy and Society*, 1 (4), pp. 425–56.

Wolpe, H. (1975) 'The theory of internal colonialism: the South African case', in I. Oxaal, T. Barnett and D. Booth (eds) *Beyond the Sociology of Development*, London: Routledge & Kegan Paul, pp. 229–52.

Young, T. (1988) 'The politics of development in Angola and Mozambique', *African Affairs*, 87 (347), pp. 165–84.

CHAPTER 3

The Chains of Migrancy and the Southern African Labour Commission

Jonathan Crush

Introduction

On 1 April 1980, the heads of state of nine ex-colonial territories in southern Africa met in Lusaka, Zambia, and issued a declaration of intent. The 'Lusaka Declaration' noted that southern Africa was dependent on South Africa as a focus of transport and communications, an exporter of goods and services, and an importer of goods and cheap labour. This dependence, it asserted, was 'not a natural phenomenon nor simply the result of a free market economy' but the result of a deliberate process of incorporation by metropolitan powers, colonial rulers and large corporations 'into the colonial and sub-colonial structures centring on the Republic of South Africa' (Nsekela, 1981, pp. 2–7). Thus did the founding fathers of the Southern African Development Co-ordination Conference (or SADCC) set out their analysis of regional interstate relations and the colonial inheritance in southern Africa. The argument, couched in the purest dependency rhetoric, has continued to dominate the voluminous academic literature on the activities and achievements of SADCC during the first decade of the organization's existence (Nsekela, 1981; Tostenson, 1982; Leys and Tostenson, 1982; Callaghy, 1983a; Thompson, 1985; Hanlon, 1986; Butts and Thomas, 1986; Amin, Chitala and Mandaza, 1987; Seidman, 1987; IPA, 1988; Brittain, 1988). This is a literature which lays great emphasis on South African regional hegemony, often portrays the 'frontline' states of southern Africa as passive victims, finds no reason to theorise the nature of the state or state–capital relations, and is largely devoid of any sense of internal class formation or the ambiguities which characterise interstate relations in the region (although see Weisfelder, 1983; Daniel, 1984; Davies and O'Meara, 1984; Libby, 1987).

One of the major indices of South Africa's neo-colonial domination of its hinterland is held to be the continuing flow of 'cheap labour' across international borders to the mines of South Africa. This phenomenon receives token consideration in many SADCC documents and most academic analyses of SADCC. Yet it is clear that it has never been a major item on SADCC's lengthy planning agenda for 'economic liberation' in southern Africa. Joseph Hanlon's recent survey of the organisation for the Economist Intelligence Unit, for example, details SADCC's achievements and prospects in such areas as foreign aid, trade, transport and communications, energy, food and agriculture, and industrial development (Hanlon, 1989). He has little to say about the movement of migrant workers into apartheid South Africa from throughout the region, or any strategies which SADCC might adopt to halt the flow. Anglin (1985, p. 169) refers to the 'curious omission' of migrant labour from SADCC's agenda (see also Anglin, 1988). Similarly, de Vletter (1985a) suggests that, 'for reasons which are unclear', SADCC has deliberately refused to consider the question.

To some extent, the issue of neglect is an institutional one. There already exists in the region a separate body charged with addressing the migrant labour question. The Southern African Labour Commission (SALC) was set up just before SADCC and operates quite independently of it. SALC has tried for over a decade to reach a consensus on migrancy to South Africa. SADCC has always seemed quite content to defer to SALC on labour questions, arguing that any other policy would involve an unnecessary duplication of effort. Since the early 1980s, however, SALC has tried repeatedly to get SADCC to take over responsibility for the migrant labour issue. SALC has argued that in order for the independent states of southern Africa to break the colonial inheritance and successfully disengage from South Africa's migrant labour system, a co-ordinated planning strategy is required. Only SADCC, they say, is in a position to mobilise international support for such an effort. To date, though, SADCC has refused to accede to SALC's request (de Vletter, 1985b; Setai, 1986). A consideration of the history of SALC and its failure to break the chains of migrancy in southern Africa provides important insights into the reasons for SADCC's recalcitrance.

The first section of this chapter examines the construction of the mines' migrant labour empire during the colonial period and, in particular, its dramatic geographical expansion in the post-1930 period. The second section examines the mixed success of those states in the region which did mount a unilateral strategy of disengagement from the empire at independence. This is followed by a consideration of the signal failure of attempts by the remaining states (through the Southern African Labour Commission) to devise a co-ordinated strategy of disengagement. In the final section issue is taken with the argument that the South African mining industry has been systematically dismantling its colonial labour empire since the early 1970s. It is suggested that although the empire is no longer needed in the way it once was, there remain persuasive reasons why the South African mines continue to maintain foreign workers on their employment rolls.

The Making of an Empire

The regional labour empire centred on the South African gold mines developed through three historical phases: (a) construction (1886–1920), (b) entrenchment (1920–70), and (c) restructuring (1970–present). Considerable scholarly attention has been devoted to the first of these phases (Johnstone, 1976; Lacey, 1981; Marks and Rathbone, 1982; Jeeves, 1985). In some Marxist accounts, the longevity of the migrant labour system is attributed to the benefits which it brought to mining capital (Wolpe, 1972; Levy, 1982). The labour was cheap, it was disposable, and it regularly displayed the kinds of ethnic and regional loyalty which could be manipulated by management. As Saul and Gelb (1986, p. 64) have observed, 'the migrant labour system and the practices of tight control over the freedom of Africans . . . were locked into place at the very heart of the economy. The African reserves . . . subsidized South African enterprises, facilitating the holding-down of wages.' There is some merit to such arguments in drawing attention to the coercive practices of the mines' labour empire. But they do not provide a sufficient explanation for why the empire came into being nor do they show how its form was crucially affected by the actions of migrants, homesteads and rulers in the supplier areas (Crush, 1984).

A more sensitive approach has subsequently emerged which sees the construction of the migrant labour system as an uneasily negotiated compromise between a dominant and powerful mining sector and a subservient but far from powerless countryside. In this vein, Cooper (1981) has suggested that the emergence of migrancy may just as well represent the resistance of rural cultivators to the work rhythms of wage labour as a perfectly functional part of a superexploitative system. Cooper argues that an approach which sees migrancy as purely derivative of the requirements of mining capital fails to consider the struggles of workers to shape the timing and conditions of labour and cultivation, the problems of disciplining and socialising workers, and the 'tension that beset migratory labour systems' (see also Cooper, 1983). This perspective, with its emphasis on African agency and supply-side dynamics, runs the danger of underestimating the coercive character and destructive effects of colonial migrancy. But it does suggest that while the mines' migrant labour system may have been the best available option, it was not a perfectly functional creation of mining capital.

One generalisation on which both schools of thought agree is that the migrant labour policies of the South African mining industry have been remarkably stable over time (Yudelman and Jeeves, 1986, p. 103). Other labour empires were certainly more coercive and brutal, but these never claimed to be voluntary systems operating under modern industrial norms (Conquest, 1978; Wolf, 1982; Lovell, 1988; Johnstone, 1989). The ability of the South African mining industry to sustain its labour empire was in part a testimony to its coercive capacity. As significant was the ability of labour recruiters constantly to expand the geographic pool from which migrants were drawn, and the existence in these supplier areas of various interests which benefited from the system. Then, as today, the system could not have endured without them.

By 1920, after three decades of intense struggle, the South African mines had in place a low-wage empire of migrant labour which spanned the southern portions of the subcontinent. Through an employers' monopoly (or 'monopsony'), the Chamber of Mines eliminated wage competition, centralised labour recruiting, and conducted quasi-diplomatic negotiations with supplier states (Jeeves, 1985). The colonial governments of the region had no intention of allowing their subjects to move permanently to South Africa. Usually operating under severe fiscal constraint, colonial state accumulation was heavily dependent on the ability to appropriate a portion of the migrant wage. This was much easier to do if the workers were forced to return home periodically. Similarly, figures of authority in the countryside (such as chiefs) encouraged participation in wage labour but also wished to make sure that their followers remained under their control. The colonial state and rural chiefs shared a common interest in perpetuating migrancy, though they often conflicted with the migrants over who should control the fruits of labour migration (Beinart, 1982; Harries, 1983; Crush, 1988).

After 1920, domestic labour shortages pushed the South African mining industry to campaign vigorously and commit considerable resources to the development of new sources of migrant labour. There was growing evidence that the gold mines were increasingly uncompetitive in the domestic labour market and, in the 1930s, the industry embarked on a major expansion programme. Between 1913 and 1932 the South African state prohibited recruiting north of 22 degrees SL. In 1932, after persistent supplication, the tropical labour ban was rescinded and the mining industry began a major push northwards for labour (Chanock, 1977; Jeeves, 1986). Under the direction of the Chamber's labour 'czar', William Gemmill, the Witwatersrand Native Labour Association (WNLA) moved into the relatively untapped rural areas of Central and East Africa. Northern Bechuanaland (Botswana) became the lynchpin of Gemmill's strategy. By establishing bases there, he was able to syphon off labour from the entire region. WNLA built over 1,000 kilometres of roads in the area, ran motor-barge transport and established air links with South Africa (Jeeves, 1986, pp. 87–8). Clandestine migrants from the north made their way to the WNLA bases from where they were whisked southwards. In other parts of the region, such as northern Nyasaland (Malawi) and Barotseland (in western Zambia), WNLA also invested heavily in transportation and medical facilities.

The British and Portuguese colonial states of the region did not meekly submit to the South African mining industry. Employers within the various colonies of the region resisted the disruption of their labour markets. Local colonial states were also unhappy about the haemorrhage of labour and tried to stem or control it. The Portuguese, for example, consistently enforced limits on the number of migrants going from Mozambique to South Africa (First, 1983). As a result, the numbers remained relatively constant for much of the postwar period and rarely went much above 100,000 (Table 3.1). The Rhodesian government fought even harder to protect the labour supplies of local mines and farms. Jeeves (1986, pp. 84–6) has detailed the protracted negotiations between Gemmill and the Rhodesians between 1930 and 1950 over access to the country's black labour.

In 1938, the Rhodesian government established a *cordon sanitaire* along the border with South Africa in an attempt to police the flow of clandestine labour to the south (Jeeves, 1986, p. 84). It also refused to allow WNLA to establish recruiting bases in the country. Nevertheless, in the 1940s the number of blacks from Rhodesia in the mines increased steadily (Table 3.1). It was only in the 1950s that the flow was staunched. The battle for control

Table 3.1 *The Mines' Labour Empire, 1930–88*

	Mozambique	Malawi	Zimbabwe	Zambia	Tanzania	Angola	Botswana	Lesotho	Swaziland
				Average number of workers employed					
1930	77,828		44		183		3,151	22,306	4,345
1931	66,941		42		142		3,149	29,662	4,738
1932	58,891		38		125		4,304	29,949	4,945
1933	48,521		29		99		5,150	32,494	6,131
1934	51,437		32	767	101		6,475	33,626	6,227
1935	62,576	49	27	570	109		7,505	34,788	6,865
1936	67,622	629	216	201			7,799	39,637	7,356
1937	81,165	1,735	2,336	1,132			8,964	39,666	6,874
1938	80,844	3,691	6,277	2,011			11,365	43,759	7,062
1939	75,676	6,563	6,959	2,402			12,038	45,575	6,791
1940	74,693	8,037	8,112	2,725		698	14,427	52,044	7,152
1941	80,369	3,621	8,459	3,294		2,949	13,731	50,950	7,749
1942	89,350	8,145	9,378	2,783	59	3,337	11,544	47,514	6,195
1943	79,910	2,438	9,767	1,367	314	4,555	9,948	39,066	5,694
1944	84,163	4,829	8,534	46	641	6,088	8,657	36,483	5,716
1945	78,588	4,973	8,301	27	1,461	8,711	10,102	36,414	5,688
1946	78,002	7,521	6,763	680	2,605	9,248	9,681	37,317	6,036
1947	81,691	8,304	5,583	4,104	2,497	8,461	10,850	34,210	6,331
1948	80,234	9,403	4,778	3,479	4,449	10,517	10,723	30,330	6,298
1949	85,975	9,196	4,638	3,468	5,609	10,032	11,905	35,275	6,614
1950	86,246	7,831	2,073	3,102	5,495	9,767	12,390	34,467	6,619
1951	91,978	7,717	654	3,108	6,542	8,467	12,246	31,448	6,322
1952	95,485	6,971	380	3,327	6,484	7,485	13,071	32,777	5,866
1953	91,637	5,456	207	3,013	6,869	7,232	12,135	30,843	5,988

Table 3.1 contd.

				Average number of workers employed					
	Mozambique	Malawi	Zimbabwe	Zambia	Tanzania	Angola	Botswana	Lesotho	Swaziland
1954	102,974	8,595	136	3,427	7,961	8,279	13,268	31,705	6,631
1955	99,449	12,407	162	3,849	8,758	8,801	14,195	36,332	6,682
1956	99,189	14,035	392	3,689	12,138	9,083	14,727	39,037	6,400
1957	103,008	14,227	482	4,147	13,178	9,727	15,749	38,586	6,507
1958	99,277	16,129	483	4,535	13,396	9,932	17,067	41,222	6,405
1959	103,125	20,314	596	5,929	14,601	11,566	19,219	48,896	6,766
1960	101,733	21,934	747	5,292	14,025	12,364	21,404	48,842	6,623
1961	100,678	30,002	900	7,078	13,856	11,825	20,218	49,050	6,784
1962	101,092	24,425	917	6,720	6,147	12,893	20,044	51,169	7,179
1963	89,694	25,517	887	6,116	3,035	17,010	19,947	52,279	6,688
1964	87,418	35,658	565	5,650	2,165	14,806	21,277	53,292	5,862
1965	89,191	38,580	653	5,898	404	11,169	23,630	54,819	5,580
1966	88,949	39,014	758	6,038	9	9,922	25,175	56,558	4,880
1967	91,797	38,182	76	2,140		6,732	21,507	57,853	4,800
1968	90,580	47,446	3	17		5,282	21,353	59,325	5,183
1969	88,117	53,315	4			4,335	19,571	59,661	5,586
1970	93,203	78,492	3			4,125	20,461	63,988	6,269
1971	95,431	92,782	3			4,136	21,539	65,639	5,840
1972	82,487	111,768	3			3,444	21,407	69,167	5,015
1973	86,696	119,141	2			2,600	22,799	78,995	5,301
1974	85,489	108,431	3			2,792	19,406	74,606	5,811
1975	97,216	27,904	2,485			3,431	20,291	78,114	8,391
1976	73,863	571	16,778			2,910	23,765	84,873	10,835
1977	40,153	4,272	20,787			1,043	23,695	95,414	10,259

Table 3.1 contd.

				Average number of workers employed					
	Mozambique	Malawi	Zimbabwe	Zambia	Tanzania	Angola	Botswana	Lesotho	Swaziland
1978	37,280	20,452	12,829			190	20,024	95,165	9,014
1979	41,914	17,914	8,256			23	19,857	98,563	8,624
1980	41,586	15,863	6,300			5	19,923	100,458	8,566
1981	42,263	14,905	3,262			2	19,633	102,993	9,207
1982	44,583	15,358	125			2	18,199	99,441	9,543
1983	44,487	16,149	1			2	18,620	99,740	10,834
1984	46,462	17,124	2			2	18,734	98,797	11,039
1985	52,631	19,031	2				17,765	101,119	12,760
1986	56,237	17,923					19,106	103,742	14,239
1987	45,917	17,620					17,939	105,506	15,743
1988	44,084	13,090					17,061	100,951	16,171

Note: The italicized numbers represent the number of workers employed in the year of political independence. Source: Chamber of Mines.

of northern labour spread to the Colonial Office and the International Labour Organisation, where Gemmill portrayed the South African mining industry as the champion of free labour against the restrictive practices of the colonial governments (Crush, Jeeves and Yudelman, 1991). Further south, in Swaziland, the postwar period also saw a major upsurge in competition for labour between local and South African employers. Here too the colonial state tried first to help satisfy local needs (Booth, 1986).

During the colonial period, therefore, the supplier states were far from hapless collaborators of the South African mines. The colonial states of the region and local capitalist employers were often unable to match the bargaining power of the mining industry or stem the leakage of labour lured by the promise of higher wages in South Africa. Hungry peasants, then as now, had scant respect for international boundaries and conventions. In response, colonial states throughout the region worked as hard as any post-colonial government has done to control the flow in their own interests. They tried to ensure that as great a proportion as possible of the mine wage went back home, they levied taxes and pass fees, and they sold licences only to approved labour recruiters.

In the 1940s and 1950s, the numbers of migrants from distant regions such as Nyasaland (Malawi), Tanganyika (Tanzania), Northern Rhodesia (Zambia), and northern Mozambique escalated dramatically (Table 3.1). These workers replaced South African migrants who were moving out of mine employment in increasing numbers towards other more remunerative and less hazardous forms of urban employment. Replacement labour from the north consequently allowed the mining industry to resist pressure for wage increases for black miners (James, 1987a). Again in the 1960s, the mines were able to use their far-flung empire to defuse pressure for higher wages at home (Jeeves, 1986). The constant enlargement of the mines' labour empire, and the deployment of recruiters on the outer tier of the subcontinent, gave the South African mining industry no cause to consider alternatives to migrancy. The migrant labour system was consistently expansionist and, like most empires, the system persisted because it could expand (Yudelman and Jeeves, 1986, p. 105).

Unilateral Disengagement

At independence, the new post-colonial governments of the region were forced to assess their role in the South African labour empire. Most had long been suppliers of labour to South Africa but in the post-1945 period, just as the 'winds of change' were gathering pace, their integration into the system intensified. Immediately after independence three states, none of them major suppliers, summarily withdrew their labour. Approximately 14,000 workers were affected by the Tanzanian decision (in 1961) but only 6,000 by the Zambian (in 1966) (Table 3.1). In the Zimbabwean case (in 1981), most of the miners were very recent recruits and the numbers had in any case been falling steadily for some time (James, 1988). In all three cases, there is little evidence

53

of resistance on the part of the workers themselves. The move was politically popular and economically feasible and most repatriated workers probably had the prospect of alternative employment at home. None of the larger suppliers made any effort to disengage. In the case of Malawi and Lesotho, the number of workers in the South African mines grew rapidly after independence (in Malawi's case from 25,000 in 1963 to 120,000 a decade later). Similarly, the post-colonial governments of Botswana and Swaziland showed little inclination to follow the example of Zambia and Tanzania.

There were three instances of unilateral disengagement in the 1970s, one deliberate (Malawi) and two largely inadvertent (Mozambique and Angola). In 1974, an aircraft ferrying Malawian miners back home from South Africa crashed in Francistown, Botswana, killing 74 of them. The Malawian president, Hastings Banda, suspended all mine recruiting in Malawi. A commission of inquiry blamed technical incompetence in Francistown for the crash. Banda denounced the mines and ordered the repatriation of all Malawian miners. The decision sent shock waves through the South African economy. Conventional wisdom held that the major supplying areas needed to send the labour more than the mines needed to receive it (Yudelman and Jeeves, 1986).

During the months that followed, the Chamber of Mines and the South African government sent high-level delegations to Banda (McNamara, 1985, pp. 92–5). He repudiated all offers of conciliation and the number of Malawians recruited for the mines plummeted from 120,000 to less than 1,000 within eighteen months (Table 3.1). The Chamber of Mines used its labour empire, as it had in the past, to secure replacement workers from throughout the subcontinent. Recruitment in Mozambique jumped from 86,000 in 1974 to 115,000 in 1975. Foreign labour from the 'inner crescent' (Botswana, Lesotho and Swaziland) increased from 96,000 recruits in 1973 to 134,000 in 1975. The mines also targeted Angolan and Rhodesian labour. The unexpectedness of the Malawian decision graphically exposed the industry's vulnerability to disengagement. In response, the Chamber of Mines instituted policies to recruit more domestic labour. The most important of these were sizeable wage increases for black miners, made possible by a dramatic surge in the gold price from US$36 an ounce in 1970 to US$159 an ounce in 1974. Thousands of black workers, many from South Africa's massive rural resettlement slums, signed on at the mines (Crush, Jeeves and Yudelman, 1991).

Various theories have been advanced for Banda's actions. The Chamber of Mines tended to focus on his quixotic personality since they could see little political or economic rationality to the move. Subsequent commentators have tended to see the move as entirely rational, relating it to the growing manpower needs of the plantation sector in Malawi. From the late 1960s, the Malawian bourgeoisie, spearheaded by Banda himself and his company, Press Holdings, began to realise the possibilities for substantial accumulation through investment in export crops such as tobacco, tea and sugar (Kydd, 1984; Mhone, 1987). Production of all three crops expanded dramatically so that, by the mid-1970s, 'Malawi was transformed . . . into an economy which had large-scale estate agriculture as its leading component of development' (Christiansen and Kydd, 1983, p. 311). As the estates grew, employment opportunities in Malawi improved, and there was a substantial informal drift of workers back to the country from Rhodesia and South Africa (Boeder, 1974, 1984; Christiansen and Kydd, 1983). Further expansion required a major infusion of cheap labour which was not easy to acquire locally. Most of the new estates were being opened up in the north of the country, and local Tambuka-speakers were extremely reluctant to work there. Why Banda waited as long as he did to recall Malawians working in South Africa has not been explained. The plane crash undoubtedly came at a fortuitous moment, however, since it allowed Banda to launch a fierce public assault on the South African mining industry and portray return to Malawi as an act of patriotism and protest.

While many returning mineworkers did find work on the estates, the sector did not absorb all of them. Some refused to work for rates that were even lower than those in the mines (Christiansen and Kydd, 1983, pp. 324–5.) Others returned clandestinely to South Africa, making their way to Johannesburg or the northern Transvaal where the Chamber of Mines established a reception depot. By the late 1970s, as estate expansion slowed and domestic unemployment grew, Banda had changed his mind. He went back to the Chamber of Mines and asked them to re-employ the Malawians. Now the mines were in a much stronger position. They re-engaged fewer than 20,000 workers and sent most of them to the poorer, lower-grade mines of the Witwatersrand. In an agreement signed in 1977 (and ratified in 1983), the Chamber of Mines did agree to allow the Malawian Department of Labour to recruit and vet all Malawian miners. Banda had successfully tightened his hold on the flow of Malawians to South Africa and raised the financial benefits to his own government. On several subsequent occasions in the 1980s, the Malawian government pushed for an increase in the flow of labour to South Africa.

The other example of unilateral disengagement in the 1970s came after the April 1974 military coup in Portugal which led directly to independence for Angola and Mozambique. In the Angolan case the number of workers in the South African mines had been declining steadily since the early 1960s (Table 3.1). Most of these workers were recruited clandestinely in northern South West Africa (Namibia) by the South West Africa Native Labour Association (SWANLA). When the South African government closed down SWANLA's operations in the area there was no easy way for workers to get to the mines. Between 1967 and 1973 there were protracted negotiations between the South African and Portuguese governments on an agreement to regulate the flow of mine labour from Angola at about 5,000 men each year. In 1974, after the news from Malawi, the South African government and the Chamber of Mines made secretive attempts to rescind the agreement. In the interim, the Chamber established a recruiting office on the Angolan border to recruit Angolans who could pass themselves off as Namibians. The numbers were small (fewer than 3,000 in 1975) and dwindled rapidly with the advent of the civil war in Angola.

In Mozambique, the reduction in migration to South Africa in the mid-1970s was far more significant. In late 1974, the Portuguese handed over power to the liberation movement, FRELIMO. In the first year of FRELIMO rule, the mines were flooded with Mozambicans eager to replace the departing

Malawians. In early 1976, however, the South African Chamber of Mines became convinced that a politically motivated withdrawal of Mozambican mineworkers was imminent. It responded with a contingency plan to replace departing Mozambicans. The Chamber believed that if FRELIMO ordered its workers home, the mines could count on 30,000 workers disobeying the order. The shortfall could be made up from a variety of foreign and domestic sources.

The Chamber's plan suggested that as a matter of policy the mines should develop a longer-term strategy to reduce the industry's heavy dependence on Mozambican workers (Crush, Jeeves and Yudelman, 1991). The decision about implementation was taken out of the hands of the Chamber by events in Mozambique. It is now generally agreed that FRELIMO never seriously countenanced a policy of disengagement from the migrant labour system. However, in 1976, the number of Mozambicans in the mines did fall dramatically. Scholars have disagreed on who was responsible, some laying the blame at the door of FRELIMO (First, 1983), others castigating the Chamber of Mines (Callaghy, 1983b; Isaacman, 1987).

In a sense, both are correct; if FRELIMO had not inadvertently reduced the flow, the Chamber of Mines would probably have done it for them. In 1976, FRELIMO set up new administrative procedures for controlling the flow of labour to South Africa. For several months Mozambican output was negligible. It later picked up again but numbers had fallen from 114,000 in January 1976 to 48,000 by the end of the year, as Mozambican miners were unable to get the papers to return to the mines. A flood of applicants from across the subcontinent quickly replaced the Mozambicans. The Chamber of Mines got the reduction it wanted but without the political fallout. Since the late 1970s, the number of Mozambicans working in the mines has remained relatively constant.

Unilateral disengagement from the mines' labour empire by Malawi, Mozambique and Angola threw the South African mining industry into a short-term crisis (Yudelman and Jeeves, 1986). In some mines production dropped sharply, there were temporary labour shortages and a dramatic increase in labour turnover with many new recruits absconding as soon as they could. By the late 1970s, the labour crisis was resolved. Since then the mines have had little trouble finding enough labour. These supply-side withdrawals were not, however, political decisions made in the heady days of independence. The Malawian action was specifically related to labour demands at home and within three years the government had effectively reversed its decision. The Mozambican and Angolan withdrawals were unplanned and inadvertent. In Mozambique, as in Malawi, the government has tried ever since to get the South African mines to take more workers (Centro des Estudos Africanos, 1987a). A decade after independence, the other foreign suppliers (Botswana, Lesotho and Swaziland) had made no moves at all to reduce the flow of labour to South Africa.

Into this basically unfavourable climate, the United Nations (UN) and ILO – as part of a broader political strategy to increase international pressure on South Africa – introduced the idea of a planned, co-ordinated regional strategy of disengagement from the migrant labour system. Soon afterwards, the Southern African Labour Commission came into existence in an effort to impose labour 'sanctions' on South Africa (de Vletter, 1985b).

Labour Sanctions and the Southern African Labour Commission

In 1978, the UN Economic Commission for Africa (ECA, 1978) and the ILO sponsored a conference on migratory labour in Lusaka, Zambia. Representatives of twelve states attended and listened to a series of academic papers by exiled South African scholars highly critical of the migrant labour system (Marks and Unterhalter, 1978; Innes and Malaba, 1978; Legassick and de Clerq, 1978; Beinart, 1978; Davies, 1978; Hemson and Morris, 1978). The conference reached two important decisions. First, the delegates adopted a charter of rights for migrant workers, aimed at improving the position of foreign workers in South Africa. Second, they passed a resolution committing themselves to a concerted, collective effort to withdraw from the migrant labour system and abolish the supply of labour to South Africa. Abolition was viewed not only as a desirable goal in itself but, in the words of the Angolan Minister of Labour, as a way of overcoming 'one of the heaviest burdens inherited from the colonial period' and of 'liquidating' apartheid (ECA, 1978).

In support of the conference resolutions, the participating states agreed to establish a 'labour committee' known as the Southern African Labour Commission (SALC). SALC had four goals: (a) to find ways and means of eliminating the migratory labour system, (b) to ensure that all migrant workers were withdrawn from South Africa, (c) to co-ordinate policies aimed at eliminating the migratory labour system, and (d) to implement the Charter of Rights for migrant workers adopted by the conference. In pursuit of the first three goals, the ILO drew up plans for a suppliers' cartel, to be called the Association of Home Countries of Migrants (AHCM), which would commit itself to a phased withdrawal of mine labour from South Africa (Stahl and Bohning, 1981). The proposal caused sufficient concern in South Africa to attract a detailed rebuttal by the Chamber of Mines (Parsons and Mashaba, 1980).

SALC primarily comprised representatives from Departments of Labour of the front-line states who met annually. Unlike SADCC, SALC had no secretariat and no permanent bureaucracy. Indeed, its profile was so low that most studies of interstate relations in southern Africa do not even mention it. At its annual meetings, SALC engaged in ritual denunciations of migrancy but made little concrete progress towards a common policy. A critical review of SALC by the ILO in 1985 noted that the organisation had failed to deliver on its commitments to orchestrate the withdrawal of workers from South Africa and improve the welfare of foreign workers in South Africa (de Vletter, 1985a, pp. 1–2, 14–15). The report pointed out that none of the SALC countries were pursuing a policy of disengagement. In his speech to SALC in 1984,

Rui Baltazar, Minister of Finance in Mozambique, denounced the migrant labour system and argued that 'effective ways and means have to be found to enable us to break out of the dependency of the system of migrant labour' (SALC, 1984). He made no reference to simultaneous high-level attempts by his own government to get the South African mining industry to triple the number of Mozambican miners to 120,000. Government representatives from the other front-line states would have known of their own attempts to strike unilateral deals with the South Africans to the same end (James, 1987b).

The inability, and unwillingness, of these states to mount a systematic and co-ordinated withdrawal campaign was a major reason for the shelving of the AMHC plan and the ineffectiveness of SALC in achieving any of its objectives. One somewhat cynical explanation is that these governments 'love power more than they detest apartheid' (Adam and Moodley, 1987, p. 176). In fact, disengagement may well have been a desirable political goal, but the argument lost much of its force in the early 1980s. By then it had become apparent to most observers that foreign labour was no longer a necessity for the South African mines and could be replaced with domestic labour (de Vletter, 1985a; Cobbe, 1986; Crush, 1987a). Labour sanctions were consequently an extremely blunt instrument for effecting change in South Africa. Even then, there were certainly no compelling domestic reasons why labour sanctions against South Africa were desirable. By the mid-1980s, even the ILO appeared to have dropped the idea of co-ordinated disengagement (of which it was the primary architect in the 1970s). A 1985 report placed greater emphasis on co-ordinated action to improve the welfare and working conditions of foreign workers in South Africa and ensuring that the supplier states did not bargain unilaterally on maintaining or increasing labour complements (de Vletter, 1985c).

As in the colonial period, most of the supplier states depend to a greater or lesser extent on migrant remittances for revenue. For some of them, such as Lesotho and Mozambique, summary withdrawal would aggravate an already severe fiscal crisis. The cash flow from South Africa through compulsory deferment and voluntary remittances rose dramatically in the early 1980s (Table 3.2). The supplier states have become more, not less, dependent on this

Table 3.2 *Mine Deferred Pay and Remittances to Frontline States, 1975–84*

| | Amount (R million) | | | | | | | | | |
	1975	1976	1977	1978	1979	1980	1981	1982	1983	1984
Lesotho	16.8	20.4	20.2	31.0	31.4	34.9	52.0	106.6	154.2	182.3
Botswana	5.9	9.6	8.2	13.1	10.8	13.6	17.1	21.0	22.1	22.5
Swaziland	3.1	4.4	5.2	6.8	6.2	7.8	9.6	10.6	12.2	11.3
Malawi	22.4	2.1	1.0	10.6	9.2	13.5	14.9	17.3	21.9	24.3
Mozambique	33.1	40.3	25.9	28.7	29.3	32.9	52.8	50.7	69.7	69.1
Zimbabwe	0.0	0.6	8.5	9.5	6.5	6.3	5.9	2.5	0.0	0.0
Total	81.3	77.4	69.0	99.7	93.4	109.0	152.3	208.7	280.2	309.5

Source: Chamber of Mines.

source of revenue. The increased cash flow coincided with a decline in alternative revenues for many, as commodity prices slumped on world markets. In Mozambique, the economic havoc wrought by the civil war and South African destabilisation made it imperative for FRELIMO that the miners continued to go to South Africa, though it would be incorrect to see this as a primary motive for destabilisation (Saul, 1987).

Like that of their colonial predecessors, the main aim of the post-colonial supplier states has been to ensure that a significant proportion of the migrant wage comes home. Strict compulsory deferred pay schemes have been instituted by most of the suppliers (60 per cent of the wage in the case of Mozambique, Malawi and Lesotho). These policies are usually justified by an emphasis on the need to maximise the local benefits of a labour repressive system. However, most were instituted without consultation and are extremely unpopular with the miners themselves. In the 1970s, for example, the introduction of a compulsory deferred pay scheme for Basotho miners led to major mine riots, several deaths and the dismissal of more than 15,000 workers (McNamara, 1988). Nevertheless, the benefits to the local state and merchants are such that the policies remain in place.

The dependence of states is mirrored in the homesteads which supply the labour. Tens of thousands of rural families throughout the region depend on mine income for survival. To order the return of migrant workers, without providing alternative sources of income, would be politically dangerous. None of the supplier states have been particularly anxious to confront their own working class in this way. Disengagement would require, at the very least, the provision of new employment opportunities at home. With rising domestic unemployment, these enabling conditions simply do not exist.

The major difference between the situation in the colonial and post-colonial periods is the growth of a sizeable regional labour surplus in recent years. In the colonial period, attempts to stop or stem the flow of migrants to South Africa were motivated by the calls of local capitalist employers for labour. Since independence, high population growth rates, low rates of job creation and an agrarian crisis in the countryside have conspired to create an abundant supply of labour (de Vletter 1982; Wilson and Ramphele, 1989). With the partial exception of Malawi's move in the early 1970s, local demands to bring back labour from South Africa have been non-existent. Most states are privately far more concerned about keeping the labour flowing and dissuading their subjects from action which might jeopardise their chances of continued employment. The more relevant concern is whether South Africa intends to dismantle what remains of its colonial labour empire.

State, Capital and Foreign Labour

The literature on the role of foreign labour in the South African goldmining industry has been heavily influenced by the notion that the South Africans have been engaged (since the early 1970s) in a systematic and relentless withdrawal from the supplier states (Clarke, 1977, 1978; Stahl, 1981; Taylor, 1982; Setai, 1986). According to this argument – dubbed 'the internalisation thesis' – foreign labour is no longer needed to sustain mining operations and the supplier states should therefore resign themselves to the inevitable and rapid loss of employment opportunities in South Africa. This thesis rests on several questionable assumptions. First, it assumes that there are no longer any good reasons why South African employers might still want to employ foreign workers. Second, it assumes a congruence of interest among the various mining companies and between the mining industry as a whole and the South African state. Finally, it assumes that the pressures for dismantling all emanate from the South African side and that the supplier states are uniformly threatened by South African withdrawal.

Statistical data for the 1980s provide little evidence that the South African mining industry has been pursuing a systematic policy of withdrawal from the ex-colonies of the region (Crush, 1987a). With minor fluctuations, the number and proportion of foreign workers has remained virtually constant for most of the decade. This situation has persisted despite the existence of massive domestic unemployment and the large number of South African and foreign workers seeking work in the mines (Thabane and Guy, 1984; Taylor, 1986; Crush, 1987b; Centro de Estudos Africanos, 1987a). This chapter has argued that between 1920 and 1970, because of domestic labour shortages and uncompetitiveness, the South African mining industry could not have survived without the spatial expansion of its colonial labour empire. After 1970, however, what was necessary became discretionary. With abundant domestic labour, foreign labour was no longer needed as it once had been, but the mining industry still had reasons for employing it.

First, the Chamber of Mines took two lessons from the events of the 1970s: cultivate multiple sources and avoid undue reliance on any one source (Yudelman and Jeeves, 1986). The General Manager of the Chamber's recruiting organisation noted that the mining industry's objective was to 'encourage interdependence between the countries of southern Africa [while] reverting as much as possible to the situation 40 years ago when nearly sixty per cent of mine labour was South African'. There is no evidence at all that the Chamber of Mines has ever wanted to displace all foreign labour (as some have claimed) or mount a systematic withdrawal from the supplier states. Diversified sourcing was the guiding principle for the 1980s. Under this principle, no foreign supplier could expect a major increase in orders but, equally, their existing position was protected.

Officially, the mining industry remains wedded to foreign labour. In practice, the degree of commitment varies across the mining industry. All mines employ some foreign labour, but the proportion varies from as low as 24 per cent to a high of 75 per cent. Only two of the six mining houses adhere at all closely to the Chamber's guideline of 40 per cent foreign labour. Individual mines have considerable autonomy on decisions about labour composition. To determine the precise mix of factors operating on every mine is beyond the scope of this chapter. It is clear, however, that foreigners are disproportionately concentrated in many of the industry's oldest and most dangerous mines.

Second, it is sometimes asserted that the South African state wishes to see

Table 3.3 **Skill Levels in Anglo-American Mines, 1985**

Job grade	Foreign labour		South African labour	
	Number	%	Number	%
1	4,741	28.1	12,139	71.9
2	9,757	29.0	23,905	71.0
3	12,852	35.8	23,006	64.2
4	25,556	46.8	29,004	53.2
5	2,534	53.5	2,203	46.5
6	2,041	50.4	2,006	49.6
7	2,898	65.7	1,510	34.3
8	4,354	70.7	1,804	29.3
9	2,734	27.7	7,123	72.3

Note: Job grade 1 = unskilled, job grade 9 = most skilled. Workers in job grade 9 are mostly clerical and other skilled surface workers. Job grade 8 is the highest level of skilled production worker. Source: de Vletter (1985a, p. 206).

the end of foreign migrancy to the mines. This, too, is disputable. The South African mining industry exists in a symbiotic relationship with the South African state (Yudelman, 1987). The South African state is far from being an instrument of mining capital, but it is dependent on mining revenues and is therefore responsive to the industry's claims about its own welfare. The state bureaucracy has itself consistently divided on the foreign-labour question (Yudelman and Jeeves, 1986). The section of the bureaucracy dealing with black labour and domestic unemployment has consistently opposed the continued use of foreign labour. The foreign-affairs bureaucracy, conscious of the value of political leverage in a regional context, has tended to support the mining industry's arguments for continued use of foreign workers. Bureaucratic cleavages have provided the mining industry with the space to continue with its long-standing independent policy on labour matters. In 1986, when P.W. Botha in a fit of pique ordered the expulsion of all Mozambican workers, the mining industry marshalled its considerable resources to contest and eventually defeat the plan (Leger, 1987; Centro de Estudos Africanos, 1987b).

Third, as de Vletter (1985a) has pointed out, foreign workers are currently amongst the most skilled and experienced in the mine labour force (Table 3.3). There is little doubt that South African replacements could be found for these workers, but the mining industry has no real incentive to displace them and engage in relatively costly training and retraining procedures. In a more recent analysis, the ILO has argued that this is an unstable equilibrium (de Vletter, 1987). The ILO predicts an imminent and rapid decline in the number of foreign workers as a result of a process of attrition. The prediction is based upon Anglo-American employment data which show a heavy concentration of workers with between five and ten years of service (64 per cent) and very few with more than ten years of service (under 2 per cent) (Table 3.4). The ILO infers that foreign workers will leave the mines in droves as they reach ten

Table 3.4 **Work Experience of Foreign Miners in Anglo-American Mines, 1986**

| Length of service | Number of workers with experience | | | |
| | In Anglo mines | | In industry | |
	Number	%	Number	%
< 1 year	4,271	5.9	11,768	16.0
1–2 years	7,751	10.7	4,408	6.0
2–5 years	12,905	17.7	7,578	10.3
5–10 years	46,563	64.0	24,371	33.2
10–15 years	956	1.3	16,165	22.0
> 15 years	315	0.4	9,165	12.5
Total	72,761	100.0	73,455	100.0

Note: Anglo Mines figures are for June 1986, Industry figures are for October 1986.
Source: Anglo-American.

years of service. Within five years, they estimate, the foreign component of the workforce could fall from 40 to 19 per cent.

The analysis has two main problems. First, it assumes that foreign workers with between five and ten years of service will exhibit the same behaviour in the future as they have in the past. It is actually more likely that they will not, and that the next five years will see a dramatic increase in the number of workers with more than ten years of service. In today's crowded labour market, where alternative job opportunities are non-existent, workers may well choose to stay on for as long as they can. Second, the ILO assumes that their figures are representative of the mine workforce as a whole. In fact, the data refer purely to the length of service of Anglo-American employees in Anglo-American mines. Many of these workers have work experience in mines not in the Anglo group. If total work experience is considered, a very different profile emerges from the same sample. Thus, 33 per cent of foreign workers have between five and ten years of industry experience and 35 per cent already have more than ten years of service (Table 3.4). These data show no dramatic fall-off after ten years of service and tend to reinforce the notion that, all other things being equal, the rate of attrition of foreign labour will be much slower than that predicted by the ILO.

A fourth reason for the continued attachment of the South African mines to foreign labour is of mixed comfort to the supplier states. Since the late 1970s, the mines have shown a distinct preference for a type of 'commuter migrancy' (Crush, 1987b). Migrants from sources close to the mines are now free to return home for weekend leave and frequently do so. In Lesotho, for example, miners on the neighbouring Orange Free State fields are now known as 'weekenders'. Lesotho, and to a lesser extent Botswana and Swaziland, are clear beneficiaries of the move to commuter migrancy. Migrants from more distant sources are clearly less desirable in this respect.

Since 1986, and the abolition of the pass laws and influx control in South Africa, the mining companies have unveiled ambitious plans to settle black labour in family accommodation on or near the mines (James, 1988; Crush, 1989a). Foreign workers are to be excluded from this process. This does not mean that they will be declared redundant. The evidence to hand suggests that stabilisation is likely to be an extremely slow process, and that foreign migrants are assured of employment well beyond the 1990s.

Finally, according to South African mine management, workers from certain foreign suppliers are supposed to be 'uninterested' in union activity. Given the growth of mine militancy in the 1980s, and the emergence of the powerful National Union of Mineworkers, this is clearly a factor of importance (Leger, 1986, 1988; Crush, 1989b). With labour in abundance, workers started to behave as if ethnicity did in fact determine distaste for the union, once this idea was put forward. In addition, the governments of most of the supplier states have all pressured their workers to conform to the stereotype. As a reward, since the 1987 strike the mines hardest hit by mass dismissals have replaced hundreds of South African workers with Mozambicans judged more 'loyal' to management (James, 1990).

Conclusion

For a hundred years, migratory labour to the South African mines has served the economic and social interests of considerably more than South African capital. This is not to deny that the impact of migrancy on rural society was universally destructive or to downplay the exploitative and coercive practices which ensured that the labour remained cheap. It is simply to reassert that there were classes and political institutions on both sides of the South African boundary which saw benefits in perpetuating migrancy and attempting to maximise the benefits to themselves. In this respect there is a much greater degree of continuity between the colonial and post-colonial states of southern Africa than many observers would care to admit.

Attempts to control, manipulate and even stem the flow of labour to South Africa are by no means a post-colonial phenomenon. Colonial states throughout the region are often portrayed as the willing agents of the South African mining industry. The reality was far more complex. These states had their own interests and class constituencies and these did not always lie in encouraging unbridled labour migration to South Africa. There were local employers to appease and labour shortages to satisfy. Some colonial states, such as Portuguese-controlled Mozambique, set limits on the volume of labour migration. Others, such as Rhodesia, consistently tried to stop workers going to South Africa at all. Always there were individual migrants willing to avoid these restrictions and exercise choice about their place of employment.

Despite the rhetoric, post-colonial policy towards migrant labour to South Africa has not been marked by any particular desire for disengagement. Only three foreign suppliers completely withdrew their workers at independence (Tanzania, Zambia and Zimbabwe). In each case the numbers were small, the decision was politically feasible, and the economic consequences were minimal. The other examples of unilateral disengagement were more complex. In the case of the two ex-Portuguese suppliers (Mozambique and Angola) disengagement was inadvertent and partial. Malawi's withdrawal between 1974 and 1977 was a clear act of disengagement but it had nothing directly to do with the country's political independence a decade before. Banda's actions were a response to the labour needs of the Malawian plantation sector in the 1970s. In this respect he behaved completely consistently with earlier colonial policies, throughout the region, to deploy migrant labour locally. Like them, he found he could not live without the mines.

Since the mid-1970s, none of the major post-colonial supplier states has shown any inclination to withdraw their labour from South Africa's mines. All have tried to bargain unilaterally with the South Africans to maintain or increase the existing flow of labour. In this context, the failure of these states to mount a co-ordinated strategy of disengagement through SALC is hardly surprising. It also explains why SADCC is reluctant to consider an issue which would require clear sacrifice and be politically unpopular with migrant workers. The argument for co-ordinated disengagement as a form of labour sanctions against South Africa has always had more appeal in the corridors of the UN and the ILO than it has in the region itself.

Even a co-ordinated bargaining strategy to improve the welfare and working conditions of their workers in South Africa seems to have been beyond the capacity of the supplier states (de Vletter, 1985b). Unilateral policy initiatives have been aimed more at ensuring that the state increases its control over the migrant labourers, thereby raising the benefits to itself. In this, too, there are notable continuities with colonial state policy. The colonial state was never noted for its deference to the wishes of the working class. Similarly, in this area at least, few of the post-colonial states of the region have shown that they put worker interests above those of local capital accumulation.

The persistence of South Africa's colonial labour empire is now in a real sense completely discretionary. Probably for the first time, profitable gold mining could continue without any labour from outside the country. As this chapter has argued, however, the South African mining industry has not itself disengaged from a single ex-colonial supplier, though it has sought since 1974 not to be over-dependent on any one supplier. What is left of the colonial labour empire has remained very useful to mining capital for the last decade.

One recent and unforeseen development, however, which could fundamentally affect the future of foreign migrancy to South Africa is the spread of AIDS. In 1986, the Chamber of Mines introduced HIV screening and discovered significant rates of infection among Malawian miners. The Chamber put pressure on Malawi to have workers tested before leaving for South Africa. Banda refused and the Chamber responded with threats not to re-employ returning migrants. AIDS could either be used as a pretext to withdraw from Malawi or it could become important enough in its own right to force the mines to abandon what remains of the northern labour empire (Jochelson, Mothibeli and Leger, 1988). Here too there is a colonial precedent. The ban on tropical labour between 1913 and 1932 was a response to pneumonia which decimated the mine workforce in the first decade of the century (Jeeves, 1985). Subsequently, medical advances neutralised the pneumonia threat and the ban was rescinded. The Chamber of Mines is unlikely to lobby as intensely for Malawian labour in the 1990s as it did in the 1930s, but a medical breakthrough on AIDS prevention would certainly make the mines more likely to hold on to what remains of their northern labour empire.

Acknowledgements

This chapter is based upon arguments developed at greater length in Crush, Jeeves and Yudelman (1991). I would like to thank the SSHRC of Canada for their research support. Various co-workers in this field deserve special thanks for their assistance. They include Wilmot James, Alan Jeeves, Jean Leger and Fion de Vletter.

References

Adam, H., and Moodley, K. (1987) 'Interstate relations under South African dominance', in W. James (ed.) *The State of Apartheid*, Boulder, Colo.: Lynne Rienner, pp. 173–96.

Amin, S., Chitala, D., and Mandaza, I. (eds) (1987) *SADCC Prospects for Disengagement and Development in Southern Africa*, London: Zed.

Anglin, D. (1985) 'SADCC after Nkomati', *African Affairs*, 84, pp. 163–82.

Anglin, D. (1988) 'Southern Africa under siege: options for the frontline states', *Journal of Modern African Studies*, 26, pp. 549–66.

Beinart, W. (1978) 'South Africa's internal labour supply with special reference to Transkei and Bophuthatswana', paper presented at the Conference on Migratory Labour in Southern Africa, Lusaka, Zambia.

Beinart, W. (1982) *The Political Economy of Pondoland*, Cambridge: Cambridge University Press.

Boeder, R. (1974) 'Malawians abroad: the history of labour emigration from Malawi to its neighbours', unpublished Ph.D. thesis, Michigan State University.

Boeder, R. (1984) 'Malawian labour migration and international relations in Southern Africa', *Africa Insight*, 14, pp. 17–25.

Booth, A. (1986) 'Capitalism and the competition for Swazi labour 1945–60', *Journal of Southern African Studies*, 13, pp. 125–50.

Brittain, V. (1988) *Hidden Lives, Hidden Deaths: South Africa's Crippling of a Continent*, London: Faber & Faber.

Butts, K., and Thomas, P. (1986) *The Geopolitics of Southern Africa: South Africa as Regional Superpower*. Boulder, Colo.: Westview.

Callaghy, T. (ed.) (1983a) *South Africa in Southern Africa*, New York: Praeger.

Callaghy, T. (1983b) 'Apartheid and socialism: South Africa's relations with Angola and Mozambique', in T. Callaghy (ed.) *South Africa in Southern Africa*, New York: Praeger, pp. 267–302.

Centro de Estudos Africanos (1987a) *The South African Mining Industry and Mozambican Migrant Labour in the 1980s: An Analysis of Recent Trends in Employment Policy*, International Migration for Employment Working Paper No. 29, Geneva: International Labour Office.

Centro de Estudos Africanos (1987b) *Mozambican Migrant Workers in South Africa: The Impact of the Expulsion Order*, International Migration for Employment Working Paper No. 37, Geneva: International Labour Office.

Chanock, M. (1977) *Unconsummated Union: Britain, Rhodesia and South Africa, 1900–45*, Manchester: Manchester University Press.

Christiansen, R., and Kydd, J. (1983) 'The return of Malawian labour from South Africa and Zimbabwe', *Journal of Modern African Studies*, 21, pp. 311–26.

Clarke, D. (1977) *Foreign Labour and the Internalization of Labour Reserves in South Africa, 1970–77*, Geneva: International Labour Office.

Clarke, D. (1978) 'Foreign labour inflows to South Africa and unemployment in South Africa', in C. Simkins and D. Clarke (eds) *Structural Unemployment in South Africa*, Pietermaritzburg: University of Natal Press, pp. 51–82.

Cobbe, J. (1986) 'Consequences for Lesotho of changing South African labour demand', *African Affairs*, 85, pp. 23–48.

Conquest, R. (1978) *Kolyma: The Arctic Death Camps*, New York: Viking.

Cooper, F. (1981) 'Africa and the world economy', *African Studies Review*, 24, pp. 1–86.

Cooper, F, (1983) 'Urban space, industrial time, and wage labor in Africa', in F. Cooper (ed.) *Struggle for the City: Migrant Labour, Capital and the State in Urban Africa*, Beverly Hills: Sage, pp. 7–50.

Crush, J. (1984) 'Uneven labour migration in Southern Africa: conceptions and misconceptions', *South African Geographical Journal*, 66, pp. 115–32.

Crush, J. (1987a) 'The extrusion of foreign labour from the South African gold mining industry', *Geoforum*, 17, pp. 161–72.

Crush, J. (1987b) 'Restructuring migrant labour on the gold mines', in G. Moss and I. Obery (eds) *South African Review: 4*, Johannesburg: Ravan, pp. 283–91.

Crush, J. (1988) *The Struggle for Swazi Labour, 1890–1920*, Montreal and Kingston: McGill-Queen's Press.

Crush, J. (1989a) 'Accommodating black miners: home-ownership on the mines', in G. Moss and I. Obery (eds) *South African Review: 5*, Johannesburg: Ravan, pp. 335–47.

Crush, J. (1989b) 'Migrancy and militance: the case of the National Union of Mineworkers of South Africa', *African Affairs*, 88, pp. 15–23.

Crush, J., Jeeves, A., and Yudelman, D. (1991) *South Africa's Labor Empire*, Boulder, Colo.: Westview.

Daniel, J. (1984) 'A comparative analysis of Lesotho and Swaziland's relations with South Africa', in Southern African Research Service (ed.) *South African Review: 2*, Johannesburg: Ravan, pp. 228–38.

Davies, R. (1978) 'Demand trends for foreign workers and employer strategy in South Africa', paper presented at the Conference on Migratory Labour in Southern Africa, Lusaka, Zambia.

Davies, R., and O'Meara, D. (1984) 'The state of analysis of the Southern African region: issues raised by total strategy', *Review of African Political Economy*, 29, pp. 64–76.

de Vletter, F. (1982) *Labour Migration and Agricultural Development in Southern Africa*, Rome: FAO.

de Vletter, F. (1985a) 'Recent trends and prospects of black migration to South Africa', *Journal of Modern African Studies*, 23, pp. 667–702.

de Vletter, F. (1985b) *The Rights and Welfare of Migrant Workers: Scope and Limits of Joint Action by Southern African Migrant-sending Countries*, International Migration for Employment Working Paper No. 23, Geneva: International Labour Office.

de Vletter, F. (1985c) *Issues Affecting the Welfare of Foreign Migrant Workers on the South African Gold Mines*. Unpublished report, International Labour Office, Geneva.

de Vletter, F. (1987) 'Foreign labour on the South African gold mines: new insights on an old problem', *International Labour Review*, 126, pp. 199–218.

ECA (1978) United Nations Economic and Social Council, Executive Committee Meeting, *Report of the Conference on Migratory Labour in Southern Africa, 4–8 April 1978*, Lusaka: ECA.

First, R. (1983) *Black Gold: The Mozambican Miner, Proletarian and Peasant*, New York: St Martin's Press.

Hanlon, J. (1986) *Beggar Your Neighbours: Apartheid Power in Southern Africa*, London: James Currey.

Hanlon, J. (1989) *SADCC in the 1990s: Development on the Front Line*, London: Economist Intelligence Unit.

Harries, P. (1983) 'Labour migration from Mozambique to South Africa', unpublished Ph.D. thesis, University of London.

Hemson, D., and Morris, J. (1978) 'Black working class residence on South African mines', paper presented at the Conference on Migratory Labour in Southern Africa, Lusaka.

Innes, D., and Malaba L. (1978) 'The South African state and its policy towards supplier economies', paper presented at the Conference on Migratory Labour in Southern Africa, Lusaka.

IPA (International Peace Academy) (1988) *Southern Africa in Crisis: Regional and International Responses.* London: Martinus Nijhoff.

Isaacman, A. (1987) 'Mozambique and the regional conflict in Southern Africa', *Current History*, 86, pp. 213–16.

James, W. (1987a) 'Grounds for a strike: South African gold mining in the 1940s', *African Economic History*, 16, pp. 1–22.

James, W. (1987b) 'The politics and economics of internalisation', paper presented at annual meetings of Association for Sociology in Bellville, Southern Africa, 1987.

James, W. (1988) 'Urban labour in the gold industry', *South African Journal of Industrial Relations*, 8, 31–52.

James, W. (1990) 'The group with the flag: class conflict, mine conflict and the reproduction of a labour force', in A. Zegeye *et al.* (eds) *Repression and Resistance: Insider Accounts of Apartheid*, London: Hans Zell.

Jeeves, A. (1985) *Migrant Labour in South Africa's Mining Economy: The Struggle for the Gold Mines' Labour Supply*, Montreal and Kingston: McGill-Queen's Press.

Jeeves, A. (1986) 'Migrant labour and South African expansion, 1920–1950', *South African Historical Journal*, 18, pp. 73–92.

Jochelson, K., Mothibeli M., and Leger, J. (1988) 'HIV and migrant labour in South Africa', unpublished report, University of Witwatersrand, Johannesburg.

Johnstone, F. (1976) *Class, Race and Gold: A Study of Class Relations and Racial Discrimination in South Africa*, London: Routledge & Kegan Paul.

Johnstone, F. (1989) 'Rand and Kolyma: Afro-Siberian hamlet', *South African Sociological Review*, 1, pp. 1–45.

Kydd, J. (1984) 'Malawi in the 1970s: development policies and economic change', in *Malawi: An Alternative Pattern of Development*, Centre of African Studies, Edinburgh: University of Edinburgh, pp. 303–9.

Lacey, M. (1981) *Working for Boroko: The Origins of a Coercive Labour System in South Africa*, Johannesburg: Ravan Press.

Legassick, M., and de Clerq, F. (1978) 'The origins and nature of the migrant labour system in South Africa', paper presented at the Conference on Migratory Labour in Southern Africa, Lusaka.

Leger, J. (1986) 'Safety and the organisation of work in South African gold mines: a crisis of control', *International Labour Review*, 125, pp. 591–603.

Leger, J. (1987) 'The Mozambican miners' reprieve', *South African Labour Bulletin*, 12, pp. 29–32.

Leger, J. (1988) 'From fatalism to mass action: the South African National Union of Mineworkers' struggle for safety and health', *Labour, Capital and Society*, 21, pp. 270–93.

Levy, N. (1982) *The Foundations of the South African Cheap Labour System*, London: Routledge & Kegan Paul.

Leys, R., and Tostenson, A. (1982) 'Regional co-operation in Southern Africa: the Southern African Development Co-ordination Conference (SADCC)', *Review of African Political Economy*, 23, pp. 52–71.

Libby, R. (1987) *The Politics of Economic Power in Southern Africa*, Princeton, NJ: Princeton University Press.

Lovell, G, (1988) 'Surviving conquest', *Latin American Research Review*, 23, pp. 25–57.

Marks, S., and Rathbone, R. (eds) (1982) *Industrialisation and Social Change in South Africa: African Class Formation, Culture and Consciousness 1870–1930*. London: Longman.

Marks, S., and Unterhalter, E. (1978) 'Women and the migrant labour system in Southern Africa', paper presented at the Conference on Migratory Labour in Southern Africa, Lusaka.

McNamara, K. (1985) 'Black worker conflicts on South African gold mines: 1973–1982', unpublished Ph.D. thesis, University of Witwatersrand, Johannesburg.

McNamara, K. (1988) 'Inter-group violence among black employees on South African gold mines, 1974–1986', *South African Sociological Journal*, 1, pp. 23–38.

Mhone, G. (1987) 'Agriculture and food policy in Malawi: a review', in T. Mkandawire and N. Bourenane (eds) *The State and Agriculture in Africa*, London: CODESERIA, pp. 59–86.

Nsekela, A. (ed.) (1981) *Southern Africa: Toward Economic Liberation*, London: Rex Collings.

Parsons, J., and Mashaba, W. (1980) 'The recruitment of black workers for the South African gold mines in the 1970s', unpublished report, Human Resources Laboratory, Johannesburg.

SALC (1984) *Report of the Sixth Meeting of the Southern African Labour Commission, 18–19 October,* Maputo: SALC.

Saul, J., and Gelb S. (1986) *The Crisis in South Africa.* New York: Monthly Review Press.

Saul, J. (1987) 'Mozambique destabilization and counter-revolutionary guerilla warfare', *Studies in Political Economy,* 23, pp. 5–40.

Seidman, A. (1987) *The Roots of Crisis in Southern Africa,* Trenton: Africa World Press.

Setai, B. (1986) 'Implications of sanctions against South Africa on SADCC: focus on migrant labour', paper presented to SADCC Secretariat, Lesotho.

Stahl, C. (1981) 'Migrant labour supplies, past, present and future', in W. Bohning (ed.) *Black Migration to South Africa,* Geneva: International Labour Office, pp. 7–44.

Stahl, C., and Bohning, W. (1981) 'Reducing dependence on migration in Southern Africa', in W. Bohning (ed.) *Black Migration to South Africa,* Geneva: International Labour Office, pp. 147–78.

Taylor, J. (1982) 'Changing patterns of labour supply to the South African gold mines', *Tijdschrift voor Economische en Sociale Geografie,* 73, pp. 213–20.

Taylor, J. (1986) 'Some consequences of recent reductions in mine labour recruitment in Botswana', *Geography,* 71, pp. 34–46.

Thabane, M., and Guy, J. (1984) 'Unemployment and casual labour in Maseru', paper presented at the Second Carnegie Inquiry into Poverty and Development in Southern Africa, University of Cape Town.

Thompson, C. (1985) *Challenge to Imperialism: The Frontline States in the Liberation of Zimbabwe,* Harare: Zimbabwe Publishing House.

Tostenson, A. (1982) *Dependence and Collective Self-Reliance in Southern Africa: The Case of the Southern African Development Coordination Conference.* Uppsala: Scandinavian Institute of African Studies.

Weisfelder, R. (1989) 'SADCC as a counter-dependency strategy: how much collective clout?', in E. Keller and L. Picard (eds) *South Africa in Southern Africa,* Boulder, Colo.: Lynne Rienner, pp. 155–78.

Wilson, F., and Ramphele, M. (eds) (1989) *Uprooting Poverty: The South African Challenge,* Cape Town: David Philip.

Wolf, E. (1982) *Europe and the People Without History,* Berkeley: University of California Press.

Wolpe, H. (1972) 'Capitalism and cheap labour power in South Africa: from segregation to apartheid', *Economy and Society,* 1, pp. 425–56.

Yudelman, D. (1987) 'State and capital in contemporary South Africa', in J. Butler, R. Elphick and D. Welsh (eds) *Democratic Liberalism in South Africa*, Middletown: Wesleyan University Press, pp. 250–70.

Yudelman, D., and Jeeves, A. (1986) 'New labour frontiers for old: black migrants to the South African gold mines, 1920–85, *Journal of Southern African Studies*, 13, pp. 101–24.

CHAPTER 4

Environmental Degradation, Soil Conservation and the Colonial and Post-Colonial State in Rhodesia/Zimbabwe

Jenny Elliott

Direct experience of environmental decline and its social and political–economic ramifications has confirmed the interdependence of the environment and development for many African governments in the 1980s. The media have also brought images of the African environment into the living rooms of individuals in the Western world. The roots of the popular portrayal of a crisis in Africa, however, may lie beyond the state of the African environment *per se*. For example, Anderson and Grove (1987, p. 4) suggest that it was the perceived contrast between the wild and 'natural' Africa and the domesticated and 'despoiled' European landscapes which stimulated many colonial development policies and 'continues to stimulate many of those who wish to intervene in the way the environment is managed in Africa'.

Conceptions of environmental degradation are multifaceted and are shaped by historical, political, psychological and cultural as well as physical forces. The shape of such conceptions influences, in turn, the range of possible conservation options available. In Zimbabwe, a leading researcher on soil erosion in the country reported in 1983 that the problem had reached crisis proportions: 'There is absolutely no doubt whatsoever that malnutrition and death through starvation of the Communal Land population is inevitable if present rates of soil erosion are allowed to continue' (Elwell, 1983, p. 45).

Although measurements of soil loss throughout Africa are notoriously complex, the quality of information is improving and there is little doubt that the problems are serious and getting worse (Stocking, 1987). A national erosion survey effected in Zimbabwe in 1988 concluded that 21 percent of the country was experiencing erosion levels described as 'moderate' to 'very severe' (Whitlow, 1988). Yet an ecological crisis in the country was first deemed imminent in the early 1930s. Fifty intervening years of colonial conservation separate the two predictions.

This chapter overviews the emergence and development of a conservationist orthodoxy in Rhodesia amongst the colonial administration at the national level, and the translation of the associated conservation structures to the local level. The analysis focuses on the conservation framework, natural resource legislation and the nature and content of the erosion control model put forward during the period 1890–1980. The strength of the colonial conservation legacy is then assessed through an analysis of the continuity and change evident within post-colonial conservation structures. A critical analysis of the contemporary conservation framework is effected, elements of change over the decade of independence identified, and insights from the local level are used to reflect and extend the promulgations of policy and practice made at the national level.

Colonial conservation policy and practice in Rhodesia cannot be separated from the colonial encounter as a whole and events within the international community generally at the time. In turn, the operation at the local level cannot be fully understood without appreciation of the motivations and aspirations of individual officers. The relative importance of events at each hierarchical level, and the strength of political–economic or environmental factors in shaping the timing, nature and content of conservation policy at the local level, inevitably vary between and within colonies as well as over time. With such a large degree of complexity, there is a danger of overgeneralisation, although international comparisons and chronologies are popular. For example, Blaikie (1985, p. 53) outlines a 'colonial' approach to conservation identified on the basis of a 'syndrome of implicit assumptions'. Anderson and Millington (1986, p. 2) similarly present a broad chronology of environmental awareness which they suggest 'might be applicable to all of Anglophone Africa'.

Historical analysis at this scale is important for contextualising the current concern for the African environment and highlighting the pervasive but fluctuating nature of such concern. At the national level it is essential for understanding contemporary physical conditions as well as the way current problems are viewed and tackled. Many conservation policies of independent African governments show strong continuity with those of the colonial state in Africa and, as suggested above, Europeans continue to exert their ideas on the African environment today. The adoption of a political–economic perspective in general (Blaikie, 1985) and Zimbabwe-specific (Elliott, 1989) literature has enhanced understanding of the various structural, environmental and cultural factors which shape the conception of conservation problems held by those who intervene in land-use decisions. All have views about the way society does and should operate which influence their perceptions of conservation options and conservation failures. The primary focus of this chapter is the national level, although details of case-study research effected by the author in Marondera district is used to contrast or extend patterns identified at this level.

Colonial Conservation in Rhodesia

The first published reference to soil erosion in Rhodesia appeared in the *Rhodesia Agricultural Journal* in 1909 (Cripps, 1909). By 1913, nearly every settler farm was reported to be suffering from gully formation (Watt, 1913), and many were experiencing dramatic declines in yields (Haviland, 1928). The agricultural and irrigation journals of this period contain many references to the destructive impact on the soil of settler practices such as herding of stock, kraaling and improper tillage. In the same literature, 'experts' recommended various practices for conserving the soils of the colony. The control of stocking levels, the preservation of timber at stream margins, the regulation of grass burning, contour ploughing and minimisation of cattle tracking were identified as essential measures if the conditions created by the white civilisation in South Africa were not to be replicated in Rhodesia. In fact, the implementation of such conservation structures prior to 1930 was minimal. Ordinances covering water use and herbage preservation were passed in 1913, but were rarely enforced and served only a cosmetic function with respect to the emerging problem of soil erosion.

In the 1930s, there was a transfer of official conservation concern from the state of the environment under settler use to that under indigenous husbandry. It has been argued that this marked switch was more a reflection of international events, in particular the dustbowl experiences of the American Mid-West and the political–economic ramifications of the Depression, than an objective worsening of the environmental situation nationally in Rhodesia (Beinart, 1984). Local-level analysis on the basis of oral testimonies (Wilson, 1986) and sequential air photograph analysis (Elliott, 1989), has further confirmed this assertion. It was from the 1930s onwards, however, that the main conservation structures were established in terms of the conservation organisation, the legislative framework and the content of the conservation model. These structures often varied substantially between the European and African sectors.

Throughout the colonial period, the content of the conservation model remained stable, both within and between the two agricultural sectors, European and African. In 1927, a model for erosion control was introduced into the European sector which came to dominate the physical environment throughout the country. From 1936, the same model was introduced into the African farming areas. It focused on the control of moving water via a series of parallel contour banks and associated storm drains aimed at minimising rill and gully formation on cultivated soils. This model was designed in America but adopted wholesale in Rhodesia throughout subsequent decades.

The selection of this mechanical model for erosion control had an immediate spatial and racial bias on introduction into Rhodesia. Alienation of land for settler production during the early Chimurenga wars and via the Land Apportionment Act of 1931 and its subsequent amendments left a distinct spatial pattern of land tenure according to racial group. European lands were largely confined to the high-veld areas in which soil and rainfall conditions were suited to intensive production of most crops. African farming areas, in contrast, occupied the drier middle- and low-veld regions in the main, and were suited only to the production of drought-resistant crops or extensive cattle ranching. The selection of a conservation model for the country focusing on water control rather than moisture conservation was therefore far more appropriate to the requirements of European than to indigenous farmers.

In addition, the conservation layouts associated with the American model were more readily assimilated into European patterns of cropping and mechanised systems of operation. In conditions of mounting land shortage in the African farming areas throughout the twentieth century, a conservation model which took out of production substantial areas of land for barriers and drainage networks was clearly unsuited to the political–economic as well as the environmental conditions of the indigenous sector. In addition, the labour demands for the construction and maintenance of these physical structures were more problematic for the African farmer. Not only did the European farmers have access to tractors and hired hands, many African households had restricted family labour, as male members increasingly took up jobs on European farms, in urban centres, in railway construction or in the mining industry.

Clearly, despite the vastly different environmental, socio-economic and political conditions and needs of each agricultural sector, the content of the conservation model during the colonial period remained constant. Despite criticisms from experienced officers within the technical services of the time, at home and abroad, concerning both the environmental and social limitations of this model, the content of the conservation model remained unchanged. The arrogance underlying such persistence stemmed from, and reinforced, the technocentric conception of soil erosion which dominated official thinking throughout the colonial period. Soil erosion was portrayed as an environmental problem to which a technical solution was available in the American model. Structural causes were not considered and the colonial conservation effort was forwarded as a politically neutral activity. Increasingly interventionist policies in the African sector were therefore justified on the basis of spreading the adoption of this conservation model.

The organisation created for colonial conservation in terms of the administrative framework, staffing levels and local institutions differed substantially between farming sectors. From 1923, the European farming sector was served by a Ministry of Agriculture with responsibility for soil and water conservation falling under the Department of Water Irrigation. In 1948, a separate Department of Conservation and Extension (CONEX) was formed and took over this responsibility. In contrast, a Department of Native Agriculture was not formed until 1944. Although soil conservation in the African sector came under the responsibility of this department, water conservation remained in the Department of Water Irrigation. It was not until 1962 that soil and water conservation in the African sector came together within one department after the dissolution of the Federation and the amalgamation of African and European conservation within CONEX. The joint administration of conservation across the two sectors in Rhodesia lasted only six years. Responsibility for conservation in the African farming areas was transferred on two further occasions prior to independence, when the Agricultural and Technical Extension Service (AGRITEX) became responsible for conservation nationally.

In addition to the contrast in terms of the continuity of personnel within the colonial conservation organisations with responsibilities for the European and African sectors, respective staffing levels also varied substantially. The early activities of the Department of Agriculture focused on research rather than extension, although 'advisory work became more systematic as the various officers became more experienced' (Kennan, 1971, p. 116). Lectures, the *Rhodesia Agricultural Journal*, farm visits and private communications were the means for communication between farmers and agricultural officers. In 1912, the government even had plans to introduce rural telephones to facilitate communication between settler farmers and technical experts.

In 1934, two Soil Conservation Advisory Councils, one for Matabeleland and one for Mashonaland, were set up to help to co-ordinate conservation advice and satisfy the demand for such guidance on behalf of the European farmers. Technical assistants were appointed from 1936 to assist the irrigation engineers with advisory work. With the establishment of CONEX, settler farmers had an organisation with sole responsibility for advising them, backed by a Department of Research and Specialist Services. By the end of the year, fifty-eight conservation officers from CONEX were active in soil and water conservation in the European sector. By 1953, this number had increased to 146, mainly fully trained professionals with a degree in conservation. In-service training was also established within CONEX.

The optimism present within CONEX during the 1950s dissolved in the early 1960s with the breakup of the Federation and the creation of a new Southern Rhodesian Ministry of Agriculture embracing African and European agriculture. Eighteen professional officers resigned fron CONEX in 1962. In 1964/5, 120 staff left the service and only 89 were appointed. In addition to falling staff levels *per se*, morale worsened with the application of sanctions, and extension activities were limited by restricted mileages for officers and competing demands on their time. Extension activities in both sectors inevitably deteriorated as the security situation in Rhodesia worsened during the 1970s.

Extension activities in the African sector started with the establishment of the Department of Native Affairs in 1894. African 'development' as a whole was the responsibility of the Native Commissioners at this time: 'The earliest vehicle tracks, if they were not made by elephant or rhino, were made by Native Commissioners. They were pioneers in the field of human relations' (Chief Native Commissioner, *Annual Report*, 1961, p. 18). In 1927, E.D. Alvord was appointed to the Department of Native Affairs as Agriculturalist for the Instruction of Natives, and a programme of demonstration in the reserves was planned:

> The principal method is analogous to the extension system
> successfully practised among negroes in the States. While
> opinions differ as to the probability of success, it is felt that the
> experiment is justifiable. (Chief Native Commissioner, *Annual Report*,
> 1926, p. 1)

Native demonstrators received training in agriculture, and by 1927 one agricultural demonstrator was posted in each of the nine districts. It was not until 1936 that the first soil conservation officer was seconded to the Division of Native Affairs (his appointment was to the Department of Water Irrigation). At this time, there were sixty-four agricultural demonstrators and three erosion control demonstrators in the division. In 1944, some decentralisation of activities of the newly formed Department of Native Agriculture was effected through the posting of a land development officer (LDO) with each Native Commissioner. Land development officers soon became '*ipso facto* soil conservation officers' (Chief Native Commissioner, *Annual Report*, 1945, p. 233). In 1955, there were seventy-seven LDOs, each 'responsible for' 500,000 acres of land and 3,650 farmers (Secretary for Native Affairs, 1955, p. 1).

The incorporation of African agriculture within the directive of the newly created Ministry of Agriculture in 1962 was aimed at improving both the quality and quantity of extension in the African sector:

> The objective of the Ministry is to provide an agricultural development and extension service to the African farmer in Southern Rhodesia which is in all respects complementary to the agricultural service provided for the European farmer. (Chief Native Commissioner, *Annual Report*, 1961, p. 6)

As highlighted above, however, resignations and internal reorganisation, such as the transfer of responsibility from the Department of Tribal Agriculture to the Department of Agricultural Development (DEVAG) in 1978, led to staff losses for agricultural and conservation extension in the African sector.

In addition to this clear divergence in the level and continuity of staff with responsibility for conservation between the two sectors during the colonial period, another primary distinction between the colonial conservation organisation was in the creation of conservation institutions at the local level. The Natural Resources Act (NRA) of 1941 established provisions for the election of Intensive Conservation Area (ICA) committees within the European farming sector. The first of these voluntary institutions was formed in 1944. These committees enjoyed close contact with governmental technical and extension services as well as with the Natural Resources Board. They received financial assistance for administration, travelling, purchase of equipment, and until 1956 received subsidies for the construction of conservation works. By 1953, eighty-five ICAs had been formed. Although the rate of formation was most rapid during the first decade of the programme, new ICAs continued to be established into the 1970s.

It was not until 1966 that any institutions similar to the ICA organisation were proposed for the African sector. Nine 'tribal land authority conservation committees' were established in that year. By 1972 there were 111 such committees affiliated to the Natural Resources Board. Many committees existed in name only. In 1968, the annual report of the Natural Resources Board reported: 'It is significant that the new committees are formed almost entirely in areas served by the Board's Assistant District Secretaries and not elsewhere' (p. 12). These local institutions did not constitute a forum for information and communication comparable to that offered to commercial farmers by the ICA network. As well as problems of staffing and commitment with government departments at this time, relations between the Ministry of Internal Affairs and the Natural Resources Board were poor and culminated in the disbandment of the Board's Tribal Trust Land Committee in 1970.

The most important piece of colonial legislation with respect to conservation was the Natural Resources Act of 1941, which covered a wide range of 'natural resources' throughout the country including soil, water, minerals, animal life and vegetation. The Act was a direct product of a Commission of Inquiry into the State of the Natural Resources of the Colony (Southern Rhodesia, 1939, p. 12) which had reported that 'as was to be expected, rarely was the native alive to the importance of conserving the soil'. Although the problem of soil erosion was not confined to the African farming areas, the official conception of the problem of erosion in the European sector was substantially different. In the European farming areas, soil erosion was conceived in terms of staff shortages and lack of information rather than wilful neglect and indifference as it was framed with regard to the African sector. The Commission reported the example of European tobacco farmers who found that contour banking concentrated water and aggravated the problems of eelworms. In this light, 'hesitation on the part of many to spend money on a programme which might, after all, be found to be disadvantageous in another direction' was understood and condoned (Southern Rhodesia, 1939, p. 16).

The Natural Resources Act 1941 had separate sections applicable to European and African farming areas although common elements outweighed differences between the sectors. In all areas, the Natural Resources Board had the power to acquire land for conservation works, to order the construction of works and apportion the costs to the owner or user of the land, to order the cessation of any activities deleterious to natural resources and ultimately to prosecute defaulters under the Act. A Conservation Inspectorate and a Natural Resources Court were also established under the Act. Some statutes, like the Water Act and the Forest Act (c 125) dealt directly with the conservation of specific resources while others, such as the Mines and Minerals Act (c 165) were indirectly concerned with environmental issues.

Although the majority of colonial conservation legislation was applicable across both sectors of the farming community in Rhodesia, the interpretation of this legislation at the local level inevitably varied between and within the two sectors (Bell and Hotchkiss, 1989). Furthermore, wide-ranging national policies such as the 1951 Native Land Husbandry Act (NLHA) and the Land Tenure Act 1970, with substantial conservation elements incorporated within them, referred specifically to the African sector. Legislation within these policies became progressively more interventionist and tied to Western conceptions of resource use and management. For example, the Natural Resources Act 1941 was an attempt to make individuals accountable for their actions and their land; the Native Land Husbandry Act changed the whole structure of landholding on the assumption that individuals would not invest in their land unless they had a title to it.

Resource trusteeship and African development were used to justify many land-use policies in the African sector which were clearly not replicated in the European sector. The period immediately after the 1931 Land Apportionment Act has been termed the 'technical development phase' in native policy (Chief Native Commissioner, *Annual Report*, 1961). Once the racial division of land had been formalised (although it had effectively existed for many years prior to 1931), the colonial state was compelled to implement land management and conservation policies in the African sector which would underwrite this division. The centralisation policy, for example, implemented from 1936 onwards, was justified in terms of the rationalisation of resource use and the enhancement of conservation. By emphasising the 'destructive' use of land by Africans in the reserves, African demands for more land could be refused, state control over African production extended and attention simultaneously diverted away from European environmental mismanagement.

Forces external to the colony were also important in shaping the nature of interventions during this technical development phase. Apart from the aforementioned Depression and dustbowl experiences, the colonial ideology depended on the belief in modernisation and the extension of technocratic rationality, and as such demanded state intervention in African production. Under such beliefs, indigenous production systems were technically classed as primitive and persistence with such techniques exhibited ignorance. 'Native development' during this period took on a new urgency and a new meaning with the extension of the Western, modernist vision into Africa.

As colonial policy in the native reserves became increasingly centralised throughout the 1940s and 1950s in Rhodesia, the capacity for local definition or modification became restricted. The primary difference in colonial conservation identified at the local level was with respect to the timing of interventions, although some divergences in content were isolated (Elliott, 1989). With the adoption of the increasingly broad-brush approach to the African sector, the role of local officers in shaping the nature and impact of colonial conservation structures at the local level was also progressively limited. Furthermore, this incapacity was not confined to conservation structures; the Native Commissioner for Marandellas lamented as early as 1929 the loss of indigenous knowledge within European education programmes:

> Surely one would think the first attempts at education would be directed towards the European to teach him the fundamental principles underlying native life and society. Is not our ignorance of such matters the root of many difficulties and troubles?. . . Is it necessary that the whole of native institutions and all cultures be destroyed to make room for the implanting of ideas, our learning and our civilisation? Surely the stock could remain and some twig be grafted on which would bring forth good fruit in due season. (Marandellas Native Commissioner, *Annual Report*, 1929, pp. 6–7)

Despite such sensitivity in local officers, as colonial conservation structures became more wide-ranging and entrenched within the African sector the mistrust for the peasant option in Rhodesia actually increased. The technical, moral and spiritual superiority of the Europeans was ensured by their faith in Western science and Christianity; salvation for indigenous societies was based on replacement rather than reciprocity (Elliott, 1989).

This analysis of the colonial conservation model, organisation and legislation has highlighted some of the forces underlying the formulation and entrenchment of conservation thinking and its associated structures in Rhodesia. The conservation framework in the country was unrivalled elsewhere in Africa during this period and it served the needs of the European farming sector very well. The conservation of soil is, however, a political issue: 'it is because the state becomes involved in soil conservation that soil erosion has already become a political–economic issue' (Blaikie, 1985, p. 2). Whatever level of the administrative hierarchy under consideration, from international advisor to district commissioner, intervention cannot avoid 'enmeshing itself in the contradictions within society' (Blaikie, 1985, p. 2). In Rhodesia, the most fundamental contradiction within society was the inequitable access to productive resources according to race. In consequence, although soil erosion in the African sector was persistently promoted as an environmental issue and conservation programmes as politically neutral activities, in fact environmental degradation was symptomatic of these more fundamental cross-sectoral inequalities and conservation measures served further to undermine the position of particular groups in society.

A history of colonial conservation must necessarily be contextualised. For example, the trigger for the marked switch in conservation concern from settler to indigenous production in the early 1930s came from forces external to the peasant sector. These were seen to lie in the modernist colonial vision internationally and the need for protectionist and segregationist policies to ensure the position of white agriculture nationally. The failure to consider soil erosion in the African sector as symptomatic of underlying structural inequalities within colonial conservation limited such efforts to palliatives at best. The rigid persistence with, and eventual enforcement of, the mechanical model for erosion control has been shown to have been insensitive to the needs of both local environments and local peoples. In fact, there were few attempts to establish what these local needs in the African sector were with respect to colonial conservation. Conservation programmes were determined centrally on the basis of emotive reports from Native Commissioners and coloured by reports of what was happening elsewhere in the colonies and internationally.

The land-use schemes, the recommended husbandry practices and the legislation forwarded subsequently in the African sector served to remove the environment further from the hands of individual farmers and communities. In the process, farmers were increasingly brought under the control of Western science and, ultimately, the colonial state. African farmers were told what to grow and how to grow it; where to cultivate and where to live; what stock to keep and how many; and what the problem of soil erosion was and how to deal with it. Traditional rights to resources were replaced with alien concepts of ownership and distributed by government appointees on the basis of Western conceptions of rational resource use.

At all stages, there was little communication between parties. In contrast to other colonies in Africa where populist policies were more prominent, in Rhodesia 'there is the theme of rejection, a general denial that there was anything good in the former system of native cultivation and resultant ways of life' (Floyd, 1959, p. 290). The extension model used in the native reserves was drawn from America and assumed 'homophily' between the extension agent and farmer; they differed only in their relative scientific education. Innovations were communicated vertically from the top (the research stations and government departments) to the bottom (the farmers). There was little two-way communication within this model. Conservation extension during the colonial period was effectively the dissemination and utilisation of scientific knowledge only.

As the environment became further removed from the hands of the land-users themselves, traditional life became divided into discrete concerns for agriculture, education and conservation. The synergism of indigenous cultures in Rhodesia was lost: 'one now goes to school to learn, to the cinema to be entertained and the church to pray. Life has ceased to be a long winding robe but a series of hops, steps and jumps' (Makina, 1983, p. 2). In the process, former structures for regulating resource use such as religious and spiritual belief systems also broke down. The pressure for such change inevitably led people to 'circumvent the old rules' (Jungerius, 1985, p. 6). New rules were introduced by the colonial government but referred to a substantially different game in which Africans were forced to play on unequal terms. This same process of 'conservation–dissolution' was perceived to be occurring with respect to education by the Native Commissioner for Marandellas: 'we have deprived these gentry of their own code of manners, but have not taught them anything of our own' (*Annual Report*, 1940, p. 78).

The independent government of Zimbabwe inherited not only a compounded problem of soil erosion, but also a great deal of entrenched conservation thinking, legislation and established orthodoxy. Aspects of this legacy are clearly visible in the physical landscape of Zimbabwe today; others persist in the minds of politicians, conservation officials and farmers (Elliott, 1989). Many more exist in the blueprints which Cliffe suggests are 'waiting on the shelves ready to be dusted off and slightly repackaged to fit the new political circumstances' (Cliffe, 1988a, p. 51).

Post-Colonial Conservation in Zimbabwe

Within months of the declaration of independence, the Prime Minister, Robert Mugabe, pledged his government's support for the conservation movement, in the form of the Natural Resources Board and the Intensive Conservation Area organisation, and confirmed his commitment to extend this movement rapidly into the communal areas: 'This area has been seriously neglected over the years in every way by successive governments which has led to the very poor state of conservation and productivity in this area generally' (Mugabe, 1980, p. 288).

Immediately on independence, soil erosion and other forms of environmental degradation in the communal areas were framed by both academics and practitioners within a set of interrelated agro-ecological, socio-ecological, socio-economic, infrastructural and institutional problems inherited from the past. Conservation in Zimbabwe was quickly linked to the wider issues of administrative reorganisation and land reform; the communal areas were to be brought fully into the political sphere for the first time and land was to be redistributed to the hitherto marginalised peasantry for development along socialist lines.

Mugabe's 'conciliatory speech' to the nation on independence, however, made it clear that the attainment of socialism in Zimbabwe was to be transitional rather than revolutionary; existing structures were to be transformed rather than replaced and all groups were to have a future in Zimbabwe. In addition, the Lancaster House agreement, promises of international aid and the conditions attached to these, as well as the threat from South Africa as a direct force and through control over trade routes, all served to work against the adoption of more radical policies. Furthermore, it has been argued that there was no coherent ideology for social change amongst the guerrilla movements in the run-up to independence (Phimister, 1988).

The major programme for structural transformation in independent Zimbabwe was through the resettlement policy, initiated in 1981. The resettlement of 162,00 families over three years was targeted (Republic of Zimbabwe, 1982). In the event, the pace of resettlement was slow. By mid-1984, the government had acquired approximately 2.5 million hectares of land at a total cost of Z$52 million, but only 36,000 families had been resettled by the end of the following year. The people resettled were largely ex-combatants, war-displaced families and the landless. Under the restrictions of the Lancaster House agreement, the acquisition of lands for this programme by the government was constrained by the guarantees on the inviolability of private property which restricted purchases to a 'willing seller–willing buyer' basis. In this way, limits were set on the quantity, quality and location of land to be redistributed. Targets for land redistribution within the most recent policy statement have been lowered to the resettlement of 15,000 families annually (Republic of Zimbabwe, 1986).

Administrative reform was also initiated quickly after independence with major implications for the organisation of conservation. In 1981, all ministries and departments became responsible for sectoral development irrespective of land holding. The Departments of Conservation and Extension (CONEX) and Agricultural Development (DEVAG) were amalgamated to form the Department of Agricultural and Technical Extension Services (AGRITEX) in the Ministry of Lands, Agriculture and Rural Resettlement, responsible for soil and water conservation in both European and African farming areas. In addition, in 1982 the District Council Act initiated the process of delineation of new district council areas on which the future administrative restructuring of the country would hinge. A hierarchy of development institutions from village to provincial level was created; the former authoritarian and interventionist character of the inherited administrative system was replaced by one in which provincial governors replaced commissioners. Rather than a single 'chain of command', development committees were established at the various levels in the hierarchy, each one responsible for co-ordinating needs at that level and forwarding them to the level above. 'The ordinary peasant has to be our object and if he is our object then we must have machinery which will affect him' (Mugabe, 1984).

Under this same Act, provision was made for the establishment of conservation committees within each district council area. These were to form the primary means for the promotion and diffusion of the conservation message in independent Zimbabwe. They would constitute elected councillors and appointed representatives, and were encouraged to hold monthly meetings which officers of the Natural Resources Board, AGRITEX and district departments would also attend.

Despite this large-scale reform of the administrative organisation in Zimbabwe, modifications to the extension framework post-independence were predominantly of a quantitative rather than a qualitative nature. Since independence, the number of extension workers in the communal areas has been increased, local housing for officers upgraded and mobility for extension workers improved, all raising the level of contact between extension worker and farmer and in these areas. However, the nature of the extension relationship within AGRITEX and the Department of Natural Resources, the two main agencies with responsibility for conservation, has remained closely tied to the 'classical' approach inherited from the past. Innovations are still disseminated from the 'top' with very little opportunity for two-way communication. Extension workers from both departments give advice to farmers on conservation practices at the local level, commonly working with farmers' groups. Local AGRITEX officers receive communications regarding latest recommendations from research establishments and are encouraged to attend refresher courses in conservation. How and when conservation is addressed with villagers, however, is left to the individual officer.

There have been attempts made to modify this model for extension at the regional level. The Communal Areas Management Programme for Indigenous Resources (CAMPFIRE) is in operation in several test areas and is a flexible approach to communal resource management which emphasises community direction and control and in which the extension officer is both teacher and learner. A programme in Wedza communal area also makes use of an intermediary group of 'farmer extension promoters' (FEPs). Committees elect a local farmer to act as an FEP, who then assists in the formation of farmers' groups, is given some basic training and acts as a link between farmers and the extension service.

The legislative structure in independent Zimbabwe remains closely tied to the colonial past with respect to natural resource use, the Natural Resources Act remaining the linchpin. The policy of the Department of Natural Resources in the early years of independence was very much one of persuasion rather than prosecution:

> It is over-legislation in the communal lands which has left those areas in a very sad state. It is better to communicate with the people and create an atmosphere that is conducive to enforcement. (Chitepo, 1986)

Recent developments, however, suggest that the policy of education rather than persuasion is changing. Convictions of both commercial and communal farmers under the National Resources Act are occurring. In the words of one inspector, 'eight years for education is enough' (Regional Land Inspector, Marondera District, 1989).

In addition to the substantial number of statutes concerning the conservation of natural resources in the country inherited from the past, under the Communal Land (Model) (Grazing and Cultivation) By-laws Act of 1984, district councils may establish by-laws concerning particular aspects of natural resource use in their areas. Councils have the power to make orders concerning the control of grazing and cultivation, schemes for improving stock and crops, and even for fixing standards of soil conservation in the area. The advantages of district definition of such legislative control is the flexibility to respond to ecologically specific conservation concerns at the local level. The danger is they may generate insecurity and resentment. Although proposed by-laws are to be discussed at village level, the Act does not stipulate that they should necessarily be approved at this level. Control of the local environment therefore remains in the hands of the district councils. In practice, few councils have to date defined local by-laws under this Act.

Despite these changes in the organisation for conservation and within the broader administrative and legislative frameworks, the model for erosion control promoted within conservation programmes in the post-independence period remains closely tied to the past. The Transitional National Development Plan (Republic of Zimbabwe, 1982, p. 61) recommended an 'active' soil conservation programme 'involving technical measures and education of the people'. The technical measure required was the same mechanical conservation layout of contour banks and storm drains as promoted throughout fifty years of colonial conservation. The content of the independent conservation model remains arable-based and centred on water control and gully erosion rather than moisture conservation and sheet loss. This restricted emphasis is at odds with the findings of research both within Zimbabwe and elsewhere concerning the conservation value of tie-ridging and mulch tillage, for example: 'The salvation of arable land in both the commercial and communal areas is to place a great deal more emphasis on moisture conservation techniques' (Elwell, 1985, p. 28). There has been little indication to date that the formal extension service has broadened the restricted inherited conservation message in the communal areas. Although mechanical conservation structures have a role to play in the prevention of soil erosion on arable plots, recent research suggests that soil and nutrient loss via sheet erosion is a far more serious problem in these areas (Stocking, 1987). Yet this is not prioritised within contemporary programmes. This model for erosion control, which was dominant during the colonial period, has left substantial legacies not only in the physical environment, but also in the socio-cultural landscape (Elliott, 1989). These may prove debilitating in the future at the local level.

The context for an assessment of the degree to which inherited conservation structures have been transformed in Zimbabwe lies within the broader challenges of independence and socio-economic development. This context has changed significantly over the ten years of independence. The First Five Year National Development Plan was published in 1986 and outlined the government's official framework for managing socio-economic development over the period 1986–90. The maintenance of a balance between the environment and development was one of the six major development objectives identified for the period. In continuity with the Transitional National Development Plan of 1982, the First Five Year National Plan reaffirmed the commitment to increasing state ownership of resources, raising agricultural productivity and enhancing standards of living. In contrast to the Transitional National Development Plan, targets for average growth rates of GDP were scaled down from 8 to 5.1 per cent per annum and employment generation became a major target in the later plan, (Republic of Zimbabwe, 1986).

Drought, world recession and the progressive deterioration in investment activity were isolated within the First Five Year National Plan as limiting factors in the achievements of the first five years of independence. Despite the need for widespread supplementary feeding programmes in many of the drier regions of the country during the poor rains of 1982–5, the rising contribution of communal farmers to grain marketing boards since independence has been referred to as Africa's 'success story' (Cliffe, 1988b). GDP grew by 15 per cent in 1981 as 'one-off' gains in the economy were made with the lifting of sanctions and the reactivation of resources underutilised during the war. In subsequent years, inflation, falling mineral prices, foreign exchange difficulties and problems of external debt servicing all contributed to decline in GDP. Levels rose again in 1984 and 1985, but fell back once more in 1986.

The main challenge of the latter part of the 1980s for the independent government remains the circular one of not earning enough foreign exchange both to service debts and to invest for expanded exports. In 1989, the president announced measures to further relax the investment code in Zimbabwe: 'The government recognises the need for a more rational and market-orientated method of determining price and incomes' (Mugabe, 1989). The role of foreign capital in the development plans of a country committed to socialist development has, not surprisingly, attracted much debate: 'At times, the juxtaposition of socialist aims and the need for investment produces the bizarre implication that foreign capital may be attracted to help achieve such a revolution' (Stoneman, 1988, p. 55).

Current agrarian strategy in Zimbabwe is shaped by political forces just as it was in colonial Rhodesia. Although race is no longer the basis for political division in the country, European farmers continue to influence agrarian strategy through crop prices and wage levels. Their position is further reinforced by the view, perpetuated by international reports, that resettlement on a large scale would cause a decline in output, and in the numbers employed in agriculture. In addition, there has been much realignment and realliance of class forces in the country. Commercialisation of the peasant sector is now accommodated by European farmers and there has been some 'Africanisation' of the bourgeoisie, although the 'exact extent of this is a matter of speculation' (Stoneman and Cliffe, 1989, p. 57).

The peasantry represent the second major influence on agrarian policy. Despite early concessions made to this class on independence, Cliffe (1988b) suggests that they are now represented by only a minority of politicians and civil servants. The peasant class itself is highly differentiated. Even during the nationalist struggle, inequalities between rural classes were rising and their unity within the liberation movements was ensured by the fact that all Africans were disadvantaged in some way under settler policies. The 'land question' is now substantially different to that articulated by the liberation movement. Objectives for transformation have been stated more cautiously or implemented more 'pragmatically', resulting in a 'much more complex configuration of issues, realities and determinations of the "land question"' (Moyo, 1986, p. 165).

The distribution of land in Zimbabwe continues to be highly skewed. In 1982, the average land area per capita in the communal areas was 4.1 hectares in contrast to 148 hectares per capita on average in the large-scale commercial farming areas (Central Statistics Office, 1984). To date, the resettlement programme has assisted less than 5 per cent of the estimated 800,000 peasant families in the communal areas and taken up only 16 per cent of the commercial farm land. Chimombe (1986, p. 139) refers to progress with fundamental reforms of the inherited economy such as land reform as being 'dismal'.

The constitutional constraints on land redistribution through the Lancaster House agreement, under which all land compulsorily purchased had to be paid for in foreign currency and that which was bought on a 'willing seller–willing buyer' basis had to be acquired at full market price, made the early resettlement programme an extremely costly exercise:

> The cost of buying the estimated 40–60% of European land not being fully utilised would be so high that even if a new government of Zimbabwe were committed to implementing a comprehensive land resettlement it would find it well nigh impossible to carry it out. (Astrow, 1983, p. 155)

As the supply of willing sellers began to dry up, land prices rose. Between 1980 and 1985, land purchase prices in the country rose by 48 per cent (Mubengegwi, 1986, p. 212). The Land Acquisition Act (1986) now gives the government first refusal on all land sales and sets procedures for the compulsory purchase of 'underutilised' lands, which in combination with the constitutional changes of 1990 will widen the government's options for land reform. Land availability may not, however, prove to be the only constraint on the success of the resettlement programme in Zimbabwe.

The organisation for conservation in Zimbabwe is now substantially different from the inherited model in terms of the institutional framework. As discussed, however, continuities persist, particularly in terms of extension relationships. The administrative restructuring at the local level has created a hierarchy of development institutions and provision for conservation committees at the district level. As a result of the District Council Act, more than 250 former African Councils became consolidated into fifty-five District Councils, with further restructuring planned through the Rural District Councils Act. This Act will for the first time bring the former Rural Councils of the European sector into direct administrative contact with District Councils. The success of the new structure in operation has yet to be determined.

At the local level, successful conservation will depend on the coordination of these district institutions with farmers and extension personnel and the coherence of the activities of the various parties. Communication will be paramount. At present, in Marondera district, there are no effective lines of communication between farmers and the conservation committee, between district extension and administrative officers, and between extension departments and local institutions. At the local level, different institutions have responsibility for different aspects of community life such that officers are unsure who to deal with: 'there are at least three leaders in each village and six villages in each Vidco [village development committee]' (Regional Land Inspector, Marondera District, 1989). Proposed reorganisation within the 'villagisation' programme threatens further confusion and lack of continuity: 'people are continually being pushed around. Such insecurity leads to poor conservation' (Regional Land Inspector, Marondera District, 1989). The multiplicity of new conservation organisations, in addition to the proposed new committees at higher levels in the hierarchy (for example, the inter-ministerial committee proposed within the National Conservation Strategy), raises financial questions quite apart from those of coherence and co-ordination.

Despite the quantitative changes in the extension relationship since independence, the nature of that relationship remains essentially constant. For example, in the light of inevitable restrictions on mileage and time, there is a tendency for extension officers to select a manageable number of farmers whom they can visit regularly, and these remain typically the better-off farmers (Cliffe, 1988b). This perpetuates the bias of colonial extension in which extension was focused on the 'master farmers': 'those who had "made the break" from "native" husbandry' (Cliffe, 1988b, p. 7).

The legislative framework for conservation in Zimbabwe shows strong continuity with the past in terms of those statutes associated directly with natural resource use. Divergences from the past were with respect to the implementation of this legislation both nationally with respect to the early policy of education rather than enforcement, and at the local level in terms of the flexibility of interpretation. Although local variation persists, recent trends suggest a reversion to legal enforcement. The devolution of some control to the district level raises additional problems of penalties and means of operation if alienation and resentment at the local level are to be avoided.

The model for conservation in independent Zimbabwe remains closely tied to that inherited from the past. It continues to be biased both spatially and according to socio-economic status. Focusing on water control rather than conservation, the mechanical model for erosion control is more suited to the environmental challenges of high-veld farmers than those in the drier, southern sections of the country. The labour demands pose problems for those households with limited access to such resources. Although several new models are being developed at the regional level, the American model for erosion control transferred to Rhodesia in the late 1920s remains the central tenet of the independent conservation model: 'A more or less standard technique has been applied whether the soil is a heavy clay loam or a loose coarse sand, whether the land is nearly flat or steeply sloping; in high or low rainfall areas' (Alvord, 1944).

The conception at the national level of environmental degradation and soil conservation in the communal areas is now showing increasing continuity with the technocentric conception forwarded by the colonial authorities identified above. Resettlement is no longer the major programme of reform in the communal areas. The relative emphasis on land redistribution with respect to other agrarian reform options is undergoing substantial and continuing change. The source of, and solution to, agrarian and conservation problems is now seen within policy statements as lying internally to the communal areas in reorganisation and restructuring programmes, rather than within external resettlement policies. This fundamental switch in emphasis from statements early in the independence period is encapsulated in the National Conservation Strategy (NCS) published in 1987 (Ministry of Natural Resources and Tourism, 1987). It was recognised that performance between the resettlement schemes and between settlers had been uneven and achievements in productivity in the communal areas had been regionally and socially limited:

> These various considerations of the unmet needs and the complex problems of the most disadvantaged areas and households point to the need for a more intensive and broader-based strategy to promote rural development and one that will require restructuring of existing patterns of land use. (Ministry of Natural Resources, 1987, p. 12)

The nature and content of this rural development strategy have yet to be finalised, although pilot projects from the Ministry of Lands, Agriculture and Rural Resettlement and the Ministry of Local Government, Rural and Urban Development are under way. The NCS frames the conservation of resources as resting on the activities of AGRITEX through their preparation of 'resource planning models' (p. 23) in both the communal and resettlement areas. It is through the implications of such models for the spatial reorganisation of farming activities and settlement patterns in the communal areas that these proposals have become commonly referred to as 'consolidation' or 'villagisation' programmes.

> The concept of consolidated villages stems from the need to restructure and reorganise the existing dispersed and isolated peasant settlements, to make for cost effective provision of social and physical infrastructure and services and to release additional land for agricultural development. (Ministry of Lands, Agriculture and Rural Resettlement, 1986, p. 52)

Currently, at the national level in Zimbabwe rationalisation of and efficiency in resource use are seen as the bases for sound management of resources and for agricultural development in the communal areas. In the latter years of independence in Zimbabwe, the 'basic scepticism' (Cliffe, 1988b) concerning peasant farming systems has re-emerged and stands in stark contrast to the early conception of agricultural and conservation problems in the communal areas as a function of systematic colonial exploitation of this sector. The similarities between this contemporary programme for communal land reorganisation and those within colonial policies of centralisation or the Native Land Husbandry Act suggest that the 'old blueprints' identified by Cliffe (1988a) are indeed being repackaged. Environmental conservation in Zimbabwe has once again become bound up with far-reaching programmes for land-tenure reform, resource rationalisation and internal reorganisation. In the return to centralised 'models', rural development becomes reduced to an exercise in town planning (Cliffe, 1988b). The needs of local environments or local peoples inevitably suffer as they did within colonial structures.

References

Alvord, E. D. (1944) Memo to Chief Native Commissioner, National Archives of Zimbabwe, S160 sc.

Anderson, D., and Grove, R. (eds) (1987) *Conservation in Africa: People, Policies and Practice*, Cambridge: Cambridge University Press.

Anderson, D. A., and Millington, A. (1986) 'Political ecology of soil conservation in Anglophone Africa', paper presented at the Annual Conference of the Institute of British Geographers, January 1986, Reading.

Astrow, A. (1983) *Zimbabwe: A Revolution That Lost Its Way*, London: Zed.

Beinart, W. (1984) 'Soil erosion, conservationism and ideas about development: a Southern African exploration, 1900–1960', *Journal of Southern African Studies*, 11 (1), pp. 52–83.

Bell, M., and Hotchkiss, P. (1989) 'Political interventions in environmental resource use. Dambos in Zimbabwe', *Land Use Policy*, Oct., pp. 313–23.

Blaikie, P. (1985) *The Political Economy of Soil Erosion in Developing Countries*, London: Longman.

Central Statistics Office (1984) *1982 Population Census. A Preliminary Assessment*, Harare: CSO.

Chief Native Commissioner (1926–61) *Annual Reports*, Salisbury: Government Printer.

Chimombe, T. (1986) 'Foreign capital', in I. Mandaza (ed.) *Zimbabwe: the Political Economy of Transition 1980–86*, Codesira, Senegal.

Chitepo, Cde. (1986) 'Africa's problems not beyond hope', *Sunday Mail*, 15 June 1986.

Cliffe, L. (1988a) 'The conservation issue in Zimbabwe', *Review of African Political Economy*, 42, pp. 48–57.

Cliffe, L. (1988b) 'Zimbabwe's agricultural success', *Review of African Political Economy*, 43, pp. 48–58.

Cripps, L. (1909) 'The erosion of soil', *Rhodesia Agricultural Journal*, 6, pp. 669–70.

Elliott, J.A. (1989) 'Soil erosion and conservation in Zimbabwe: political economy and the environment', unpublished Ph.D. thesis, University of Technology, Loughborough.

Elwell, H.A. (1983) 'The degrading soil and water resources of the communal areas', *Zimbabwe Science News*, 17 (9/10), pp. 145–7.

Elwell, H.A. (1985) 'An assessment of soil erosion in Zimbabwe', *Zimbabwe Science News*, 19 (3/4), pp. 27–31.

Floyd, B.N. (1959) *Changing Patterns of African Land Use in Southern Rhodesia*, Lusaka: Rhodes–Livingstone Institute.

Haviland, P.H. (1928) 'Soil erosion', *Rhodesia Agricultural Journal*, 24, pp. 329–33.

Jungerius, P.D. (1985) *Perception and Use of the Physical Environment in Peasant Societies*, Geographical Papers No. 93, Department of Geography, University of Reading.

Kennan, P.B. (1971) 'The development of the extension service among the European farmers in Rhodesia', *Rhodesia Agricultural Journal*, 68, pp. 116–20.

Makina, J.C. (1983) 'A preliminary survey of mass adult conservation education using broadcast media with special emphasis on four selected radio programmes', unpublished B.Ed. dissertation, Department of Education, University of Zimbabwe.

Ministry of Lands, Agriculture and Rural Resettlement (1986) 'Conceptual framework for the Communal Lands Development Plan', draft plan, Harare.

Ministry of Natural Resources and Tourism (1987) *The National Conservation Strategy*, Harare: Ministry of Information, Posts and Telecommunications.

Moyo, S. (1986) 'The land question', in I. Mandaza (ed.) *Zimbabwe: the Political Economy of Transition 1980–86*, Codesira, Senegal.

Mubengegwi, C. (1986) 'Continuity and change in agricultural policy' in I. Mandaza (ed.) *Zimbabwe: The Political Economy of Transition 1980–86*, Codesira, Senegal.

Mugabe, R. (1980) 'Opening address of the First National Conservation Congress of Zimbabwe', *Zimbabwe Science News*, 14 (12) pp. 287–9.

Mugabe, R. (1984) quoted in Ministry of Information, Posts and Telecommunications, *Provincial Governorship of Zimbabwe*, Harare: Government Printer.

Mugabe, R. (1989) 'Mugabe to woo foreign investors in policy U-turn', quoted in *Daily Telegraph*, 19 April 1989.

Native Commissioner Marandellas (1929–40) *Annual Reports*, Salisbury: Government Printer.

Natural Resources Board (1968), *Annual Report*, Salisbury: Government Printer.

Phimister, I. (1988) 'The combined and contradictory inheritance of the struggle against colonialism', in C. Stoneman (ed.) *Zimbabwe's Prospects: Issues of Race, Class, State and Capital in Southern Africa*, London: Macmillan.

Regional Land Inspector, Marondera District (1989) personal communication, 20 March 1989.

Republic of Zimbabwe (1982) *Transitional National Development Plan 1982–1985*, Ministry of Finance, Harare: Government Printer.

Republic of Zimbabwe (1986) *First Five Year National Development Plan 1986–1990*, vols. 1 and 2, Ministry of Finance, Economic Planning and Development, Harare: Government Printer.

Secretary for Native Affairs (1955) 'Conservation and Development in Native Areas', National Archives of Zimbabwe 35537.

Southern Rhodesia (1939) *Report of the Commission to Enquire into the Preservation etc of the Natural Resources of the Country*, Salisbury: Government Printer.

Stocking, M.A. (1987) 'Recognising environmental crisis in Africa', paper presented at Conference of Developing Areas Research Group, Institute of British Geographers, December 1987, London.

Stoneman, C. (ed.) (1988) *Zimbabwe's Prospects: Issues of Race, Class, State and Capital in Southern Africa*, London: Macmillan.

Stoneman, C., and Cliffe, L. (1989) *Zimbabwe: Politics, Economics and Society*, London: Frances Pinter.

Watt, W.M. (1913) 'The dangers and prevention of soil erosion', *Rhodesia Agricultural Journal*, 10, pp. 667–75.

Whitlow, J.R. (1988) *Land Degradation in Zimbabwe: A Geographical Study*, Department of Natural Resources/University of Zimbabwe, Harare: Government Printer.

Wilson, K.B. (1986) 'History, ecology and conservation in southern Zimbabwe', paper delivered at a seminar, Department of Sociology, University of Manchester, 12 February 1986.

91

CHAPTER 5

Missions and Migration in Colonial Kenya

W. T. S. Gould

Missions and the Colonial Space Economy

The space economy of colonial Kenya was structured round a functional dichotomy between the settler 'core' on the one hand, the 'Scheduled Areas' of European settlement and commercial activity which were expected to generate export income and internal development, and the peripheral 'reserves' on the other, areas of African farming communities whose main function for the colonial state was to provide a labour force for the productive sectors, both rural and urban, of the core. John Overton (1987) has clearly placed the contradictions inherent in that spatial order into a wider context of the role of the colonial state in generating and mediating the spatial interactions across the Scheduled Areas/Reserves boundary. The net effect of these interactions of people, produce and capital in the early period, 1895–1920, was to exacerbate the structural inequalities on which the system was premised. Social capital, particularly transport, was allocated; revenue was extracted, through taxation; and there was labour migration. Each of these had effects disproportionately in favour of the areas of European settlement. Overton focuses his attention on the direct role of the colonial state in creating a space economy based on structural inequalities that are evident in Kenya at the present time, nearly thirty years after independence. The modern state has inherited contradictions that it has failed to resolve (Gould, 1987; Kitching, 1980; Leys, 1975; Obudho and Taylor, 1979).

It is not the purpose of this chapter to dispute the general thrust and conclusions of such a perspective; indeed the argument presented here reinforces Overton's claims. However, it considers in much greater detail one aspect of the contradictions he identifies: why the forces within the state that were relatively well-disposed to a parallel African development alongside European development remained weak, and, in particular, why some of the institutions established in the Reserves to promote development in the Reserves themselves were ineffective against the broader structures of the colonial space economy. While most attention in the recent historiography of Kenyan development has been directed to elaborating the essentially negative role of the colonial state in coercion, taxation and land and crop regulation in the Reserves (Berman and Lonsdale, 1980; Stichter, 1982), Overton himself draws attention to the limited attempts by the state directly to encourage development in the Reserves, even if this was 'only . . . when it complemented, or operated independently from, an inherently weak settler sector' (Overton, 1987, p. 268).

Within the Reserves, however, the missions were much more directly involved in development activities than was the state, especially in the early decades of this century. Christian missions were very active in Kenya from the late nineteenth century, in many areas before the formal control of the colonial state was established, and their work was almost entirely in the Reserves (Oliver, 1952). They brought the Gospel, but with that came men and materials, innovations and ideas, that were the raw material of modernization. As far as the settlers and the colonial government were concerned the missionaries promoted the African interest. Missionaries were nominated to represent Africans on the legislative council, and were often far from silent in promoting a liberal and non-racial perspective on the main policy issues of the day such as labour coercion and child labour (Oliver, 1952). However, their activities in development were severely constrained by shortage of finance. They could not command the financial resources available to the colonial state and received grants-in-aid from government only for a limited range of activities, notably education and health. They were also constrained by the legal and developmental restrictions imposed by the state, for example in not being permitted to promote cash cropping in certain areas, notably in the Kikuyu areas of Central Province, to the north of Nairobi. Thus the missions could operate only within the parameters of the structures imposed by the colonial order. They seemed to offer the possibility of a distinctive and independent economy in the Reserves, but sustained the settler and colonial interest in the longer term by their adherence to these structures, for they were dependent on them for their financial support. The missions were major actors in the articulation between the core and the periphery, and exacerbated, however inadvertently, its spatially differentiated consequences. They are therefore a proper subject of concern for the geography of development, not merely in terms of the location and land-use of mission stations (Johnson, 1967), but also as actors who helped to fashion the space economy of Africa.

Missions and African Education

The impact of the missions was probably greatest in the field of education. The state was happy to leave African education primarily in the hands of the missions throughout the colonial period, particularly before 1913, while the state established and funded schools for Europeans and Asians. Missions were given grants-in-aid to run their own schools, but expenditure on the education of Africans was much lower than expenditure on the education of Europeans or Asians, and the racial basis of educational provision reflected the more general patterns of allocations and priorities in the colony (Furley and Watson, 1978).

African education provided by the missions was in part strictly Christian, based on catechistic proselytisation developed in various ways by all Christian denominations. However, it was also 'relevant', and designed to be of practical value both in the reserve and beyond. It could be directed to the needs of local farming and village communities, but it could also increase the supply of labour from the Reserves. While the great demand by the state and the settlers in the earliest period was for unskilled and, by implication, uneducated labour, increasingly the colonial state and the European farmers needed skilled tradesmen and clerks, people with a background of some formal education. Mission schooling could be 'relevant' to the settler economy by training African workers and thereby lessening its dependence upon Asian clerks and *fundis* (craftsmen), considered by the Europeans to be expensive and unreliable. Those Africans who received an education in mission schools in the Reserves needed to migrate to towns or settler farms to use and benefit from that education, and so schooling became closely associated with migration. It was a factor promoting and encouraging the system of circular mobility of wage labour, a component of the broader processes of peripheral underdevelopment in which the benefits of production accrued in the core but the costs of reproduction of the labour force, including the direct and indirect costs of schooling, were borne in the Reserves.

While it is generally recognised that in Britain's African colonies and dependencies policies towards native education were ambivalent in the choice between education primarily for African advancement and education in the colonial and European interest (Whitehead, 1982), in Kenya, at least until 1929 when H. Scott succeeded J. R. Orr as Director of Education for the colony (Furley and Watson, 1978, p. 184), the missions, the settlers and the colonial government all agreed that practical training was to be preferred to an academic education. Formalised and institutionalised instruction was preferred to on-the-job training, for the latter would have required substantial involvement of the Asian urban craftsmen as trainers and employers.

The missions had been anxious to introduce practical training from the beginning of their work in education. The Church of Scotland Mission, the largest Protestant mission among the Kikuyu, early developed technical training workshops in many of its schools, a lead that was followed, though to a lesser extent, by Roman Catholic and other major Protestant groups (King, 1977). These early initiatives before the First World War had the effect of integrating the core and periphery in a national labour market in which the supply of labour to the urban and rural areas of European settlement, a major concern of the colonial state, was enhanced by the mission schools in creating a pool of labour with some skills, and an even larger pool of people made increasingly aware of opportunities for individual advancement outside the Reserves.

By the 1920s, however, there was a shift in government emphasis towards a concern for the role of education in the development of the Reserves. This was promoted in Kenya, as elsewhere in British Africa, by the Phelps-Stokes Commission to Kenya in 1924, which followed the 1920 Commission to West and South Africa. These Commissions drew heavily upon the experience of black education in the United States to promote rural self-sufficiency through education and training. The benefits of rural development based on African farming in the Reserves would then allow the Reserves to become integrated into the wider economic structures of the colony on a more equal and com-petitive footing. African education would still be essentially practical, but directed primarily to the needs of the Reserves. In addition to the Phelps-Stokes Commission, there were strong and influential voices in government in favour of the emphasis on development in the Reserves. J.R. Orr, Director of Education from 1911 to 1929, had been strongly influenced by the ethos of the Phelps-Stokes Commission's approach (and had been instrumental in its being invited to work in Kenya) (Abbott, 1970). However, initiatives by the colonial state and missions for training for rural self-sufficiency, such as the training of teachers for service in rural communities, the so-called Jeanes teachers, were small in comparison with measures to provide industrial train-ing, notably at the Government Native Industry Training Depot at Kabete, near Nairobi, and other mission schools in the 1920s. Kenneth King's major study of the Phelps-Stokes Commission and its impact in Kenya confirms the nature of the continuing dilemma of training, 'whether it should be directed towards the European labour market or the African reserves' (King, 1971, p. 115). In practice, the needs of the settler economy predominated.

Kenyan settlers were not granted internal self-government in 1923, as Southern Rhodesian settlers were, and the Devonshire White Paper concluded that 'primarily Kenya is an African colony and . . . that the interests of the African natives must be paramount'. That interest, however, was interpreted by the colonial state to be best served by closer integration into the settler economy. The settler ascendancy and the space-economy were confirmed and were reflected in the role of education as a training for migrants at the time. For the remainder of the colonial period education remained largely in the day-to-day control of the missions, and remained the servant of the commercial economy. The bias by the 1930s and 1940s was shifting from practical to academic education, as public demand for training for white-collar jobs grew and missions responded, often reluctantly, to that public pressure (Ranger, 1965). In the minds of the African population there was a direct link between education and migration, and the mission made that link possible. In their promotion of modernisation through education, missions strengthened the articulation of the Reserves with the commercial labour market, at the expense of the potential impact of education and training in the Reserves themselves.

Such a broad conclusion ascribes to the missions a largely uniform approach and objectives, and implies that they were passive clients of the colonial state and invariably pursued policies in education, as in other aspects of their work, that furthered the settler interest, whether deliberately or by default. The missionaries were themselves 'Europeans', the majority of them British, and shared many of the settlers' economic and cultural premises and objectives. Their work was imbued with a strong sense of cultural if not racial superi-ority, by a firm paternalistic intent to bring light to darkest Africa. For evan-gelicals this meant a mission to lead the fallen natives to a Christian life; for others it meant seeing the noble savage as deserving redemption in the next world and better health and education in this; for yet others it meant promoting positive development among African populations and in African areas.

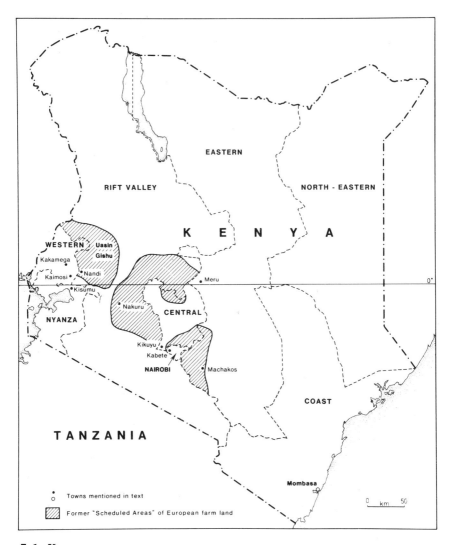

5:1 Kenya.

Clearly, missions and missionaries could be very different in their approaches and objectives, and their work brought them into varying degrees of conflict with the settlers and the colonial state. Many of these conflicts, over curriculum, land and wages for example, have been elaborated elsewhere (Anderson, 1970; Oliver, 1952; Ranger, 1965; Van Zwanenberg, 1975). In the rest of this chapter, however, there is a focus on the different ways in which two missions, the Church of Scotland Mission, operating mostly among the Kikuyu in Central Province, and the Friends Africa Mission (FAM), operating in what is now Western Province, perceived the relationship between the core and the periphery, the Scheduled Areas and the Reserve (Figure 5.1). The discussion will illustrate how their training and education policies differed, and concludes that, despite these differences, their policies, however vigorously pursued, had similar outcomes. The Reserves and their populations were increasingly enmeshed in the wider processes of articulation between core and periphery.

The Church of Scotland Mission

The earliest Christian missions in Kenya were established by the mid-nineteenth century in the coastal zone. However, the main period for the establishment of mission stations was in the first decade of the twentieth century, and was associated with the building of the Uganda Railway from Mombasa to Port Florence (Kisumu) on Lake Victoria, 1895–1904. Many mission groups established themselves in what was by then Kenya Colony, chiefly in the areas established as Reserves for the African population, and mostly in geographically concentrated areas (Oliver, 1952). Only the largest groups, the Roman Catholics and the Anglican Church Missionary Society, sought a colony-wide distribution. Most of the many smaller Protestant missions confined their activities to one area, jealously guarding that area from 'poaching' by rival missions. The Church of Scotland Mission (CSM) was one of the largest of these localised missions, early established among the Kikuyu, to the north and north-west of Nairobi in what is now Central Province, and also in nearby Meru District (Anderson, 1970, p. 15).

The Presbyterian Church of Scotland by the early twentieth century had had considerable mission experience and motivation. In the earlier part of the nineteenth century it had been much exercised by missionary work at home in the Highlands of Scotland that had the purpose of direct evangelisation (Meek, 1987). By the end of the century, however, much had changed, thanks in no small measure to the reputation of David Livingstone and his missionary activities and exploration in Central Africa, and his belief that evangelisation alone was not sufficient. The missions had to be seen to bring practical advantages to the African population (Anderson, 1970, p. 14). The early CSM stations were immediately associated with agricultural developments as well as schools and health care, and the mission quickly became well established throughout the Kikuyu population. The Presbyterian style of church government was well suited to the acephalous traditional authority structures of the Kikuyu. By the second decade of the century there was a great demand from the Kikuyu for training in CSM schools, and that demand was supported by the government, which sought to establish a trained African labour force to support the growing European settler economy in Nairobi and the Scheduled Areas surrounding it. The settler interest required a labour force at much lower cost that the growing number of Asian immigrants were providing, and the colonial authorities responded by offering grants-in-aid to missions for training. In 1913 they directly established a training school in Machakos, this being the first direct investment in African education by the Kenyan government (Anderson, 1970, p. 38; King, 1971, p. 105).

The CSM was well placed to become a principal focus for this training. It had a distinct geographical advantage in that its area of concern was near

Nairobi, the largest urban labour market by far, and also near the coffee farms of the growing settler populations. In addition, however, the mission itself had its roots in urban and industrialised Scotland, and many of the missionaries were themselves from urban and artisanal backgrounds. For them, a training in urban and industrial skills was familiar and appropriate for young African men to allow them to become better integrated into the economic life of the colony. The CSM established trade training schools with government grants-in-aid to train masons, carpenters and others on an indentured labour basis. This model, styled by Kenneth King as 'the school as factory' (King, 1977, p. 22), persisted into the 1930s both in CSM and other mission schools and in government institutions such as the Native Industrial Training Depot (NITD), established in 1924. In these 'schools' apprentices were taught basic numeracy and literacy, but also manual skills that were directly applied in work gangs as part of a practical apprenticeship. These arrangements were very different from the minimal teaching of practical skills in the formal curriculum in Scottish schools at that time, but in the UK as a whole there was a strong emphasis on on-the-job training in formal apprenticeships with private employers:

> The instructor who moved, for example, from Aberdeen primary schools in the 1920s to being an instructor missionary in the Church of Scotland's main primary schools in Kenya went from a situation where manual instruction was something of an educational extra, not the least related to production, to a factory system where schools indentured their technical students for the first three years of a five year apprenticeship. Such students worked daily as masons, carpenters and blacksmiths, from 7.30 a.m. to 4 p.m. for their last three years of school, and were encouraged to partake of night school for two further hours after work. (King, 1977, p. 183)

Johnstone Kamau, later Jomo Kenyatta, first President of Kenya, was one of the early trainees in the CSM at Kikuyu (King, 1971, p. 105).

Although rural work was certainly not ignored in CSM schools, for example in Meru (Anderson, 1970, p. 21), there was an explicit objective in the higher training to provide a skilled labour force for the urban and rural commercial labour markets, and the availability of government finance ensured its survival for several decades. King argues that the use of the schools system to produce African artisans 'stemmed from the larger politics of East Africa at the time' (King, 1977, p. 23). The CSM had become, probably unwittingly or at least with sound and benign intentions, a critical contributor to the political environment within which it had to operate.

The Friends Africa Mission

Unlike the major mission groups, many of the Protestant missions that were active in the Western Reserve were American in origin, largely from the 'bible-belt' of the Mid-West, and promoted a distinctly fundamentalist set of religious attitudes transferred directly from the small farming communities of the American prairies. Such a group were the Friends Africa Mission of Quakers (FAM) with their headquarters in Richmond, Indiana, who established a mission at Kaimosi, Kakamega District, in 1902, some 250 kilometres west of Nairobi and west of the main area of European farming land. Although this was outside the area formally designated for land alienation, the mission was granted freehold of 1,000 acres (405 ha) of forested land in an area which was sparsely populated at the time, a no-man's land between the Nandi and Maragoli (Gilpin, 1976, p. 6). At that time, however, the African population was spreading eastwards from Maragoli and soon the area round the mission land, still largely forested, was densely settled. Today, the area of Kaimosi and the surrounding locations of Tiriki and North Maragoli are among the most densely populated areas of Kenya (Gould, 1985).

The American Friends are not silent worshippers, like East Coast American or British Quakers, but evangelical fundamentalists with strong anti-urban and anti-modern sentiments. Their roots are in God-fearing, self-sufficient and isolated rural communities in the USA, and the early missionaries brought to Kaimosi the precepts and practices of the prairie homesteader. Willis Hotchkiss, one of the original missionaries, wrote after retirement in 1937: 'generally speaking it does not take a long sojourn in a town to spoil any Native' (Hotchkiss, 1937, p. 69). The archives of the FAM, deposited at independence in the Kenya National Archives, offer a rich insight into the attitudes, objectives and methods of the mission and individual missionaries over a period of sixty-one years (1902–63). They have been used by Clifford Gilpin (1976) to explore the social and political relationships between the church and the community in and around Kaimosi. He shows how 'the Friends missionaries transferred the concept of "pastoral idyll" and the "good life" to Western Kenya' (p. vi). They have also been used by the present author to explore the development of technical education in Kaimosi (Gould, 1989).

The three original missionaries founded a mission with four departments – evangelisation, education, medical and industrial – and each was pursued vigorously. The industrial mission was prominent from the early years, and from 1912 to 1946 was the main responsibility of one man, Fred Hoyt, now a substantial, if somewhat notorious, legend in the area. Hoyt was born in Iowa in 1879, was farming in Oklahoma in 1905, and in Imperial Valley, California, in 1910 when he was recruited by Hotchkiss, explicitly to 'build houses, schools and churches' and to 'train young Africans along these lines', as described by Alta Hoyt, his wife, in a family biography (Hoyt, 1971, p. 22). This he did with enormous vigour and great success, and many of the major buildings in the mission at Kaimosi and surrounding areas at the present time were built by Hoyt and his men. They built roads and bridges, and developed water supplies, water mills and a host of other practical works in forest management and crop development. Hoyt embodies the pioneer spirit, and was enormously practical and self-confident, with scant respect for authority, whether of the FAM in the USA or the colonial authorities in Nairobi. He sought to establish self-sufficient rural communities in the surrounding villages, each with their own builders and craftsmen, contributing to communities that were to be similar in many respects to Nyerere's vision of *ujamaa* villages at a later period of Tanzania (Gilpin, 1976, ch. 3).

The training Hoyt provided was essentially on-the-job training in the practical skills of carpentry, masonry and machinery, similar to King's 'school as a factory' model. From 1928 he ran a technical school with government support for his salary, and by the 1930s his was the only technical school given official support in the colony other than the official Native Industry Training Depot. Hoyt's intention and also his expectation, as is indicated by the correspondence in the archives, was that each trainee, provided with a tool box, would 'take them home and set up his own carpenter shop in the village market, or take a building job for a farmer or a chief on a Government project' (Hoyt, 1971, p. 91). That he had established a national reputation for training and that the colonial government was prepared to support his work is suggestive of how the impact of his training, designed to be primarily local in the home village, was felt elsewhere and in the areas of the commercial economy, despite relative remoteness from it, certainly compared with Kikuyu trainees from the CSM schools. Hoyt's trainees, with enormously marketable skills that were in short supply, were able to find good jobs on the settler farms and in urban areas, and found very little direct use for their skills in the impoverished villages of the Reserve.

Hoyt's objectives were similar to those of the Phelps-Stokes Commissioners and the Director of Education in the 1920s. He had visited Hampton and Tuskegee Colleges in the USA where the experience of practical black education, on which the ideology of the Phelps-Stokes Commission was based, had been developed. But he was operating in an economic and political vacuum. There is no sense in the archive materials, or in Alta Hoyt's biography, of his being sensitive to the realities of the political economy of the colony, or to the spatial dichotomy of the Reserve and the Scheduled Areas. He and the FAM authorities implicitly assumed that a viable economic development was possible in the Reserves and that his own work in the industrial mission and in the training of skilled craftsmen would permit that parallel and competing development, as it had done in the USA, where the small farmer was, in the late nineteenth and early twentieth centuries, apparently well able to thrive alongside larger and more capitalist operations.

Furthermore, even though Kaimosi was technically in an African Reserve area and surrounded by African farming communities, Hoyt was able to operate the industrial mission as a viable commercial enterprise in the colonial economy, with good supplies of land, materials, labour and capital. He undertook commercial work for the government (building roads and schools and providing furniture under contract), for settler farmers (the neighbouring districts of Nandi and Uasin Gishu were Scheduled Areas), for mining companies (providing pit props and supplying food for workers, especially during the Kakamega gold boom of the 1930s), and for urban commercial concerns (notably in Kisumu, on Lake Victoria, some 45 kilometres from Kaimosi and the main commercial centre for the west of the country). The forest reserves of the mission land provided plentiful building materials, and he was able to experiment in agriculture, growing cash crops, including tea and coffee, denied to Africans in Western Province until the 1940s. The school as factory concept gave him access to labour. In many respects he operated as a settler in the settler's economy, exhibiting the mission's products at agricultural shows in Nakuru and elsewhere and generally being well known among the settler and official community. His commercial success could certainly not be replicated by Africans in the area, who had no access to the technology or materials available to the mission and could not obtain the capital to acquire them.

Hoyt's success in technical training promoted the culture of migration rather than slowing it down. In such a poor and, by the 1930s, land-scarce area, opportunities for viable commercial agriculture were distinctly limited, by colonial policy towards cash crops as well as by land shortage. Family survival depended on cash incomes being generated elsewhere. The area of southern Kakamega in which the Friends Mission was active became at an early period one of the main areas of labour supply in the colony, and classic circular patterns of male labour migration were established (Moock, 1973). In the absence of local cash-earning opportunities any training or education could only enhance wants and expectations of those trained, and these could only be satisfied by migration. Hoyt's trainees found work at first on the settler farms and then, from the 1930s, in towns and particularly in Nairobi. The links with Nairobi were maintained by the continuous interaction implicit in the labour migration system, and the wider objective of the mission in establishing self-sufficient Christian villages was itself rejected by the local population. The FAM itself by the 1940s was more inclined to promote academic education rather than technical training, for its adherents wanted access to government and other well-paid jobs in the rapidly growing towns. In the eyes of the missionaries, contacts with towns brought undesirable social and cultural influences, corrupting the noble savage and diverting him or her from the rural idyll. Amongst other influences brought to Kaimosi from Nairobi by returning migrants was a further mission group, the Salvation Army, originally strongly urban-based, but from the 1940s a strong rival for the allegiance of the rural African population in Kaimosi (Sangree, 1966). For a community so strongly integrated into the urban economy, the more positive approach of the Salvation Army to towns and to migration generally was attractive and easily broke the Friends' local dominance of Christian adherence.

Conclusion

The cases of the Church of Scotland Mission and Friends Africa Mission provide further support for a structuralist interpretation of the space-economy of colonial Kenya. These were missions which pursued very different objectives: one which fitted well with the model offered by the colonial state, and the other which was inconsistent with it. The FAM tried to generate an independent, viable rural economy in an area which was seen by the state primarily as a source of labour. At one level it tried, through training and example, to counteract the colonial structures, but was unable to do other than strengthen these structures by moulding the selectivity of migration and accelerating the out-migration of trained workers. The FAM provided no real threat to the colonial spatial economy, and ultimately served to reinforce it through the migration system. Both missions, however, developed institutional structures that were well integrated into the economic life of the colony by providing building and other engineering services, as well as skilled labour. They operated within the structures of the state and were co-opted into it through grants-in-aid.

The failure of the alternative development model was confirmed by the African population itself in its rejection of technical training and agriculture as a basis for development, and by successfully promoting expansion of academic education in the last twenty-five years of colonial rule in all parts of Kenya, through the missions as well as directly by government and in independent schools. Academic education ensured that the populations of the Reserves had better access to the labour market and to higher incomes in the commercial economy. Only through the migration system could household viability, even survival, be guaranteed. The missions could not prevent migration, however much they may have wanted to, but through the education they provided they lent legitimacy to the separation of sources of labour from areas of demand for labour that were at the heart of the colonial spatial system. Core and periphery were integrated into a system of unequal exchange.

Since Kenya's independence in 1963 the migration system has remained largely unaltered in its essential features. In the decade immediately after 1963 there was some permanent resettlement of African farmers from the then overcrowded Reserves into the former European farming areas, but the national migration system remains characterised by circular migration between the impoverished and land-hungry periphery and the rapidly growing urban areas and commercial farms. The continuity in the migration system between the early decades of the twentieth century and the closing decades of the twentieth century reflects the continuity in the space-economy between early colonial Kenya and neo-colonial independent Kenya, between the national core, now dominated by a bureaucratic bourgeoisie, and a fragmented periphery of districts of limited economic opportunity characterised by out-migration.

The education system has expanded rapidly since independence, more than keeping up with high rates of growth of the school-age cohorts. There has been some slight restructuring to include a limited amount of practical study in the primary school curriculum, but the system remains heavily biased towards academic education rather than practical training. This bias has been demand-driven. Pupils and their parents seek education for white-collar employment, even though such employment is increasingly difficult to find. Where government has not been able to provide sufficient schools, 'harambee' self-help efforts have allowed a community-based solution, largely for academic schooling. International agencies, such as the World Bank and the International Labour Organisation, and bilateral donors have tried to encourage expenditure on industrial and technical education but these have remained relatively unimportant, given little more than lukewarm support by the Kenyan government in a range of ways. In the formal technical secondary schools, limited development of a diversified practical curriculum has not benefited those exposed to it. When compared with those who have been exposed to a standard academic course, technical school leavers have similar chances of finding a job, after leaving school (Lauglo and Narman, 1987). The village polytechnic movement was developed expressly to provide Kenyan school leavers with skills that will be useful to them in rural areas and thus help to reduce urban migration, but evidence both from Central Province (Barker and Ferguson, 1983) and from Western Province (Gould, 1989) suggests that a village polytechnic training may raise rather than reduce migration propensities of trainees.

The lessons of the colonial experience of skill training have not been well learned by policy makers, and successful alternatives in training and education must await a more fundamental restructuring of the national space-economy. The Kenyan strategy has in the past been dependent on top-down diffusionist assumptions, and, while there has been more evident trickle-down from the core to Central Province than there has been in western Kenya, the state's attempts to accelerate the spread of development from the core have had limited impact. Successive development plans have reiterated the need for regional incentives for industrial relocation to smaller centres away from Nairobi, but success is limited since the incentives available have been small. Current policies for decentralisation in a 'district-focus' for development are similarly weakly supported by additional resources (Obudho, Akatch and Aduwo, 1988). The structures of the early colonial space-economy remain largely unchallenged in principle, and the migration system, which began in these early days in part as a result of the efforts of missionaries to facilitate African advance, continues to maintain the mutual complementarities, but also confirms the unequal exchange between the neo-colonial core and the periphery.

Acknowledgements

The research for this chapter was supported by grants from ESRC and the British Academy. The author is grateful to Gerry Kearns, David Siddle and Charles Withers for comments on a previous draft.

References

Abbott, S. (1970) 'The African education policy of the Kenya government, 1904–1939', unpublished M.A. thesis, University of London.

Anderson, J. (1970) *The Struggle for the School: The Interaction of Missionary, Colonial Government and Nationalist Enterprise in the Development of Formal Education in Kenya*, London: Longman.

Barker, D., and Ferguson, A. G. (1983) 'There's a gold mine in the sky far away: rural–urban images in Kenya', *Area*, 15 (3), pp. 185–91.

Berman, B. J., and Lonsdale, J. M. (1980) 'Crises of accumulation, coercion and the colonial state: the development of the labour control system in Kenya, *Canadian Journal of African Studies*, 14 (1), pp. 37–54.

Furley, O. W., and Watson, T. (1978) *A History of Education in East Africa*, New York and Lagos: NOK Publishers.

Gilpin, C. (1976) 'The Church and the community: Quakers in western Kenya, 1902–1963', unpublished Ph.D. thesis, Columbia University.

Gould, W. T. S. (1985) 'Migration and development in western Kenya, 1971–1982: a retrospective analysis of primary school leavers', *Africa*, 43 (3), pp. 262–85.

Gould, W. T. S. (1987) 'Urban bias and regional differentiation: the role of rural–urban interaction in Kenya', in C. Dixon (ed.) *Rural–Urban Interaction in the Third World*, IBG Developing Areas Research Group Monograph No. 4, pp. 21–58.

Gould, W. T. S. (1989) 'Technical training and migration in Tiriki, western Kenya, 1902–1987', *African Affairs*, 88 (2), pp. 253–71.

Hotchkiss, W. R. (1937) *Then and Now in Kenya Colony: Forty Adventurous Years in East Africa*, New York: Fleming H. Revell.

Hoyt, A. H. (1971) *We Were Pioneers*, Wichita, Kans.: Friends University.

Johnson, H. B. (1967) 'The location of Christian missions in Africa', *Geographical Review*, 57 (2), pp. 168–202.

King, K. (1971) *Pan-Africanism and Education: A Study of Race Philosophy and Education in the Southern States of America and East Africa*, Oxford: Clarendon Press.

King, K. (1977) *The African Artisan*, Nairobi: Heinemann.

Kitching, G. (1980) *Class and Economic Change in Kenya: The Making of an African Petite Bourgeoisie, 1904–1970*, New Haven, Conn.: Yale University Press.

Lauglo, J., and Narman, A. (1987) 'Diversified secondary education in Kenya: the status of practical subjects and effects on attitudes and destinations after school', *International Journal of Educational Development*, 7 (4), pp. 227–42.

Leys, C. (1975) *Underdevelopment in Kenya: The Political Economy of Neo-Colonialism, 1964–1971*, London: Heinemann.

Meek, D. E. (1987) 'Evangelical missionaries in the early nineteenth-century Highlands', *Scottish Studies*, 28, pp. 1–34.

Moock, J. L. (1973) 'Pragmatism and the primary school: the case of a non-rural village', *Africa*, 43 (3), pp. 302–15.

Obudho, R. A., Akatch, S. O., and Aduwo, G. O. (1988) 'A district focus policy for rural development in Kenya: empirical application of bottom-up concept', *Regional Development Dialogue*, 9, pp. 158–88.

Obudho, R. A., and Taylor, D. R. F. (eds) (1979) *The Spatial Structure of Development: A Study of Kenya*, Boulder, Colo.: Westview Press.

Oliver, R. (1952) *The Missionary Factor in East Africa*, London: Longman.

Overton, J. (1987) 'The colonial state and spatial differentiation: Kenya, 1895–1920', *Journal of Historical Geography*, 13 (3), pp. 267–82.

Ranger, T. (1965) 'African attempts to control education in East and Central Africa, 1900–1939', *Past and Present*, 32 (1), pp. 57–87.

Sangree, W. (1966) *Age, Prayer and Politics in Tiriki, Kenya*, Oxford: Oxford University Press for the East African Institute for Social Research.

Stichter, S. (1982) *Migrant Labour in Kenya: Capitalism and African Response, 1895–1975*, London: Longman.

Van Zwanenberg, R.M.A. (1975) *Colonial Capitalism and Labour in Kenya, 1985–1963*, Nairobi: East African Literature Bureau.

Whitehead, C. (1982) 'Education in British colonial experience', in J.K.P. Watson (ed.) *Education and the Third World*, London: Croom Helm, pp. 47–60.

CHAPTER 6

Colonialism and the African Nation:
The Case of Guinea

Peter M. Slowe

Introduction

The contrast between the African and the European inheritance in Guinea is clear and stark. Guinea was at the heart of two states before the colonial era, Futa Djallon and the Mandinka Empire of Samory Touré. As the last of these, the Mandinka Empire, declined, the French completed their penetration inland and the colony of Guinée with its capital at the port of Conakry came into being, its boundaries agreed between the French and the British in 1904. This colony was later to become independent Guinea, the modern West African republic with a population of about 6 million and a territory of about 95,000 square miles (246,000 sq. km) (Figure 6.1).

Guinea spent the colonial era administratively and economically as part of French West Africa. The French imposed on Guinea a new set of frontiers which coincided only in a few places with the more flexible borderlands of the pre-colonial states and, as elsewhere in Africa, these paid no regard to ethnic boundaries. It was within these new colonial boundaries, however, that the roads and railways for moving the colony's cash crops and minerals were built, linking Conakry to the interior. These economic links combined with administrative arrangements to give some coherence to the colonial territory.

Education in French was the key for the African to being a member of the colonial elite. While 10 per cent of children received some education in French (Afrique Occidentale Française, 1958, p. 88), these were mainly ethnic Soussou living in Conakry or the families of chiefs. They were the immediate inheritors of the colony. Their elite *lingua franca* and their concept of a new Guinean state on the territory of the French colony, as well as domestic infrastructural linkages and commercial orientation towards the needs of the colonial power, made up the basic colonial inheritance of independent Guinea in 1958.

In this chapter, the development from the pre-colonial state, through the colonial era and the anti-colonial reaction under Sékou Touré, culminating in Guinea's neo-colonial position under military rule, is traced in clear stages. It is in fact this simple demarcation of contrasting approaches to development that makes Guinea a particularly rewarding case study.

6:1 Guinea.

The Pre-Colonial State: The Almamy Empire of Futa Djallon (1720–1830)

In the eighteenth century, the main political and territorial entity in what is now Guinea was the Islamic Almamy Empire of Futa Djallon. A series of small, ethnically distinct kingdoms in the Futa Djallon hills adopted Islam in the space of a few years at the start of the eighteenth century ahead of surrounding areas in the south and west in what now constitutes the rest of Guinea and Sierra Leone. Following a *jihad* in 1725, Futa Djallon became the centre of an empire stretching almost to the border of modern Nigeria; but it was an empire with only loose allegiance beyond the core area of the Futa Djallon hills, ruled by an oligarchy of political priests (*ulama*), mostly from the families of the local nobility (Dupuch, 1917). Futa Djallon became an Islamic state at a time when Islam was in retreat south of the Sahara, and was consequently geographically isolated from the rest of the Islamic world. To survive in these adverse circumstances, there had to be a degree of political, social and cultural integration in the Futa Djallon hill kingdoms, promoted by a policy of positive Islamisation.

107

First, Islamic Futa Djallon overcame internal ethnic rivalries and divisions of caste which had both played a major part in the indigenous religions, and indeed were oriented around them; they lingered for some years but were in the end irrelevant to Islamic social organisation. Furthermore the penetration of Islam in the early eighteenth century acted as a bulwark against the spread of later deviant forms of Islam which, in other parts of sub-Saharan Africa, tended to exploit ethnic, caste or territorial rivalries. Secondly, extensive Islamic educational and missionary work helped to secure Futa Djallon from disintegration by greatly increasing the number of social and cultural transactions within the core of the Almamy Empire; the *ulama* eschewed the idea of a single capital and moved court regularly, thus establishing close involvement with up to 300 Islamic centres of learning in the Futa Djallon hills (Hopewell, 1958). Thirdly, the integration of Futa Djallon made it possible for the Almamy Empire to establish a superior military organisation and hence to gain suzerainty over neighbouring areas, at least in the role of protector of Muslims living or trading there. For nearly a century Futa Djallon was a powerful empire loosely controlling extensive tracts of West Africa with very limited encounters with Europeans (Diallo, 1971, pp. 120–44). European encroachment and the dwindling of trans-Saharan trade eventually contributed to the substantial decline of Futa Djallon by the end of the 1820s.

The Anti-Colonial State: The Mandinka Empire (1870–98)

The Mandinka Empire of Samory Touré has been idolised in modern Guinean literature for its resistance to colonial powers between 1870 and 1898 (Traoré, 1962). It is notable for its political and military integration of an area roughly the size of modern Guinea (but extending into modern Sierra Leone and Liberia), although there was no attempt at the social or cultural integration so typical of Futa Djallon.

First, the Mandinka Empire united politically in one Islamic state some twenty of the tribal kingdoms, mostly of the Malinke people, over which Futa Djallon had previously established suzerainty. Unlike Futa Djallon, however, the geographical periphery, of the Mandinka Empire was important, as the suzerain approach was dependent on repelling territorial conquest by colonising European powers. Whereas Futa Djallon had been satisfied with occasional tributes from the peripheries of its empire, the Mandinka Empire's major military concerns were on its most far-flung territorial periphery. Samory Touré had to assert direct control through military governors with whom he was in regular communication, sometimes arranging mass evacuations as part of the scorched-earth policy with which he sometimes fought the French (Balési, 1976, pp. 33–5).

Secondly, while close political control was maintained over the whole empire, social and cultural control was weak. The Mandinka Empire was Muslim and even practised a loose version of the *sharia* but more traditional values and practices were also permitted; the village imam was in regular political communication with Samory Touré and took political authority away from the village chief, but permitted a variety of Islamic and other religious practices.

The Mandinka Empire was finally defeated by the French in 1898. As a model of military and political integration, it contrasts with the Futa Djallon model of cultural, social and political integration.

Guinea as a Colony (1889–1958)

The colonial era, from 1889 to 1958, was a period of disintegration for Guinea as Islamic central authority was destroyed. The Islamic leadership of the eighteenth and nineteenth centuries gave way in the 1890s to the colonial administration of French West Africa. Reports from the colonial authorities in the first decade of the twentieth century reveal the aim of building up the chiefs into reliable and viable instruments of colonial rule (Crowder, 1968a, p. 35). The focus on the chiefs was significant – as heads of clans, they were a counterbalance to Muslim officials and they were divided from each other by old rivalries and disputed boundaries which could be, and frequently were, exploited by the colonial power, sometimes in a most overt way specifically to disrupt established Muslim patterns of authority (Harrison, 1988, pp. 68–89). In other words, working through the chiefs involved a 'divide and rule' approach to ethnic diversity, the exact opposite of the impact of Islam on Futa Djallon and the political and military authority of the Mandinka Empire.

Apart from the use of chiefs for administration, the French found it useful for the economic exploitation of French West Africa, like other colonists elsewhere, to develop a small native elite. The École William Ponty and other training establishments in Senegal provided a class of *évolués* in Guinea (Diop, 1985). Although there was only a handful of native university graduates in Guinea at the time of independence in 1958, there was a significant elite of favoured technicians, teachers and others, a class apart, nearly all Soussou people from the Conakry area. The class division between these *évolués* and most of the rest of the native population was strengthened by French colonial policy after the Second World War which sought to guide colonies into a closer political involvement with France. French citizenship became the overriding aim amongst the *évolué* class.

The economic exploitation of Guinea entailed the development of a colonial economy oriented around the export of cash crops with its legacy of substantial spatial inequality, typified by heavy investment in the capital and main port, Conakry, and neglect of all but a handful of main towns elsewhere. For most of the colonial period, the planting and export of coffee and bananas, and associated railway development, constituted the main economic activities. Despite a gold rush in 1900, it was not until the 1950s that gold, along with bauxite and diamonds, were mined in significant quantities. The consistent pattern was of primary products mined or grown for export, a transportation system entirely operating for this purpose and the whole range of these activities run by foreign companies using Soussou labour from the Conakry area. The export economy extended just a few miles either side of the railways from Conakry to Kankan and from Conakry to Fria. The rest was essentially a subsistence economy with probably less inter-trading than in the pre-colonial period.

In contrast with much of French West Africa, Guinea also developed an organised working class, albeit on a very small scale consistent with the amount of industrial development. Its organisation originated with small groups of *anciens combattants* returning from the First World War, influenced by French socialists and by other aspects of their war experience (Crowder, 1968b; Summers and Johnson, 1978). *Anciens combattants* were involved in the Conakry dock strikes of 1918 and 1919. The Guinea trade union movement was the only one in French Africa to provide a post-colonial leader (Sékou Touré went from the leadership of the Confédération Nationale des Travailleurs Guinéens into the leadership of Guinean independence politics). The political importance of the Guinean trade-union movement allowed Guinea to escape political leadership dominated by the *évolué négritude* philosophy which tended to isolate African culture from politics. Touré and his fellow trade-union leaders reached the same revolutionary conclusions as Fanon (1969) and Nkrumah (1964). Their alternative to *évolué* philosophy was the psychological reconstruction of the African to a revolutionary consciousness, the devolution of maximum political and cultural power to the village (to villagers, not chiefs), and authoritative democratic criticism and self-criticism of the national political centre (Touré, 1969; Jinadu, 1978).

This political philosophy helped to bring about the circumstances of early independence for both Ghana and Guinea. The Guinean nation-state had been defined in terms of its political extent in a treaty between the British and the French in 1904, but was split economically, culturally and territorially at the local level by clan chiefs. Independence in 1958 marked the start of a period of much-needed reintegration.

Reaction against Colonialism: Sékou Touré's Guinea (1958–84)

The leader of Guinea's independence movement, Sékou Touré, took the view that Guinea's continued participation in international capitalism would lead to a continuation of the disintegration experienced under colonial rule. Although Guinea would have political sovereignty, the loss of economic sovereignty would force Guinea to put any other aims secondary to conventionally measured economic growth, the maximum output from cash crops and mineral deposits. Touré's government opted for policies consciously and specifically aimed at the establishment of Guinean nationhood through the integration of the Guinean nation-state, politically, culturally, socially and economically. This was to be at the expense, where necessary, of economic growth.

Measures aimed at the integration of the Guinean nation-state were assisted by international events over which Guinea itself had little or no control. Guinea rejected in a referendum the opportunity for semi-independence within the French African Community, and the French reaction was violent. The

French press and de Gaulle accused Guinea and Sékou Touré of being dominated by the Soviet Union (Panaf, 1978, p. 78). All French personnel and assistance were immediately withdrawn, and all administrative files were destroyed (Adamolekun, 1976, p. 44). The *évolué* elite, suspicious at first of Sékou Touré's independence from the French African Community, drew their own conclusions.

At the same time, Guinea took on all the paraphernalia of an independent nation-state: a flag, an anthem, and laws and speeches referring to 'liberty', 'dignity' and 'sovereignty'. While these all helped to establish Guinean identity within established territorial boundaries, they meant little to a disintegrated and divided nation-state until it was faced with a series of external threats to national sovereignty.

First, in 1960, there was the French Army Dissidents' Plot to regain Guinea for the French African Community. The anti-French reaction to this plot had the side-effect of bringing to an end increasingly violent clashes between the Soussou and the Foulah. The Soviet involvement in the Teachers' Plot of 1961 had a similar effect on the Malinké and the Foulah. Subsequently Guinea became more closely associated with the United States, but this involvement was to be short-lived. In 1966 the arrest of Guinean ministers on an American plane in Ghana brought about riots in Conakry and the arrest of American diplomats and Peace Corps workers.

The fourth and most serious threat to Guinea, and the single event which helped more than any other to solidify Guinea's national self-image, was the Portuguese invasion from their colony of Guinea-Bissau in November 1970. This invasion was supposed to release Portuguese prisoners of war held by the Guinea-Bissau and Cape Verde independence movements and bring about the overthrow of the Sékou Touré regime. The former objective was achieved; the latter failed and the resulting open battle was the first time the mass of the population had been faced with the choice of taking up arms to defend the Guinean nation-state or remaining passive while the country's fate was decided by outsiders. That Guineans fought in civilian militias as well as in the armed forces was to the credit of the integrating nation-building processes that had been going on in the twelve years since independence.

One of the Touré government's most urgent tasks had been ethnic integration. The French colonial authority's use of ethnic and tribal disputes to arrest a sense of national ethnic identity, with their promotion of the power of the chiefs, had been a major force for disintegration. A typical example of ethnic division was the inability of Foulah, Malinké and Soussou to agree on locations for any of the three secondary schools promised by the French for the five years prior to independence.

Even before independence, the ruling party, the Parti Démocratique de Guinée, played 'ethnic arithmetic', sending members from one ethnic group to run the party in an area dominated by another ethnic group, emulating Sékou Touré, a Malinké, who had been mayor of Soussou Conakry. After independence, a Soussou minister was given responsibility for Foulah affairs and key posts were generally distributed evenly. Special steps were taken to ensure that the national assembly contained ethnic representation in accordance with the estimated population of each ethnic group – and at the same time incidentally ensured almost total support for the Parti Démocratique de Guinée. The political patronage that arose from the consequent one-party state was distributed in a positive discriminatory way to avoid domination by the better-educated Soussou from the capital (Rivière, 1971).

Because ethnic groups in Guinea were concentrated in certain geographical areas, Sékou Touré also embarked, as part of the general aim of ethnic integration, on spatial policies based on the ethnic characteristics of different parts of the country. Ethnic equality was given such a high priority that national economic development was frequently sacrificed intentionally in favour of ethnic regional equality. For example, in 1959 bauxite production in the Foulah area east of Tougue, a major earner of foreign exchange, was reduced to 60 per cent of pre-independence output and retained at that level until 1964 when iron-ore production could be developed in the Kissi Forest Region. Similarly the pricing policy for rice favoured inland Malinké production in order to equalise its price at Conakry, despite its being some 20 per cent more expensive in real terms because of transport costs. This policy lasted from 1960 until 1985.

Colonial development, which had favoured the capital and railway towns, was reversed wherever possible, despite the high production costs resulting from inferior infrastructure in remoter locations. The 1964–71 *Plan Septennal* (République de Guinée, 1965) was intended to put into effect regional sub-plans which were audaciously biased against export orientation and in favour of spatial equality. The plan anticipated a very slow overall increase in the standard of living during the plan period of some 0.8 per cent per year. It was a conscious nation-building exercise. However, the official report (République de Guinée, 1971) indicated that the plan targets were underachieved by 20 per cent. Thus the regional emphasis of the plan meant an actual decline in average living standards in Conakry and four other main towns.

Ethnic integration policies were complemented by those aimed at the integration of classes. Here the integrating role of Islam in Futa Djallon and of the military organisation of the Mandinka Empire were copied by the Parti Démocratique de Guinée in Sékou Touré's Guinea.

The party became completely dominant. No human activity was outside the scope of party involvement from baptism to the channels of food supply, from primary education to funerals. Everything was done in the name of the party or 'for Party and Nation'. Nearly everyone in Guinea was a member of the party and attendance at party indoctrination meetings was compulsory.

The party's youth organisation (Jeunesse de la Révolution Africaine), incorporating all Guinean youth, was set up in 1959, replacing, where there had been any organisation at all, a variety of regional youth groups dominated by chiefs. The focus of its activities was Guinea as a whole – national and party culture, sport, national defence and revolutionary thought. This did not mean that ethnic origins were overlooked; it would not have been possible to effect any sort of real cultural revival in Guinea without reference to ethnic culture. Youth organisations had used French as their *lingua franca* in the colonial period; now they used all three main national languages and five minor ones, which were also used as teaching media up to the second year of secondary schooling. A new language academy translated French texts into all eight languages. The youth organisation thus had the twin aims of reducing the influence of residual *évolué* francophilia and helping to counterbalance the ethnic class distinctions promoted by the French, who had incorporated only the Soussou from the coast into their economy and society.

The objective of overcoming class distinctions by using the party machinery could also be seen in the rules governing party membership and, especially, membership of the party elite. The party was intended to be an agent of social equalisation, promoting the interests of labour (including traditional village labour) at the expense of those of capital. Indeed, at various times the party excluded tradesmen, businessmen and industrialists from any positions of rank. The party elite, with few exceptions, did four months' compulsory rural labour service each year. These measures, reinforced by the territorial decentralisation of power, ensured that during the 1970s no new party elite or cadre could become firmly established.

Following the implementation of the *Plan Septennal*, wide powers of local policy determination were given to the villages. Indoctrination had penetrated deeply enough for genuine devolution to take place, along with the real popular participation, without risk to the central government of Sékou Touré and the party. Weekly village *assemblées générales*, each with a part-time executive *comité de village*, ran the economic and judicial affairs of the village. The central government still retained control over the funding of major projects, but the *comités* and *assemblées* could decide between expenditure on, for example, cash crops and subsistence crops, roads and school buildings, and collective and hierarchical forms of organisation for work-shops and farms. This was a new departure for Guinea, for under the French and during the first decade and a half of the Touré regime all but the most minor decisions were taken in Conakry. It is significant that power in Guinea was based either at national or village level. Unlike many African states, Guinea had no ethnic regional administration. Touré favoured this approach on the grounds that regional administration was as remote as national administration and it could become a focus for ethnic rivalry (Touré, 1969, pp. 404–7).

None of these policies, aimed at the ethnic or class integration of the Guinean nation-state, was designed specifically to promote conventional economic development. The argument was that the majority of Guineans had limited economic expectations, at least in the short term, perhaps just food, clothing and shelter, all of which could be provided at reasonable standards by the Touré regime, owing in part to the happy accident of extensive mineral deposits. Touré argued that the cultural assertion of the African, and the construction of an integrated nation-state in Guinea, depended on a measure of isolation from international capitalism, which would inevitably bring with it a new emphasis on economic development over political and cultural development. Since international capitalism could not be rejected in alliance with other African states, as he and Nkrumah had hoped, it was necessary to isolate Guinea alone. Openness, he argued, would bring about the disintegration of Guinea (Touré, 1979).

Neo-Colonialism and Disintegration: Conté's Guinea (1984–7)

Three days after Sékou Touré's burial in 1984, a military *coup d'état* led by Colonel Lansana Conté took place. Conté immediately announced a programme of economic liberalisation to be piloted by the Comité Militaire de Redressement National over which he presided. Touré's policies for national integration were to be replaced by policies giving absolute priority to economic growth.

Within a few weeks the Parti Démocratique de Guinée was disbanded along with the youth organisation and its associated militia. Two months later, village organisations were also disbanded. In a succession of announcements, the new regime made it clear that economic growth was to be given a clear priority over cultural development, and both foreign and domestic private capital investment were to be welcomed.

In the first two years of this new regime, the rate of capital investment increased by 114 per cent: of total new investment, 56 per cent was in the Conakry prefecture, 31 per cent outside Conakry in bauxite mining or ancillary activities, and only 13 per cent (an approximate reduction of 25 per cent over the last two years of the Touré regime) in activities elsewhere. Agricultural investment fell back under the new regime, whereas investment in non-bauxite mining activities, particularly for gold and diamonds, increased by some 120 per cent (Cheveau-Loquay, 1987; Bureau Économique du CMRN, 1988). International aid for small indigenous enterprises has almost all been used for mining ancillary industries. These are rarely locally owned; for example, when there was an application by a local mineral prospecting consortium in Boffa for enterprise funds, it found that the contract for its area had been handed over without consultation to Arédor, a mining multinational, which had agreed to set up a locally run subsidiary.

Guinea's ethnic disintegration is reflected in the capital in various ways. For example, the dismissal of 10,000 civil servants, under an agreement with the International Monetary Fund (IMF), was carried out mainly along ethnic lines by the Soussou-dominated military government. Malinké people were overrepresented five times in the sackings with the obvious result that the new poor are nearly all non-Soussou; the sharp cuts in agricultural investment have left them little alternative but to exist on the fringes of urban life. Again, the heavy concentration of both foreign and domestic investment in the capital (with the main port and only international airport), combined with underinvestment in agricultural villages, have led to a sharp increase in the urban population by job seekers from non-Soussou rural areas.

Guinean statistical evidence is still scanty, especially for comparisons with the Touré era, but all the evidence suggests that a process of national 're-disintegration' was under way, along ethnic, class and spatial lines, as Guinea started to play a full part in international capitalism. If trends had continued, only the formal shell of the nation-state would have remained. However, during the period 1987–9 economic growth resulting from participation in the international economy began to overcome problems associated with disintegration. Indeed, it may be that the trend to disintegration has stopped.

Overall, whereas Touré's regime targeted ethnic and geographical integration, Conté's regime has aimed primarily at economic development. Touré consciously sacrificed overall economic achievement in favour of geographical class and ethnic equality of economic development, but Conté has risked, in particular, the wrath of the Malinké people of Guinea's interior in favour of his own Soussou people based around the capital city, Conakry. The Soussou have been the main political and economic beneficiaries of Conté's regime.

Conté's regime has generally gone out of its way to make itself attractive to international investors. Its reward has been IMF-related investment (on IMF terms) and a close relationship with France. But Guinea's full participation in the international system may yet fail, as Conté himself has recognised: 'We do indeed have a lot of problems here. The investors who come here aren't serious investors. They are more like invaders ... Negotiations rarely end with anything positive' (Conté, 1988, p. 23).

Neo-Colonialism and Reintegration: Conté's Guinea Since 1987

The development process in Guinea since 1987 has suggested that the geographical dispersal of Guinean economic development may overcome – by chance – some of the disintegrating effects of the Conté regime's policies. It may be that the welfare benefits of integration may be starting to coincide with the benefits of accelerated economic development.

Political events in 1987 and early 1988 were the culmination of growing ethnic tension and dissatisfaction with the economic consequences of Guinea's IMF package, which had insisted on major cuts in the civil service. Additionally, among intellectuals there was a growing frustration at the Conté government's failure to grant any political reforms. Recognising the dangers of mounting ethnic tension, Conté undertook a major programme in the August and September of 1987 to win over Malinké support for his regime with the aim of including a few more Malinkés in the higher levels of the army and government. His failure to obtain this political support resulted during October in the delivery of an angry speech in the Soussou language to a Conakry audience in which he referred to an illegal opposition movement, the 'Mandingo Union', which was active in Malinké areas and would have to be wiped out. At the same time, Conté increased his support among the Soussou by promising them increased trade-union freedom.

In December 1987, increased Malinké opposition forced Conté to cancel a state visit to France. Then, in early January 1988, he came under further pressure. Students rioted at the University of Conakry, ostensibly against their own specific problems of food and living costs. They were soon supported by both Soussou and Malinké workers in Conakry protesting about general economic conditions, especially the prices of bread, rice and petrol (and consequently transport), which had all doubled in the twelve months to January 1988 as subsidies were phased out as part of the IMF package.

Although the riot was put down with one dead and ten injured, the next day Conté climbed down. He did so under cover of an attack on economic saboteurs and unscrupulous merchants. The government announced price freezes (except on petrol) and improvements in students' living conditions. Having achieved a truce, the regime then went on the offensive. The university's rector, Aboubacar Somparé, suggested that there were political forces, controlled by Guinean exiles in Côte d'Ivoire, behind the students, and rumours of a *coup* plot in the making were given credence. The result was a purge of senior posts, with new government positions being filled by civilian and military figures considered personally loyal by Conté.

Lansana Conté has since walked a political tightrope in two major respects. The first is that his dependence on external financial support has forced him to accept an IMF package which includes phasing out subsidies, currency devaluation, wholesale sackings in the public service and a concentration on investment for export. This militates against political stability by making it impossible to give priority, as Touré's regime had done, to ethnic equality and national integration. Secondly, continuing economic liberalisation has meant a loss of wealth and power by the urban middle class who are part of, or deal with, government organisations. Yet it is they who are also inevitably responsible for putting the liberalisation into effect, through either their official or their entrepreneurial roles. Conté has called for greater administrative efficiency and greater integrity in carrying out reforms and he has tried to divert attention from his central economic and political problems by concentrating in speeches on drug trafficking and juvenile delinquency. It is an open question how long President Conté can survive the contradictions his regime has created.

While political affairs may be uncertain, economic affairs certainly are not. Economic policy in Guinea is dominated by the need to cut state subsidies to industry, agriculture and the civil service and to achieve an appropriately valued currency. Guinea's three-year development plan, initiated in 1986, is concerned with phasing out subsidies, promoting privatisation, developing economic infrastructure and controlling the exploitation of Guinea's immense mineral wealth.

Privatisation is considered especially urgent by the Conté regime. Badly managed public concerns are still a considerable burden on the Guinean economy. Some have already been put into private hands, with a preference for Guineans wherever they have the requisite capital and skill. Two agro-industrial units (producing tea and quinine), a printing works, a brickworks and a fruit-juice factory were all privatised in the first two years of the new regime and they were all taken over by Guinean nationals. But they were not the biggest firms. In these cases, the government tends to consider foreign investors, who almost all complain about the government's tardiness in its gradual revision of Touré's laws in favour of indigenisation and against foreign ownership. The government in turn considers that foreign offers are too low and some of the negotiations have been going on for more than three years. For example, the Sanoyah textile mill, the pride of Guinea's state companies, is the subject of negotiations between the government and the UCO/Schefer

Group, which has still not been finalised; the factory has been working at less than 30 per cent capacity since September 1988. Again, the Guinea National Hydrocarbons Board, another big concern which could be privatised, should soon be taken over by a consortium of Shell, Total and Agip. Negotiations have been dragging on for three years and the state is still paying the wage bill for some of the board's workforce.

The government has expressed disappointment at the poor take-up by multinational capital of its privatisation programme. It now feels that the economic infrastructure is sufficiently improved, with better roads, a good water supply, and simplified tax systems and mining and investment codes. It has therefore concluded that only policies which will assist the broader development of Guinea, improving infrastructure in rural as well as urban areas, in other words policies which had been used by the Touré regime to target national integration, will actually make the privatisation programme work. This has been the focus of substantial development assistance resulting from Guinea's agreement with the IMF.

Following the IMF agreement, concluded at the end of 1986, Guinea received 600 million French francs, becoming the second largest recipient of French aid (after Côte d'Ivoire). Japan also immediately granted Guinea a loan of 5.5 billion yen on International Development Association terms and 600 million yen in grants as part of the special IMF Facility for Africa. The IMF–World Bank programme provided US$115 million a year for the period 1988–91. Two-thirds of this funding was for development projects and the rest to finance the balance of payments deficit.

Following the Toronto economic summit of 1988, a series of debt renegotiation meetings converted short-term repayment arrangements to longer-term agreements and some long-term credits were converted to grant aid. The money freed in this way was intended, under a further agreement concluded with the IMF during 1988, to facilitate private investment in minerals and (to a lesser extent) cash crops for export.

In rural areas some £300 million of grant aid will be used over the period 1988–91 to develop health care and roads. An emergency programme of primary and secondary road rehabilitation was initiated early in 1989. This involves the asphalting of 1,200 kilometres of roads, mainly those linking Conakry with Kankan, Nzérékoré and Forécoriah (Figure 6.1). In addition, there are plans for the upgrading of 1,900 kilometres of rural tracks. By 1993 Guinea should have a dense, properly constructed primary and secondary road network, making for easy access to production areas and removing a major barrier to the exploitation of minerals and cash-crop potential. While the production of rice, coffee, oil-palm, mangoes, pineapples and bananas has begun to expand rapidly, it is in mineral extraction that infrastructural aid has had its most significant effect.

Guinea has extraordinary mineral wealth. It has the purest bauxite in the world and about a quarter of the world's known reserves, producing (under the auspices of a multinational consortium headed by Alusuisse) about 14 million tonnes a year from three sites, two of them in Foulah areas and only one in the coastal area inhabited by the dominant Soussou. There are 6.5

billion tonnes of iron-ore reserves, including very high-grade (70 per cent plus) ore from Mount Nimba in the remote forest region. Ore exports via Liberia are now planned to start at 6 million tonnes during 1990, the high quality making exploitation profitable even at low world prices. Guinea also produces diamonds of very great purity, which means that demand from the jewellery industry is heavy. The estimated reserves are 400 million carats, two-thirds of them of gem quality. The principal new capital for diamond exploitation comes from the multinational, Arédor, working mainly in Malinké inland areas. Guinean gold is historically recorded as the basis of the region's wealth from the fifteenth to the eighteenth centuries and gold is still mined mostly by craft gold workers operating individually or in small co-operatives. Union Minière, a French-based consortium, is now starting to organise the industry, again mostly in the country's interior. Investment in the exploitation of all these minerals happens to favour the spatial dispersal of development, countering some of the disintegrating impact of the first three years of economic liberalisation.

Guinea's mineral wealth is no longer regarded as the means of political and cultural self-sufficiency. Instead, Guinea has now opted for a path of maximum resource exploitation firmly rooted in international capitalism. By the chance location of mineral resources, the rapid recent increases in investment in Guinea have handed the Conté regime an opportunity to rectify some aspects of ethnic and class disintegration resulting from its liberalisation policies. International insistence on infrastructural aid and international capital's overwhelming concern with Guinea's geographically dispersed mineral wealth and cash-crop potential is now forcing the Conté regime to recover some of the ethnic and class integration achieved under Touré, and at the higher economic levels of attainment possible in the light of continuing economic development.

Conclusion

There can be few small states which offer such a clear contrast as Guinea between different approaches to development. Built on the foundations of two pre-colonial states, the French colony of Guinée in French West Africa ignored all the previous rich administrative and cultural history and allowed the African only a very limited say in local affairs. The aim was to substitute the French *mission civilisatrice* – with its ultimate objective of French citizenship for all – for African culture, and to substitute a colonial economy for regional patterns of trade and food production for local consumption. By about 1920 it was clear that the *mission civilisatrice* had failed and from then on Guinée, like most other colonies, existed principally to supply cheap tropical products to the colonising power.

The completion in 1914 of the railway from Conakry to Kankan helped to integrate the economy of Guinée, the boundaries of which had emerged from French administrative arrangements following a treaty with the British in 1904 and had never had any meaning economically or ethnically. The boundaries were perhaps the only part of the colonial legacy never questioned by the independence leader, Sékou Touré, who became president in

1958. The rest of the package of Western values was decisively rejected.

Touré wanted to create a culturally independent, modern African society. Although this ideal was shared by other African leaders such as Nkrumah and Nyerere, it was only Touré who defined the means for achieving it. Guinea would make independence from Western values its primary development aim. Conventional measures, such as economic growth, were secondary. Indeed, significant economic sacrifices were made to achieve the national integration Touré considered necessary as a basis for effective African cultural development. In his own terms he was successful, moving towards ethnic equality in a relatively classless one-party state. But poverty – and the privileges of the Touré family – brought the experiment to an end when Sékou Touré died in 1984 after twenty-six years in power.

The new military regime aimed to use Guinea's mineral wealth to attract foreign investment, rather than as a means of keeping Guinea free to develop culturally and politically separately from the rest of the world, as Touré had done. The new economically liberal approach had backing from the IMF, Western governments and multinational companies interested in mineral exploitation. It has been the good fortune of the military regime that the spread of investment has been such that ethnic equality and rural development have been promoted without state planning, and a counterbalance has thus been provided against the instincts of the Soussou-dominated army tending to promote the Soussou population of Conakry at the expense of the rest of the country.

It is ironic that the army, which ended the tyranny of the Touré family, is succeeding, despite itself, in achieving some of Touré's aims simply by economic orthodox. It is now possible for Guinea both to be an integrated nation-state and to have one of the highest standards of living in West Africa. It depends on the success of the economic and social policies of the military regime and, after 1994, its elected successor.

References

Adamolekun, 'L. (1976) *Sékou Touré's Guinea*, London: Methuen.

Afrique Occidentale Française (1958) *Afrique Occidentale Française 1957*, Dakar: Haut Commissariat de la République en Afrique Occidentale Française.

Balési, C. J. (1976) 'From adversaries to comrades-in-arms: West Africans and the French military 1885–1919', unpublished Ph.D. thesis, University of Illinois.

Bureau Économique du CMRN (1988) *Revue Économique et Financière*, Conakry: Bureau Économique du CMRN.

Cheveau-Loquay, A. (1987) 'La Guinée: va-t-elle continuer à négliger son agriculture?', *Politique Africaine*, 2 (1), pp. 120–6.

Conté, L. (1988) 'The investors who come here are not serious investors', *EEC Courier*, 108, pp. 23–6.

Crowder, M. (1968a) *West Africa under Colonial Rule*, London: Hutchinson.

Crowder, M. (1968b) 'West Africa and the 1914–1918 war', *Bulletin de l'Institut Fondamental d'Afrique Noire*, 30 (2), pp. 227–47.

Diallo, T. (1971) 'Les institutions politiques du Futa Djallon au XIXe siècle', unpublished doctoral thesis, Université de Paris (Sorbonne).

Diop, M. (1985) *Histoire des Classes Sociales dans l'Afrique de l'Ouest*, Paris: L'Harmattan.

Dupuch, C. (1917), 'Essai sur l'Empire réligieuse chez les Peulh du Futa Djallon', in Comité d'Études Historiques et Scientifiques de l'Afrique Occidentale Française (ed.), *Annuaire et Mémoires*, Paris: Comité d'Études Historiques et Scientifiques de l'Afrique Occidentale Française.

Fanon, F. (1969) *The Wretched of the Earth*, Harmondsworth: Penguin.

Harrison, C. (1988) *France and Islam in West Africa 1860–1960*, Cambridge: Cambridge University Press.

Hopewell, J.F. (1958) 'Muslim penetration into French Guinea, Sierra Leone and Liberia before 1850', unpublished Ph.D. thesis, Columbia University.

Jinadu, L.A. (1978) 'Some African theorists of culture and modernisation: Fanon, Cabral and some others', *African Studies Review*, 41 (1), pp. 121–38.

Nkrumah, K. (1964) *Conscientism: Philosophy and Ideology for Decolonisation and Development*. New York: Monthly Review Press.

Panaf (1978) *Sékou Touré*, London: Panaf.

République de Guinée (1965) *Plan Septennal*, Conakry: Ministère d'État.

République de Guinée (1971) *Revue du Développement Économique*, Conakry: Ministère d'État.

Rivière, C. (1971) *Mutations Sociales en Guinée*, Paris: Marcel Rivière.

Summers, A., and Johnson, R.W. (1978) 'World War I conscription and social change in Guinea', *Journal of African History*, 19 (1), pp. 25–38.

Touré, A.S. (1969) *La Révolution Culturelle*, Conakry: République de Guinée.

Touré, A.S. (1979) *Africa on the Move*, London: Panaf.

Traoré, D. (1962) *Samory Sanglant et Magnifique*, Conakry: République de Guinée.

CHAPTER 7

The Landscape of Colonialism:
The Impact of French Colonial Rule on the Algerian Rural Settlement Pattern, 1830–1987

Michael J. Heffernan and Keith Sutton

French rule in Algeria began in 1830 and ended, after a bloody eight-year war, in 1962. The intervening years represent the longest and, arguably, the most intensive period of continuous and direct colonial domination by a single European power over a section of the African continent. This chapter considers the impact of French colonial domination on the landscape and settlement of rural Algeria from the beginning of French rule to the late 1980s. It has two objectives. The first is to demonstrate how and why the Algerian rural settlement pattern was progressively modified, and ultimately transformed, during the colonial period. Particular attention is paid to the creation by French colonial authorities of a network of nucleated rural settlements which was superimposed on a pre-colonial pattern of dispersed settlement. The second objective is to analyse how and why the colonial geographies which were created in rural Algeria have persisted into the post-independence period.

Land and Life in Rural Algeria before 1830

Any examination of the impact of French colonial rule on the Algerian rural landscape requires some consideration of conditions prior to 1830. The basic chronology of the region's history before this date is well-established and was already understood by the French at the time of the conquest (Thompson, 1987). From the early sixteenth century, the regency of Algiers was part of the Ottoman Turkish Empire. Before that, the region had been dominated by a predominantly nomadic, tribal, Arabic-speaking population which had colonised the North African coast in two waves, the first coming in the seventh century AD and the second, more important invasion, beginning in the eleventh century AD. Earlier still, the North African coast had been an important part of the classical Mediterranean worlds of Rome and Carthage.

Recent work on pre-colonial Algeria, particularly that produced since independence in 1962, has added flesh to this skeletal outline (Abun-Nasr, 1987; Berque, 1978; Gallissot, 1975; Julien, 1970; Laroui, 1977; Valensi, 1977; Wolf, 1979). We now know that, on the eve of the French conquest, the population of the regency of Algiers was around 3 million (Yacono, 1954, 1966). Although the majority of the population lived in rural areas, urban life was well-developed and sophisticated. At least three cities – Tlemcen, Algiers and Constantine – could boast more than 20,000 inhabitants and each possessed a prosperous merchant class. Apart from the thin spread of Turkish merchants, administrators and soldiers, Algerian towns were characterised by a cosmopolitan mix of races and religions, and most possessed large and long-established Jewish communities. By 1830, the port of Algiers had declined as a centre of maritime trade as a result of the general collapse of Mediterranean piracy and privateering which had been such notorious features of the city's economy during the seventeenth and early eighteenth centuries (Sari, 1970; Stambouli and Zghal, 1976). Although it was to stagnate after 1830, the Saharan caravan trade in luxury products between the interior of the continent and the North African coast was still a significant element of the local economic system (Holsinger, 1980; Miège, 1981). The Turkish administration of the regency was characteristic of the more distant regions of the Ottoman Empire; although the local Turkish overlords in Algiers (*deys*) were theoretically vassals of the Ottoman Empire, they had become virtually independent of Constantinople by the late seventeenth century. As the economy was dominated by urban and maritime trade, most of the structures and institutions of the Turkish administration were urban in focus.

The absence of effective political control beyond the major urban centres meant that there was little systematic exploitation of the agricultural or mineral potential of the rural interior. Rural areas were dominated by a subsistence agricultural economy and rural society was ethnically diverse and tribal, reflecting the region's long history of conquest and colonisation. Around one-third of the rural population were sedentary, village-dwelling Berbers and Kabyles, most of whom lived and farmed in the more fertile valley bottoms of the upland massifs of Kabylia and the Aurès mountains. This population has generally been seen by Europeans as the descendants of the aboriginal people. The remainder of the population comprised widely distributed, nomadic and pastoral Arab tribes. These different groups created a correspondingly diverse rural landscape comprising a range of different settlement types, from relatively large villages, particularly in the foothills and valleys of the more mountainous regions, to smaller hamlets and isolated farms on the plains, the latter separated by huge tracts of apparently 'unsettled' lowland (Nouschi, 1961). The agrarian economy and society of pre-colonial Algeria was therefore varied and complex, and can be seen as an appropriate, or at least an inevitable, response to the challenging and diverse environmental conditions of the region and to the prevailing religious and cultural values of the inhabitants. Although traditional and technologically primitive, Algerian agriculture was based on a series of ecologically sensitive adaptations to the absence of abundant water supplies and to the need to limit soil erosion. The tribal nature of society, and the Muslim faith of the majority, encouraged a collective, communal attitude to land use which scarcely recognised the individual ownership of land. Following Islamic law, Algerian land was classified according to complex and overlapping criteria as either *beylick* land (in the legal possession of the Turkish administration), *habous* land (controlled by the mosques and religious foundations), *arch* land (communally controlled, tribal territory) or *melk* land (the nearest equivalent to private property)

(Pouyanne, 1895). According to this system, land was 'owned' by Allah and was used only temporarily by its earthly inhabitants (Steele, 1965; Ruedy, 1967). There were therefore few clearly defined units of land associated with either individuals, families or tribes and no established tradition of property as a commodity. The ritual of Islamic pilgrimage encouraged this conception by insisting that all Muslims must have unhindered access to land during their travels.

To the conquering Europeans, this agrarian regime was primitive, wasteful and inefficient. It created an impression of emptiness and disorder, of *un pays sans maître* which needed to be mapped, surveyed, drained or irrigated and then developed according to the rational, ordered logic of European agrarian capitalism. According to many of the standard historical, archaeological, ethnological and geographical accounts of the region produced by French colonial scholars after 1830, the centuries before the French conquest had been a retrogressive and barbaric era of despotic and corrupt Turkish Muslim administration. This had been partly responsible for a catastrophic environmental collapse which had reduced this once fertile and productive region – part of the legendary 'granary of Rome' – to a pale reflection of its former self. The 'proof' of this decline was the widespread distribution across Algeria of Roman and Carthaginian ruined settlements, many located in barren and inhospitable sites, which seemed to stand out as poignant reminders of the region's glorious past (Shaw, 1981). Linked to this environmental decay was a presumed moral and social regression. A once proud and civilised people, it was claimed, which had in ancient times spawned a prosperous economy and society, had been reduced to a tribal, nomadic and primitive state. This interpretation of Algeria's pre-1830 history generated a European discourse which sought to justify colonial conquest and colonisation in the firm belief that the imposition of a 'rational' European order onto an Algerian rural landscape which was perceived as a chaotic, disorganised wasteland would transform the region to the benefit of all (Lacoste, 1984; Lucas and Vatin, 1975; Nordman and Raison, 1980; Sahli, 1965; Said, 1978; Vatin, 1984; Wansbrough, 1968). The benign and industrious presence of France – frequently depicted as the modern heir to the values and traditions of Rome – would allow Algeria to re-emerge from its dark ages, recapture its 'natural' fertility and enter a new age of progress, civilisation and productivity.

The Conquest and Early Colonisation of Rural Algeria

French colonial involvement in Algeria began on 14 June 1830 when 35,000 troops landed at Sidi-Ferruch, to the west of Algiers. Three weeks later, the 15,000 Turkish troops defending Algiers had been defeated and the city capitulated (MG, 1838, p. 190). This intervention was motivated by a number of objectives but can be seen, at least in part, as a desperate attempt to divert public attention in France from the growing criticism of Charles X's government (Julien, 1979, pp. 1–60; Hamdani, 1985). This objective failed dismally, for a few days later the Restoration Monarchy was shattered by the revolution of July 1830. The new July Monarchy of Louis-Phillippe was preoccupied with domestic reform and showed a marked lack of enthusiasm for France's newly established North African base. To withdraw victorious French troops would have been unthinkable, however, and in the absence of any clear political directive from Parisian politicians the occupying army assumed *de facto* control over the region. Throughout the early 1830s, French control was limited to Algiers, its immediate hinterland and the major coastal towns of Oran, Bône, Kolea, Arzeu and Mostaganem, which had all fallen to French forces in the early months of the occupation.

The rural interior remained in a state of near anarchy until the arrival of Marshal Bertrand Clauzel as the new *gouverneur-général* in 1835. Ignoring an official report of 1834 which had recommended a strictly limited colonisation of Algeria – the so-called *occupation restreinte* (Yacono, 1966; Julien, 1979, pp. 109–18) – Clauzel sought to accelerate and intensify French colonial expansion. The inland towns of Tlemcen, Mascara, Miliana and Médéa were quickly seized by French troops, followed, after an initial unsuccessful attack, by the fortress city of Constantine. Meanwhile, Clauzel and his officers began – in a conscious attempt to replicate Roman imperial practice – to experiment with agricultural development projects on 'vacant' rural land. At this stage, the objective was to provide the French army with as much locally produced food as possible to reduce dependence on supplies from France. Using troops as labourers, a significant area of land, particularly in the marshy but potentially fertile region of the Mitidja to the south of Algiers, was cleared and drained (Franc, 1928). Gradually, a number of *fermes fortifiées* were established for European settlers, many of whom were army veterans who had been encouraged to return briefly to France after their tour of duty to choose a wife and had then been offered free, good-quality land and accommodation as pioneer colonists back in North Africa. In 1835 the first recognisable settler village was established at Boufarick, to the south of Algiers, where 562 small lots were cleared across nearly 200 hectares of land and eighty-three small cottages were constructed for European settlers (GGACC, 1922, p. 14; MG, 1838, p. xxiv).

The gradual expansion of French control during these years met with increasing, but somewhat localised, resistance from indigenous tribes. Although this violence may have discouraged some would-be colonists, it also displaced a significant sector of the local population from the relatively fertile coastal belt (*Tell*), thus 'liberating' large amounts of land which were promptly appropriated by the French army. The outbreak of more extensive hostilities in November 1839 simply accelerated the rate of French territorial expansion. In that month, the principal anti-French indigenous leader, Abd-el-Kader, marshalled sufficient support to declare a general *jihad* against the French invaders. Despite some early successes, the resistance forces were soon pushed onto the defensive, particularly after the arrival, early in 1841, of Marshal Thomas-Robert Bugeaud as *gouverneur-général* (Danziger, 1977). A tough, uncompromising soldier of peasant Limousin stock, Bugeaud waged a ruthless campaign through the early 1840s which eventually broke all resistance by 1847 (Sullivan, 1983).

The increasing amount of land under French control generated a vigorous debate in France about the possibilities of European civilian colonisation. According to Bernard (1930, p. 203), some 300 books and pamphlets on this topic were produced in France during the 1830s alone. Although several of these were somewhat bizarre – one project envisaged the construction of a network of medieval castles across Algeria in order to reconstitute in Africa the social and moral order of feudal France – the advocates of colonisation convinced a surprising range of opinion, including intellectuals on the radical left. Friedrich Engels, for example, spoke enthusiastically about the expansion of European power into North Africa (Heffernan, 1989, p. 381), while Prosper Enfantin, the utopian crypto-socialist and self-styled prophetic leader of the Saint-Simonian sect, was even more committed. Enfantin had been an influential, though less than diligent, member of a major government-sponsored scientific expedition to Algeria in the late 1830s (*Exploration Scientifique de l'Algérie*, 1844–67) and was convinced that the region was ideal for a programme of carefully managed European colonisation. In his view, the large-scale, spontaneous European emigration to the New World was eroding Europe's power and leading to the wholesale and barbaric destruction of indigenous peoples in North America and Australia. In North Africa, under the benign guidance of an enlightened France, Europeans could extend their influence in an ordered, rational and harmonious way leading ultimately to the creation of a superior, hybrid civilisation which would combine the best qualities of European culture with the most desirable attributes of Islamic society. The natural fertility and potential productivity of the region – so sadly unexploited hitherto – would once again flourish in this new order. This would be achieved through the creation of a dense network of small, nucleated rural settlements for European settlers, particularly those from the morally suspect environments of urban France. These centres – utopian communities on the edge of a new continent – would act as seed-beds of European civilisation and would eventually become the points of cultural interaction and intermingling between *colons* and natives (Enfantin, 1842; Émerit, 1941).

Although these mystical speculations were rarely taken seriously, the practical aspects of Enfantin's vision struck a common chord with other advocates of Algerian colonisation. Many informed observers felt that the colonisation of Algeria would serve a number of purposes, unrelated to the colony's economic development. First, colonisation would spread French language and culture into the vast continent of Africa; an important consideration in view of the rapid geographical expansion of English settlement around the world and the threat this posed to French cultural hegemony. Secondly, the Algerian countryside seemed an ideal place to resettle and rehabilitate convicts and other 'undesirable' elements amongst the 'surplus' urban poor of a rapidly industrialising France. Algeria could become a kind of enlightened 'French Australia' which would help to reduce the threat of unrest in the overcrowded, burgeoning cities of France. Thirdly, although colonisation might reduce the population of metropolitan France, the strategic incorporation of the native Algerian population into a greater France would also help to remedy France's slow population growth, already a matter of concern to French politicians who were ever mindful of the relationship between demographic power and

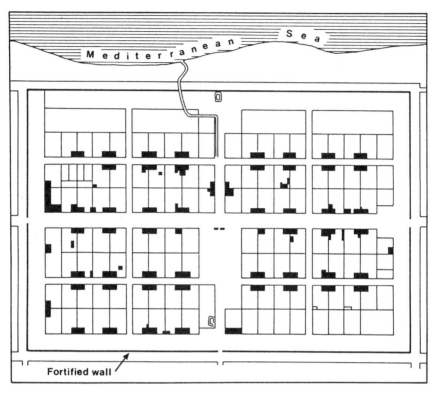

7:1 Colonial village plan, Algeria, c. 1848. *Source: Heffernan (1989)*

military prowess. This process would be greatly assisted if some of the poor and dispossessed from other European countries could be persuaded to emigrate to Algeria and abandon their native identity in favour of French nationality, culture and language.

Yet even the most optimistic colonial enthusiasts agreed that forging a new national identity within such a heterogeneous group of settlers would be a difficult and risky process, particularly as this type of social and moral cohesion seemed already to have been eroded by urban, industrial development within Europe. Most observers agreed that this would only be possible if *colons* were directed towards a carefully organised and readily surveyed rural lifestyle in small, purpose-built agricultural communities, if necessary under military control. These 'disciplinary' objectives are revealed in the preferred layout for colonial villages (Figure 7.1). In common with other pioneer colonial settlements elsewhere, the supporters of the European colonisation of Algeria advocated small, square, easily defended villages, surrounded by stout perimeter walls, with standard gridiron, orthogonal street plans and discrete family cottages with small plots of land. These nucleated villages were, of course, radically different from any form of settlement which existed in Algeria before the 1830s and were designed consciously to facilitate control over the incoming *colons* while at the same time demonstrating to the indigenous population the rational, ordering power of European social and economic organisation.

The impact of these ideas can be seen in the law of 18 April 1841 which granted free land, accommodation and passage to European *colons* wishing to settle in Algeria, on condition that they worked their land for a specified period. Despite Bugeaud's personal hostility to the 1841 law, it was during his period as *gouverneur-général*, from 1841 to 1847, that the first significant changes were made to the Algerian rural landscape and to the overall pattern of rural settlement. In 1833, there were just 7,812 European civilians in Algeria, the vast majority living in Algiers and the other larger coastal towns, together with nearly 28,000 French troops (MG, 1838, pp. 265–6). By 1840, the European civilian population had risen to 37,724 – the large majority still living in the principal towns – and the French armed presence had increased to 66,000 men (MG, 1840, pp. 52–3; Julien, 1979). Six years later, there were 109,400 European settlers in Algeria. Only 43 per cent of the European population were native-born French, the rest having come from elsewhere in Europe, particularly Spain, Italy, Malta, Switzerland, Prussia, Bavaria and Hesse (MG, 1847, pp. 191–3). About 20 per cent of this population had settled in a network of sixty-three newly established nucleated agricultural villages, most of which had been constructed on 60,000 hectares of the fertile land in the hinterland of Algiers (Figure 7.2) (MG, 1847, pp. 148–9, 184; GGACC, 1922, pp. 57–87).

By the beginning of 1848, colonisation and land appropriation had already significantly altered the nature and structure of the Algerian rural settlement pattern in the hinterland of Algiers and the other major towns. This had been facilitated by changes to the administrative geography of the country, notably the law of 15 April 1845, which had confirmed the three traditional provinces based on Algiers, Oran and Constantine but which introduced a new, threefold legal classification of all Algerian territory. Henceforth, territory was desig-nated as either *zones civiles* (areas where Europeans were in the majority), *zones mixtes* (areas where Europeans were in the minority) and *zones arabes* (where no Europeans had settled). In both the *zones mixtes* and the *zones arabes* normal civil liberties were suppressed in favour of direct military rule, exercised through an army hierarchy which culminated with the *gouverneur-général* in Algiers and the *ministre de la guerre* in Paris. Affairs relating to the indigenous population were dealt with by French soldiers and their paid Muslim assistants (*caids*) through a network of *bureaux arabes* (Yacono, 1953; Perkins, 1980). Deprived of virtually all legal rights under this system, the indigenous popula-tion was subjected to further legislation on 21 July 1847 which, based loosely on early attempts to settle native Americans in the United States, introduced the idea of *cantonnement* (Nouschi, 1961, pp. 268–84). Presented as a liberal act to secure indigenous property rights, the real objective of *cantonnement* was to undermine the nomadic, pastoral existence of local tribes by limiting the amount of land open to them and by encouraging them to settle and farm in discrete, clearly demarcated zones. Although this ran roughshod over pre-existing Muslim property rights, it released large tracts of Muslim land for European colonisation (Bouhouche, 1978; Isnard, 1950; Powers, 1989; Sari, 1977; Yacono, 1955).

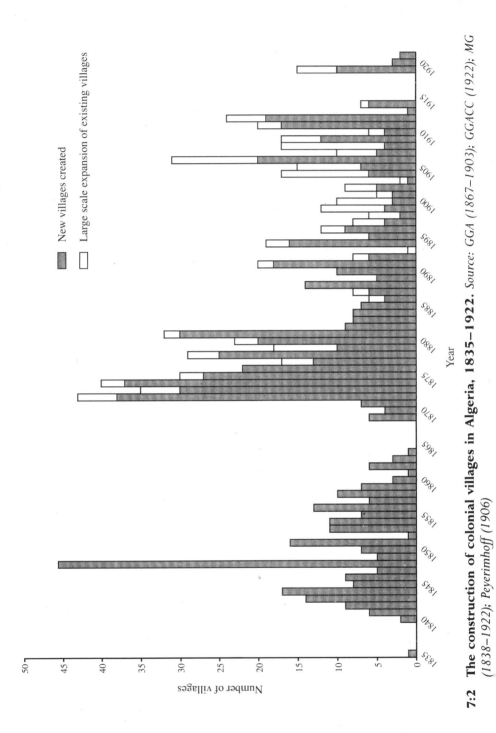

7:2 **The construction of colonial villages in Algeria, 1835–1922.** *Source: GGA (1867–1903); GGACC (1922); MG (1838–1922); Peyerimhoff (1906)*

1848 and the Colonisation of Rural Algeria

The colonisation of rural Algeria accelerated dramatically following the collapse of the July Monarchy and the declaration of the Second Republic on 24 Feburary 1848 (Heffernan, 1989). This political upheaval came after a period of deepening economic crisis in France characterised by harvest failures and food riots in the countryside, by industrial collapse in the cities and by violence on the streets of Paris, a city of more than a million inhabitants with an adult male unemployment rate of over 50 per cent. The new regime immediately put forward a number of social and political reforms in an attempt to head off further unrest. The most important palliative measure – a public works scheme involving a series of national workshops – quickly collapsed, and the resulting popular anger spilled over into a series of increasingly violent demonstrations in Paris and other major cities during the spring which culminated in a massive insurrection in Paris in June 1848 which was put down with great bloodshed and loss of life.

In this national emergency, a military government under General Eugène Cavaignac and General Christophe de Lamoricière assumed control in Paris. Both these men were veterans of Bugeaud's Algerian campaigns but, unlike their former superior officer, they strongly supported the idea of extensive civilian colonisation and instinctively looked to Algeria as a solution to the social and political crisis of urban France. On 2 March, it was announced that Algeria was to become an integral part of the new Republic and that the existing threefold classification of Algerian territory would be changed into a simple division between *territoires civiles*, where civil law applied, and *territoires militaires*, where military rule would continue. The old provinces of Algiers, Oran and Constantine were to become fully constituted French *départements* and the *territoires civiles* would be administered by nominated civilian *préfets*, complete with local and regional councils elected by the European population. The ultimate objective was to allow Europeans to govern themselves according to civil law while retaining military authority over the indigenous peoples in clearly identified areas. The stage was therefore set for a new phase of intensive colonisation.

Several prominent figures, including Alexis de Tocqueville and Alphonse de Lamartine, had proposed schemes involving state-sponsored population resettlement from urban France to rural Algeria in the months leading up to June 1848. These were hastily re-examined by Lamoricière, the new *ministre de la guerre*, and an ambitious scheme was devised to resettle up to 100,000 Parisians over a three-year period in a network of new agricultural villages in rural Algeria to be built partly by the army and partly by the *colons* themselves. Each family would be given a small plot of land and a cottage. A total of 50 million francs was set aside to complete this project and legislation was rushed through the Assemblée Nationale on 19 September. Posters were displayed around the capital, encouraging unemployed workers to emigrate. Within three weeks, over 36,000 Parisians had registered with the Ministère de la Guerre.

This rushed and ill-thought-out panic measure was doomed to failure and

129

the project was eventually abandoned. However, nearly 15,000 unemployed Parisians were shipped out to Algeria within a year of the 1848 law. They endured appalling conditions, living under military surveillance first under canvas or in badly equipped military barracks and then in jerry-built accommodation in fifty-four small, hastily constructed villages scattered across Algeria, many located in hopelessly impractical sites, with no sanitation or service roads. Ravaged by cholera and abused by hostile and insensitive army officers, around one-third of these *colons* died and a further one-third fled back to France or to the larger Algerian cities, taking with them an understandable bitterness towards Parisian politicians. By the end of 1851, in the immediate aftermath of Louis-Napoléon Bonaparte's *coup d'état* which brought an end to the Second Republic, nearly 130 new colonial villages had been created in Algeria, covering over 115,000 hectares of land. Of the 131,283 Europeans in Algeria at that time, 30 per cent had settled in the rural villages and around 20 per cent were still living under military rule.

The Advent of European Capitalism in Rural Algeria under the Second Empire

As the domestic crisis abated under the Second Empire, so the process of colonisation became less frenetic and panic-stricken. The number of *colons* continued to increase, reaching 170,000 by 1856, but the proportion living under military rule fell sharply to only 5 per cent. The number of new villages established also began to decline (Figure 7.2). According to the 1856 census – the first to record details on the indigenous population – there were around 2.3 million Arabs, Kabyles and Berbers, and 21,000 Jews. These groups were deliberately classified (and were increasingly treated) as discrete ethnic communities in a quite conscious attempt to divide and rule (Lacoste-Dujardin, 1986). Around 90 per cent of the indigenous population were living under military rule.

The late 1850s witnessed an important redirection of French policy towards Algeria. Eager to see his empire become a functioning reality and to facilitate the full assimilation of Algeria into a greater France, the Emperor Napoléon III decided to suppress the position of *gouverneur-général* and create a new, civilian ministry in Paris with direct responsibility for Algeria and the colonies, under the control of his cousin, Prince Napoléon-Jérôme. This decision – widely interpreted as an attempt to reduce the power of the military in Algeria and to limit the expansion of European power over Muslim property – was motivated by the emperor's sympathy for the Saint-Simonian ideal of peaceful contact between Europe and Africa and can be traced to the influence of Arabophilic advisers like Ismaïl Urbain. The decision was reinforced by legislation, passed in 1858 and 1860, which abandoned the practice of giving free land and accommodation to incoming *colons* on condition that they remained in occupation for a specified period. With much-reduced state support, the rate of European colonisation and village foundation was dramatically reduced (Figure 7.2; Ageron, 1980).

Unfortunately, the continuing violence in Algeria played into the hands of the military and, after a short but significant visit to the region in September 1860, the Emperor was persuaded of the need for a strong military presence under local control in Algeria. The new colonial ministry was suppressed and a military *gouverneur-général* was reinstated in Algiers. The position was occupied by Marshal Amable Pélissier, the Duc de Malakoff, a truculent Algerian veteran and disciple of Bugeaud. Pélissier used the existing *cantonnement* laws to launch a wholesale attack on Muslim property. Liberal opinion in France was dismayed by this renewed expansion and fresh legislation – the so-called *Sénatus-Consulte* laws – was eventually passed on 22 April 1863 and on 14 July 1865 which was designed to preserve indigenous land rights from European encroachment. Muslim property could no longer be confiscated without compensation, and all transfers of land to Europeans had to be paid for through the normal market mechanism. Although Pélissier tried to ignore these restrictions, they were eventually brought into effect by Marshal Patrice MacMahon, who succeeded Pélissier as *gouverneur-général* in the autumn of 1864. These laws, coupled with the earlier removal of state financial support for colonisation, greatly slowed the rate of European colonisation, and halted the establishment of colonial villages (Figure 7.2).

Although these Second Empire reforms temporarily halted the extent of European impact on the landscape of rural Algeria, they promoted a much more capital-intensive development of the areas already under European control. The process of *cantonnement*, which was extended under a new law of 16 June 1851, brought more land under European control, for which limited funds were paid out in compensation. According to Yacono (1953, p. 165), *cantonnement* led to the transfer of at least 60,000 hectares to Europeans during the early 1850s in western Algeria alone. The *gouverneur-général* at this time, General Alexandre Randon, was an enthusiastic advocate of capitalist expansion into North Africa and generous concessions to exploit forest, mineral and other resources were granted to French land companies, notably the Société Génévoise de Sétif, which acquired 20,000 hectares in 1853, the Société de l'Habra et de la Macta, which received 24,000 hectares in 1854, and the Société Générale Algérienne, which was allocated 100,000 hectares in 1865. The new settler villages which were created were also far larger than those which had previously been constructed. The 106 new settlements built between 1851 and 1870, for example, accounted for 336,000 hectares of land (Figure 7.2). An increasing percentage of the incoming *colons* settled in these and other agricultural centres so that, by the mid-1850s, over 50 per cent of Europeans were living in rural areas.

With their traditional tribal, nomadic and pastoral way of life under threat, the local population was increasingly dependent upon the European agricultural sector for survival. This unsettled the delicate balance between population and resources, and increased local susceptibility to demographic crises. Throughout the late 1850s and early 1860s, the Arab and Berber populations increased very rapidly to approach 3 million by the mid-1860s. Disasters of almost biblical ferocity ensued in the late 1860s, including cholera, typhus and smallpox epidemics, famines, earthquakes and plagues of locusts (Turin, 1976). Unable to adjust to these pressures, the indigenous population declined rapidly. By 1872, the native population had fallen to just 2.1 million (GGA, 1874, pp. 94–163).

The Third Republic and the Colonial Order of Rural Algeria

Like the upheavals of 1848, the chaotic events of 1870–1 in France had an immediate impact on Algeria (Ageron, 1979). The defeat in the Franco-Prussian war, the collapse of the Second Empire and the establishment of the Third Republic, the siege of Paris by the Prussian army, and the bloodbath of the Paris Commune all demonstrated the vulnerability of France as a great power. Aware of this, a series of uprisings against French rule broke out in Algeria, beginning in Kabylia (a region which had remained beyond French control up to the mid-1850s) and spreading throughout most of the country (Sari, 1972). The uprising was eventually put down after a savage campaign characterised by numerous massacres perpetrated by both sides. The new *gouverneur-général*, Admiral Louis de Gueydon, determined that the tribes involved in the insurrection should be forced to pay indemnities for damages to the French colonial authorities and obliged to surrender large tracts of their territory. The republican authorities in Paris had already brought forward a complex mix of reforms relating to Algeria, including granting the Jewish population the right to claim French nationality, suppressing the *bureaux arabes* and, most importantly, repealing the *Sénatus-Consulte* laws. These changes allowed Gueydon to recommence a programme of aggressive territorial expansion and to acquire yet more land for colonisation.

In part, this renewed expansion was linked to an immediate problem posed by the influx of refugees into France from Alsace-Lorraine after the region was ceded to Germany in 1871. As a partial solution to this immigration, around 100,000 hectares of newly acquired Algerian land was set aside for some of these refugees in the summer of 1871. By 1874, 877 families had settled on around half of this land in a series of newly built colonial villages (GGACC, 1922, p. 25). The acceleration in the European colonisation of Algeria after 1871 was also the result of a profound sense of national disgrace occasioned by the disasters of 1870–1. These seemed to confirm that French society had become decadent and immoral, and that the country was in danger of losing irrevocably its world position. Prophets of the 'new imperialism' – notably Anatole Prévost-Paradol (1868) – had been insisting throughout the 1860s that France would continue on a path of inexorable decline unless the country adopted a policy of aggressive imperial expansion. According to this view, France should acquire more overseas territories, French men and women should be persuaded to colonise beyond the borders of France and, crucially, the indigenous peoples of conquered areas should be assimilated into a French cultural tradition to increase the effective population of a greater France (Brunschwig, 1966).

Algeria was the obvious starting point for this imperial *mission civilisatrice* and a series of major laws was passed to encourage European colonisation, culminating in the so-called *Loi Warnier* of 26 July 1873. This law – proposed by Auguste Warnier, the *député* for Algiers and a veteran *colon* who had lived and worked in Algeria since the 1830s – represented a return to state-sponsored colonisation, or *colonisation officielle*, based on a system of free grants of land and accommodation, with obligations placed on incoming *colons* to occupy their land for five years. The law also reclassified Algerian land and removed all forms of collective property, thus reducing dramatically Muslim land rights. This brought 2,123,000 hectares of land under European control between 1874 and 1895. In 1872 there were around 260,000 Europeans in Algeria; ten years later there were more than 412,000 (GGA, 1874, 1877, 1879, 1882). The period 1871–81 witnessed the establishment of 229 new colonial villages and the expansion of a further 35 existing settlements, accounting in total for some 401,099 hectares of land. By 1901, there were around 630,000 Europeans in Algeria (GGA, 1903), an additional 169 new villages had been established and a further forty-one existing centres had been substantially expanded, covering 296,000 hectares (Peyerimhoff, 1906; GGACC, 1922) (Figure 7.2).

This continuing immigration was sustained by events in France, notably the phylloxera crisis, which decimated domestic French wine production. Unaffected by the blight, Algerian viticulture benefited considerably from the influx of skilled French workers who had been encouraged to seek a new life in North Africa (Isnard, 1951–4). While the European population rose through immigration, the indigenous population increased naturally to exceed 4 million by 1901 (GGA, 1903). Despite the enormous numerical superiority of the indigenous peoples – which oscillated between eight and ten to one throughout the remainder of French rule in Algeria – less than 15 per cent of Algerian land was legally owned by Muslims by the early twentieth century (Steele, 1965, p. 189).

Notwithstanding a temporary collapse of French investment in Algeria during the First World War (Meynier, 1981), the rate of new village foundation and expansion of existing settlements continued apace throughout the early years of the twentieth century. In 1921, there were about 800,000 Europeans, or *pieds noirs*, as they were referred to by the metropolitan French, in Algeria (Nora, 1961). Over the preceding twenty years, 123 new colonial villages had been established and a further seventy-six existing villages expanded, accounting for an extra 200,000 hectares. This process was sustained by a sophisticated propaganda exercise mounted by the colonial authorities in Algeria designed to convince public opinion that the links between Algeria and France had become indissoluble and that, in effect, the two countries had become one. 'L'Algérie', proclaimed one such propaganda booklet,

> est moins une colonie que le prolongement, au delà de la Méditerranée, de la France elle-même . . . Il y a bien plus de différence entre la Flandre et la Provence qu'entre le Sud de la France et le Nord de l'Afrique. Le vigneron de l'Aude peut se croire chez lui dans le Mitidja ou dans la plaîne de Bône; le paysan bas-alpin retrouve son décor familier en Kabylie comme le laboureur du Haut Languedoc sur les plateaux de Bel-Abbès ou de Sétif; les uns et les autres n'ont

presque rien à changer à leur vie, et, presque reprendre leurs cultures traditionnelles; ils ont à leur disposition de la terre à plus bas prix et une bonne main d'oeuvre, tandis qu'ils gardent ce même marché métropolitain privilégié et fortement défendu. (GGACC, 1922, p. 8)

Yet this vision of traditional bucolic bliss was already misleading. Throughout the Third Republic, an ordered, European, capital-intensive agrarian economy was emerging in rural Algeria. This quintessentially colonial economic system was structured around the network of relatively prosperous nucleated villages, was dominated by a few export crops such as wine, cotton, fruit and tobacco, and was controlled by a small group of successful European *colons* (Halvorsen, 1978). Although the European population was rising rapidly to reach 833,359 by 1926 (compared to 5.1 million Algerians: GGACC, 1927, pp. 206–7) and nearly 950,000 by 1936 (compared to 5.6 million Algerians: GGASE, 1936, pp. 42–67), the percentage of the European population living on the land began to decline sharply as employment in the agricultural sector declined and as job opportunities in the burgeoning urban-industrial areas of Algiers and Oran expanded. Existing agricultural villages were continuously expanded up to the Second World War, but relatively few new settlements were created (GGASE, 1937). By the 1940s around 70 per cent of all Europeans lived in the urban centres, representing about 50 per cent of the entire urban population of Algeria. This proportion was to continue rising up to independence in 1962. To begin with, the indigenous, dispossessed population was drawn into the European rural colonial economy as unskilled, manual labourers to replace departing European workers. Eventually, however, even these rural employment opportunities began to wane. By the 1950s, one in nine of the Muslim population was unemployed and a further 25 per cent were underemployed (Horne, 1987, p. 62; Smith, 1974). Increasingly, the indigenous rural workforce began to migrate to the larger Algerian towns in search of work and eventually turned their sights on the expanding industries of metropolitan France.

Through the interwar years, French control in Algeria seemed to be permanent and unquestionable. Despite several further attempts to improve the conditions of life for the Muslim majority – notably the proposals to increase Muslim political power through electoral reform in 1919, 1936 and 1944 – all reforms which seriously challenged the colonial *status quo* were defeated by a well-organised and intransigent *pied noir* lobby. The electoral system was structured such that one European vote was worth at least eight Muslim votes and the so-called *communes mixtes*, where Muslims were in the majority, remained under the control not of elected councils but of nominated European administrators (Berque, 1967). The great centenary celebrations of French rule in 1930 seemed to confirm the monolithic and immutable nature of this colonial order. As the British writer Mary Motley wrote at the time: 'In the golden glow of the centenary there seemed no reason why the existing regime should not last indefinitely' (Horne, 1987, p. 36).

Yet the winds of change which were already beginning to blow through the colonial world fanned the flames of a nascent, anti-French Algerian nationalism which drew moral and political inspiration from a complex mix of forces, including Islam and socialism. The experience of life as part of an organised, but distrusted and racially suspect, urban labour force in France; the memory of two world wars which had demonstrated the potential weakness of France and which had seen Algeria occupied temporarily by Anglo-American forces after 1942; the continuing desperate impoverishment of large sectors of the Algerian population under French rule – all these factors had a catalytic effect on the native Algerian population, particularly the younger generation, and began seriously to erode the façade of a benign, tolerant and assimilationist French colonial power (Julien, 1972; Kaddache, 1980; Stora, 1989). The depth of anti-colonial feeling was revealed by the gruesome massacre of more than 100 European settlers by local Muslims in and around the town of Sétif as the Allied victory was being celebrated in May 1945. This appalling act – reminiscent of Mau Mau assaults on white settlers in Kenya – generated even more awful and indiscriminate acts of revenge, meted out by the French army and by vigilante *colon* patrols, which left around 6,000 Muslims dead. Although a tense calm returned to Algeria thereafter, militant anti-French nationalists, eventually organised into a well-armed Front de la Libération Nationale (FLN), began the lengthy preparations for wholesale war. Inspired by the French army's catastrophic defeat at Dien Bien Phu at the end of the country's colonial struggle in Indo-China, the FLN finally declared war on the French colonial administration in Algeria at midnight on All Saints' Day 1954.

The Impact of the War of Independence (1954–61) on the Algerian Rural Settlement Pattern

During this final, bitter phase in France's long colonial involvement in North Africa, the Algerian rural landscape underwent an unprecedented era of disturbance which in some regions amounted to a major and traumatic upheaval. This resulted primarily from the French army's anti-guerrilla strategy during the savage war of independence. The history of this final era of conflict has been expertly developed in a number of places and requires no repetition here (Alleg *et al.*, 1981; Horne, 1987). Suffice it to say that in the early years of the revolutionary struggle, the armed conflict was concentrated in the countryside and it was the Algerian peasantry who supplied the ranks of the *fellagha* or guerrilla fighters and who suffered the harsh consequences of France's counter-insurgency policies. This involved the massive regrouping of the rural population by the French army, partly to protect it but also to prevent active assistance to the guerrillas. Early regrouping policies lacked any basic strategy or overall planning, amounting, between 1955 and 1957, to a 'scorched-earth policy' with the creation of extensive *zones interdites* or forbidden zones. The inhabitants were expelled from these 'free-fire zones' and the abandoned settlements were destroyed by the French troops with little or no provision being made to rehouse those expelled from their homes. According to Côte (1988a), 8,000 rural settlements were destroyed, ranging from isolated farms, hamlets and *mechtas* to whole villages. Rural housing conditions deteriorated considerably. Deprived of their traditional sturdy stone houses with tiled roofs, many families were forced to live as refugees in, or near, existing villages and towns in the foothills and plains around the forbidden zones in temporary huts constructed of earth and corrugated iron roofing which came to be known as *gourbis.*

From early 1957, a more organised regrouping policy was developed which culminated in the creation of *centres de regroupement,* entirely new villages established to resettle the displaced rural folk. The number of these *centres* increased rapidly, particularly in late 1958 when the French army constructed fortified barrages along Algeria's eastern and western frontiers and methodically cleared the territory behind them. All too often the construction of these essentially military *centres* was poorly planned and inadequately prepared. The resulting villages were therefore ill-equipped to receive large numbers of refugees. After growing concern in France at the deplorable state of these new villages, the civilian authorities in Algeria intervened and set up an Inspection générale des regroupements (IGRP) in 1959 in a belated attempt to improve conditions and foster rural development around this new network of settlements. The better-sited *centres,* constructed using permanent materials and endowed with certain basic amenities, were renamed 'new villages' as part of a propaganda exercise entitled the 'thousand new villages' programme incorporated in the 1959 Constantine Plan.

It is difficult to overemphasise the impact of this upheaval on Algeria's rural settlement system. The new settlements which were created across Algeria during the war represented a major reorganisation of traditional dispersed settlement systems and a dramatic addition to the stock of fewer than 1,000 nucleated rural settlements which had been created during the preceding generations of French rule. The IGRP's statistics indicate that, between 1954 and 1961, some 2,380 *centres de regroupement* were built. Of these new foundations, 1,217 were temporary *centres* and 1,163 'new villages' (Cornaton, 1967). In addition there were many *recasements,* whereby displaced people were resettled in adjuncts to existing settlements. For 1961, the IGRP calculated the regrouped population to number 1,958,302. Cornaton's fieldwork discovery of many more *centres,* however, supports his more valid 1961 estimate of 2,350,000 people in *centres,* which amounted to one-third of the rural population. If all those who fled or moved to *recasements* are added, his estimate rises to 3,525,000 Algerians displaced, a staggering 50 per cent of the rural population (Cornaton, 1967). Estimates by Bourdieu and Sayad (1964) support this figure and this has led them to conclude that this displacement of population was one of the most brutal known to history.

Not all these *centres* were to survive nor were many initially significant as service centres. Rural economies subjected to this resettlement upheaval were often shattered, original settlements and crops destroyed, and landscapes sometimes rendered unusable and unrecognisable through napalm bombing. While some people returned to re-establish traditional ways of life after hostilities ceased, many *regroupés* remained in the *centres,* while others migrated out or dispatched the family breadwinner to the larger Algerian towns or to cities across the Mediterranean in France itself. This rural–urban exodus was reflected in the first post-independence population census in 1966. *Arrondissements* which experienced high levels of *regroupement* tended to display below-average population growth for the period 1954 to 1966 and had already become established as the principal zones of out-migration. In contrast, the rapidly growing *arrondissements* during this period were the lowland coastal and urban regions where smaller proportions of the population had been regrouped. These became the major centres of rural–urban in-migration (Lesne, 1962; Sutton, 1972).

The local impact of this concentration of a formerly fairly dispersed rural settlement pattern has been demonstrated by several researchers. In the coastal Djebel Chénoua region, the scattered rural population was concentrated into eight *centres*, located mainly around the periphery of the upland massif (Leveau, 1975). Similarly, the *daïra* of Collo had a weak settlement hierarchy of one town and five villages before the creation of forty-six *centres*, thirty of which were still in existence in 1966 with a total population of 20,000 people (Pierre, 1966). As many of these *centres* were created in completely unsuitable locations for effective agricultural production and were constructed using inappropriate house designs and settlement layouts, it may have been expected that they would not survive after the cessation of hostilities. Yet it soon became clear that the *centres* were persisting in many regions, including the Mitidja (Mutin, 1977), Lower Kabylia (Peillon, 1970) and in the Annaba region (Tomas, 1977). This survival was confirmed by Cornaton's (1967) field surveys in 1965–6, which demonstrated that this major late-colonial upheaval had left a permanent legacy on the Algerian rural settlement pattern. Thus Côte (1981) lists seventy-seven *centres de regroupement* out of a total of 283 rural centres in his study region, the High Plains of eastern Algeria. As such they form the second most important type of nucleated settlement in that region after the 102 original colonial villages, and well ahead of the forty-four traditional villages.

A further systematic investigation of all the *centres* listed by Cornaton has been made using archival material associated with Algeria's 1977 population census (Sutton and Lawless, 1978; Sutton, 1981). Out of Cornaton's sample of 146 *centres de regroupement*, ninety-eight could be traced in the 1977 documentation and a further twelve had become suburbs of towns. Thus, at least 75 per cent of the sample had become permanent additions to the Algerian settlement pattern. This figure may well be higher when one takes into account the widespread Arabisation of the original French placenames. Furthermore, many *centres* had recorded a stable or increased population between 1965 and 1977. Despite their unpromising beginnings, many had started to acquire local service functions, especially retailing and primary schools. Indeed, by the 1987 census twenty-nine of Cornaton's sample of *centres* had evolved into commune administrative centres (*agglomérations au chef lieu*), with population sizes sometimes in excess of 5,000 (RGPH, 1989). Belatedly, then, this resettlement legacy of the final throes of French colonialism has ultimately started to have a positive impact on Algeria's rural settlement system, at least in regions such as the Collo peninsula.

Not to be outdone by the former colonial occupiers, the newly independent Algerian government after 1962 embarked on its own brief resettlement
programme, creating similar *villages de reconstruction*. These resettlement centres were built between 1963 and 1966 partly to rehouse people from the
worst and most overcrowded *centres de regroupement* and partly to regroup
rural people as part of a post-independence counter-insurgency struggle
against Kabylie rebels (Cornaton, 1967). Ironically, these villages were based
on layouts and plans almost identical to those employed by the French. Consequently, the same errors were often made relating to poor sites, unsuitable
houses, inappropriate use of breeze-blocks, and undersized villages. The new
buildings sometimes remained uninhabited or incomplete. More successful
were the reconstruction settlements which were grafted on to pre-existing
villages or *centres de regroupement* (Brûlé, 1976). Côte (1988a) thus records
twenty-three such *cités de reconstruction*, built in 1963–4, as an identifiable
component of the rural settlement system of the eastern High Plains in the
1980s.

From Colonial Farm to 'Autogestion' Estate

By the late 1950s, several decades of rural–urban migration on the part of the
European settler population had turned most colonial villages into Muslim-
dominated settlements. Refugee flows during the war of independence
hastened this transformation so that by the last months of French rule the
characteristically French colonial morphology and building styles of these
villages contrasted with an overwhelmingly Muslim population. With the
precipitous exit of 95 per cent of the French settlers in 1962, both the colonial
villages and most of the colonial farms were abandoned completely by the
remaining European residents and owners. The ex-colonial villages now took
on new post-independence functions. Swollen with rural–urban migrants, they
assumed more of a residential and welfare role and acted as staging posts in
the rapid urban-oriented flux in the 1960s. Some acquired additional local
administrative roles and in time other service functions. Others, particularly
around Oran and in the Mitidja Plain and Sahel around Algiers, became commuter villages (Mutin, 1980). Although churches were converted to mosques
and French bars became cafés, the cultural landscape remained decidedly
French, if initially rather dilapidated.

The 22,000 European farms remaining at independence were occupied by
their agricultural labourers to protect both the forthcoming crops and their
jobs. This *ad hoc* self-managed co-operativism was institutionalised by the state
into an *autogestion* sector as the colonial estates and farms were rationalised
into about 2,000 large socialist estates or *autogestion* units. In 1966, some units
were handed over to co-operatives composed of veteran guerrilla fighters or
anciens moudjahidine. Theoretically organised on co-operative lines, the
autogestion units rarely practised real worker participation and functioned
more frequently as state collective farms (Dominelli, 1986). Côte (1988b)
likens them to *kolkhozes*. Production and productivity stagnated through the
various organisational phases of centralisation and decentralisation culminating

in the 1983 shake-up when the remaining 2,099 *autogestion* units were restructured into 3,415 *domaines agricoles socialistes* which were granted greater autonomy and were organised on a more manageable scale. Côte (1988b), however, still regards them as *pseudo-fermes d'État*.

The land-use and settlement significance of the *autogestion* sector is that it maintained and to a degree fossilised colonial, commercially oriented agricultural methods over a considerable part of northern Algeria. Admittedly there were land-use modifications but generally, large-scale mechanised and modern agriculture systems prevailed. In settlement terms, the faded glory of the settlers' grand farmhouses was perpetuated as they became either new residential establishments, offices or sometimes factories. Overmanning was a problem, exacerbated by much clandestine residential occupancy as *autogestion* workers switched to urban and industrial jobs, commuting from the illegally maintained dwellings on the *autogestion* estates (Mutin and Rebbouh, 1978). It was not until the late 1970s that rural housing policies attempted to add about 15,000 much-needed dwellings to the *autogestion* units, of which 1,482 had been completed and 7,174 were under construction at the end of 1979 (ONS, 1979).

In comparison with the attention given to *autogestion*, the traditional peasant agricultural sector and its associated settlements were relatively neglected, at least until the *révolution agraire* of the 1970s. Despite all the aforementioned nucleated settlement activity, the 1966 census revealed the continued dominance of dispersed rural settlement. Seventy-four per cent of rural people still lived in small and dispersed settlements of fewer than 100 dwellings, and seventy-six of Algeria's 7,000 communes did not contain an agglomerated *chef-lieu*. These areas had also been severely disturbed by the counter-insurgency policies employed during the war of independence which had a particularly devastating effect on the pastoralists' way of life. As a result, many traditional rural settlements suffered from an increasing rate of out-migration and a growing problem of soil erosion in the more marginal lands, and generally underwent a form of *clochardisation*. Rural housing was often sadly inadequate. Out of 1.1 million rural dwellings in 1966, 160,000 were tents or shanty huts and 260,000 lacked solid construction materials. Only 5 per cent of rural dwellings were linked to the electricity networks, only 7 per cent to a piped water system, and only 9 per cent to a drain or sewer (Côte, 1988a). Only garden agriculture and small-scale irrigation development offered scope for improvement, while emigrants' remittances held together weakened rural communities especially in the over-populated upland massifs (Côte, 1988b). It was not until the 1970s that Algeria's development priorities turned to the restructuring and revival of this stagnating and neglected traditional rural settlement system.

The Socialist Villages – An Urban Solution to a Rural Problem?

From the outset, Algeria's Charter of the Agrarian Revolution, promulgated in November 1971, recognised that a more equitable and dynamic agricultural system would involve more than the mere redistribution of land. New villages were to be incorporated as part of a parallel and supporting range of restructuring institutions. By the end of the 1970s, more than 90,000 beneficiaries had received reform land and were grouped into about 6,000 production co-operatives. Together with the *autogestion* estates and private holdings these reform co-operatives were organised into over 600 service co-operatives to provide agricultural inputs and market outputs (Brûlé, 1985). As part of this restructuring, a more nucleated rural settlement pattern was deemed necessary to rehouse reform beneficiaries nearer to their newly acquired land and often to assist in locating the service co-operatives and other necessary service functions centrally within their prospective hinterlands. The largely colonial rural settlement system with its settler-oriented colonial villages and *centres de regroupement* structured and located according to military objectives was ill-suited to serve traditional agricultural areas undergoing agrarian reform; hence the launch of an ambitious and much publicised '1,000 *villages socialistes*' programme, a nomenclature unfortunately recalling the 1959 '1,000 new villages' project under the French Constantine Plan. Guidelines for these new 'socialist villages' stressed their restructuring function as technical bases for agricultural production and as centres for both the community's collective activities and the family's social life. Early surveys of reform recipients in these new settlements, however, revealed poor housing standards, inadequate services, and often excessive distances between recipients' homes and their new reform land (AARDES, 1975).

The first socialist village was inaugurated in April 1972. Sixty villages were completed by November 1976, 120 by July 1979, and 171 by late 1981 (Sutton, 1984, 1987). By the early 1980s the programme was under review and eventually ended. Altogether 400 out of a planned 1,000 villages were constructed (Côte, 1988a; Brûlé and Fontaine, 1986). Assuming an average rural household size of six or seven people and an eventual total of about 70,000 dwellings, the truncated socialist villages programme could have eventually housed over 400,000 people. Spatially the programme was truly at a national scale with, by 1981, completed villages found in all *wilayate* except Tamanrasset, where three were then under construction (MHU, 1982; Sutton, 1987). The 1987 census records many of these socialist villages with populations in excess of 1,000 and even with local administrative functions as *agglomérations au chef-lieu*. The shortcomings of these centres is demonstrated, however, by the relatively low proportions of their occupied populations working in agriculture (Table 7.1). Several regional concentrations and disparities have also emerged with more socialist villages in those *wilayate* with extensive agricultural areas, notably in the Steppe and High Plateaux, but also many in the *Tell* as in Tizi Ouzou and Annaba *wilayate*. These are often regions in which most of the redistributed agrarian reform land is located. In comparison with the French colonial bias towards the coastal *Tell*, this represents a spatial favouring of the High Plateaux and the Steppe in the allocation of infrastructure and social investment. Significantly, according to Adair (1982), the building of villages progressed faster away from the major regional centres, so benefiting small interior towns and more isolated regions. This was as much

Table 7.1 *Some Algerian Socialist Villages in 1987*

Wilaya	Village	Status	Dwellings	Population	Agricultural population (%)
Aïn	El Emir Abdelkader	ACL	250	1919	36
Temouchent	Aurès-el-Meida	AS	150	1332	40
Mascara	Sidi Mahieddine	AS	410	2684	67
	Aïn Bouras	AS	131	817	75
Batna	Oustili	AS	229	1653	38
	Legrine	AS	209	1258	40
Sétif	Akrif Bourdim	AS	157	1465	18
	Sid Ali	AS	142	818	13
	Bir Labiod	AS	174[1]	664	44
	El Mellah	ACL	242	1851	46

Notes:
ACL = Agglomération au chef-lieu.
AS = Agglomération secondaire.
Note: 1. Only 70 houses in Bir Labiod were inhabited.
Source: RGPH (1989).

a consequence of higher land prices and the lack of spare construction capacity near the main cities as the result of deliberate decentralisation.

By the 1980s, therefore, there had emerged a wide scatter of new, distinctive, nucleated settlements throughout rural Algeria. Notwithstanding variations in layout and house type, the socialist villages now constitute a separate group of rural settlements distinct in terms of their modern if uniform houses built to quite high standards and serviced along the lines of small towns. However, as a major exercise in social engineering, the socialist villages programme, along with the agrarian reform, met with setbacks and criticisms. Construction took longer than anticipated and costs were higher. Self-construction by potential villagers and the use of cheaper local building materials were infrequent. All too rarely were the opinions and collaboration of the potential inhabitants sought by the authorities. Decisions over house types and village layout were taken by technicians often with limited knowledge of the local rural society. Hence, urban values were imparted in the layout of the houses, the positioning of doors and windows, and the often symmetrical morphology of each settlement. Criticism centred on the unsuitability of such peri-urban house and settlement forms and on the standardised bureaucratic approach taken, which largely ignored local needs and regional idiosyncrasies. Even the necessity to concentrate reform co-operators in a centralised village was sometimes questioned. Instead, a standardised package was usually followed with serried ranks of identical houses and a predetermined range of service outlets. The new villagers were confronted by a 'discontinuity of modernity'. The new, unfamiliar building materials, especially concrete walls and floors, together with the more concentrated and hence more public settlement form with its lack of privacy for womenfolk, gave rise to grievances and detracted from the undoubted improvement in basic living conditions. The culturally important courtyards were too small for rural households, uniform house sizes clashed with the variable size of families, concrete and breeze-block presented unfamiliar heating problems in winter, and concentrated settlement morphologies contrasted with the traditional loosely organised *douars* or hamlet clusters, usually of kinsfolk (Sutton, 1987; Lesbet, 1983). The fundamental problem was that an urban settlement model was adopted, but, as Côte (1988b) remarks, one based on the 'West' rather than on the Arab *medina*. Designed and constructed by city-dwellers, the new village was 'urbain avant d'être "socialiste"' (Côte, 1988b, p. 294). An urban settlement model was further reflected by the way these rural houses were separated from the agricultural area, in terms of both distance and function. Most lacked sheds, barns or stables. Not surprisingly some villagers were found not to have abandoned their former residences on receipt of houses in a socialist village. Others attempted to deal with the houses' inappropriateness by modifying them and building higher courtyard walls and traditional ovens in the courtyard and bricking-up external windows. Some even abandoned their new houses and with them their reform land. Most, however, stayed and in time acquired a more urban outlook and consumer tastes. Poor income levels on the unfamiliar and hence relatively unproductive reform co-operatives made it difficult to meet these new consumer requirements. In this way, what proved to be a well-meaning but excessively 'urban' approach to meeting the housing and service needs of land reform beneficiaries probably contributed to undermining the fundamental aim of the agrarian revolution, which was to improve agricultural production and social well-being in rural Algeria.

In the wider context of the rural settlement system, this addition of 400 villages with their basic services served to reconstruct many rural localities and integrate them into the national economic space. This is well illustrated around Chelghoum Laid, in the High Plateaux, west of Constantine, where five socialist villages have supplemented earlier colonial villages to provide a reasonable structure of local service centres (Brûlé, 1985). The Mitidja Plain socialist village of Beni Chougrane-Tamesguida has been shown to serve a wider area than just its own population (Mutin, 1979). A Saharan socialist village, Akfadou near El Oued, has served to promote social life and networks, in this case with the womenfolk to the forefront (Kielstra, 1976).

So, despite criticisms and shortcomings, the socialist villages have certainly represented a more positive addition to the rural settlement system than the earlier *centres de regroupement*. However, a number of striking parallels can be drawn between these two exercises. Burgat (1982) has remarked on the resemblance between the two programmes with respect to the authoritarian management style and the sudden change in living style for the inhabitants. The possibility of similar reactions to parallel if quite different resettlement experiences has been postulated (Sutton and Lawless, 1978), and suggested as analogous by Adair (1982) in discussing the evidence of *déracinement* and *dépaysannisation* experienced by those involved in this relocation exercise to concentrate a previously dispersed rural settlement. Lesbet (1983) draws further analogies between the two '1,000 villages' programmes. Indeed, he found evidence of a more precise link in that sometimes plans of villages from the 1959 programme were merely 'dusted off' and reused when 1970s officials had to suggest sites and layouts for socialist villages.

Into the 1980s with 'Autoconstruction' and Return Migration

Lesbet's (1983) epitaph on the socialist villages programme was 'an operation born in haste, carried out with urgency, and buried in silence' (p. 332). A less cynical view would be that national policy shifts in the early 1980s mitigated against further socialist villages. The rehabilitation of the private sector in the Algerian economy generally worked against a furtherance of co-operative approaches in agriculture. Consequently agrarian reform co-operatives and the earlier *autogestion* estates have been restructured with a greater emphasis on smaller units and private initiative. Associated with this, the socialist villages programme was replaced by a wider rural-settlement policy of assisted private house construction or *auto-construction*. In this *auto-construction* policy the state provided building materials and other aid to enhance the non-remunerated work contributed by the future occupant of the dwelling, a degree of participation conspicuously absent earlier in the socialist villages programme. However, these *auto-construction* projects appear to have largely favoured the middle and upper strata of rural society rather than the theoretical beneficiaries, the underprivileged, including recipients of reform land (Haider, 1982). Perhaps as a consequence, the official *Annuaire Statistique de l'Algérie* increasingly merged the results of the socialist villages programme with the wider rural settlement statistics which cover *auto-construction*, *autogestion* estate houses and extensions to existing settlements. Compared with detailed data on socialist villages published until the late 1970s, the 1981 *Annuaire*, published in 1983–4, fails to refer separately to socialist villages in the section devoted to rural settlement, and only gives brief and outdated figures in its Agrarian Revolution section (ONS, 1981).

In his recent survey of Algerian rural settlement Côte (1988a) also notes a progressive disengagement on the part of the state from constructing dwellings in the countryside, partly for ideological reasons and partly for financial reasons following a reduction in oil revenues. Since the late 1970s the government has put less emphasis on rural dwellings, leaving that to *auto-construction*, and has focused instead on providing infrastructure such as electrification, local roads and rural schools. Côte (1988a) calls this a policy of *centres-supports*, whereby a certain number of services or infrastructure outlets are grouped in the midst of a zone of traditional dispersed settlement. He illustrates this for the Tebessa region, where earlier village-based restructuring of the rural settlement system is now being completed at this finer scale involving roads, power and schools. In regions such as this Côte detects a 'fever of construction' as rural dwellings are renewed and upgraded, socialist villages completed and *centres-supports* established.

A particular input to this *auto-construction* involves the injection of outside capital as earlier rural emigrants to French or Algerian cities seek to invest their savings in building rural houses for themselves or their rural relatives, perhaps in anticipation of retirement back in their original settlements. Long-established out-migration regions like Kabylia have received essential remittance payments for years to help keep over-populated rural economies functioning. Fontaine (1983) estimates that in the *wilaya* of Bejaia up to 450,000 people have migrated out, one-third going abroad. The return migration of a significant minority of these former residents to establish residences or businesses in the small towns or villages of the region is adding a dynamism to certain rural and interior regions. Given that some of this present and prospective return migration is from the Algerian community in France, it can be suggested that the French colonial impact on Algeria's rural settlement system is embarking on a second cycle. More significantly, perhaps, Fontaine (1983) has detected a degree of counter-urbanisation which has added commuter elements to accessible rural areas in the Bejaia region. Consequently, Côte (1988b) suggests a reversal of earlier rural–urban drift in the 1980s with a stabilisation of the population in a decidedly changed and urbanised countryside.

The 1987 census results support this suggested reversal with only relatively slow growth registered in coastal metropolises while the interior High Plains and Saharan regions have become the scene of strong, above-average population growth. While much of this new-found dynamism may be in the interior towns rather than in the countryside, it represents the first signs that the colonial legacy of coastal dominance is no longer as influential as once it was and that post-independence developments, decisions and mistakes are now the main influence on settlement evolution. This readjustment, if not yet reversal, of the coastal–interior imbalance is clearly demonstrated in Côte's (1988b) interpretation of settlement evolution in a north–south belt of eastern Algeria from Kabylia to the Hodna Basin. The pre-colonial settlement system of the coastal uplands was succeeded by the 'colonial space' in the High Plains with its colonial villages and *centres de regroupement*. This, in turn, has been linked into a 'post-colonial space' further south in the Steppe region as a dispersed pastoral settlement system has been restructured by socialist villages and *centres-supports*. Elsewhere in Algeria, the pre-colonial settlement systems were less resilient away from upland massifs and the 'colonial space' consequently more clearly associated with coastal locations and dominant, for example, around Oran or in the Mitidja Plain. As a generalised model, however, Côte's designation of 'trois espaces, trois âges' neatly encapsulates nearly two hundred years of rural settlement change, with the new 'post-colonial space' beginning to demonstrate sufficient dynamism to retain its demographic growth and to start reversing the rural imbalances of Algeria's long colonial interlude (Figure 7.3).

Conclusion

To a large extent, the landscape and settlement pattern of rural Algeria, and hence the very experience of rural life itself, is a product of French colonial rule. A central component of this rural transformation was the creation by

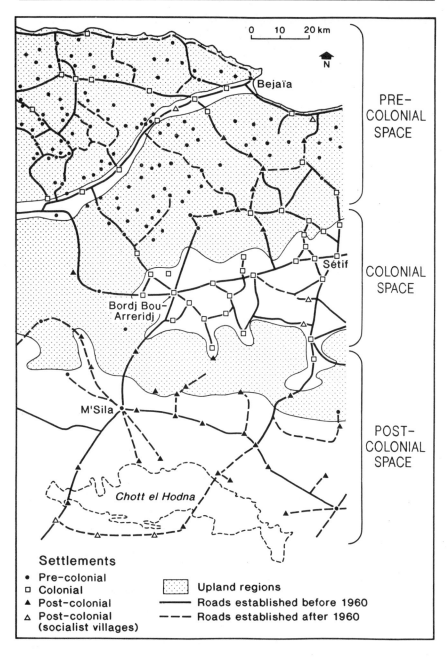

7.3 The development of rural settlement in Algeria, 1830s to 1980s.
Source: Côte (1988b, p. 328)

French colonial authorities of a network of nucleated settlements which were scattered across a rural landscape, characterised before 1830 by a mixed pattern of dispersed farms, hamlets and small villages. These colonial settlements, with their rectilinear street plans and bland uniformity, were constructed initially as secure rural depositories for European settlers who were treated, by both Parisian politicians and Algerian colonial authorities, with suspicion and hostility as the social and political outcasts of industrialising Europe. Within a generation or so, this European Algerian population had become a relatively prosperous, settled and politically influential force (Tinthoin, 1947). Once this had occurred, the focus of French colonial policy shifted towards the indigenous population who, despite their opposition to French colonial expansion, had remained a strangely invisible element to the French colonial authorities before the Third Republic. After 1870, the native Arab and Berber populations of the Algerian countryside were drawn progressively into the orbit of the commercial agrarian economy of colonial Algeria, based on the network of European settlements. This led to a gradual sedentarisation of the population (Trautmann, 1989), a process which accelerated rapidly under the exceptional conditions of the war of independence. The policy of *regroupement*, which was at the heart of the French strategy with respect to the rural indigenous Algerian population during the 1950s, was in many senses a continuation of previous colonial policies. The emphasis on creating secure, easily surveyed settlements for a suspect Muslim population directly parallels the early colonial policy of constructing rural villages under military control for European settlers. Although the specific reasons for constructing nucleated settlements varied over time, it is a striking fact that successive colonial regimes in Algeria relied on a similar type of purpose-built, nucleated rural centre as a solution to the economic, military and political problems associated with the maintenance and extension of colonial power. This rural landscape, and the attitudes which created it, has proved extremely difficult to modify, despite the ending of French rule in 1962. Like their colonial forebears, the independent Algerian authorities have shown little sympathy towards nomadism, particularly in the desert interior, or to other traditional agrarian practices, and successive regimes have pursued policies designed to settle the rural population in official, specially constructed centres which bear a distinct similarity to the strategies employed by the French. At a general level, the socialist villages represent a continuation of earlier French colonial policy. Throughout this process of rural transformation, the emphasis of both colonial and post-colonial authorities has been on the disciplined allocation of space and the creation of an ordered rural landscape, conducive to the interests of capitalist agricultural production and to the effective surveillance of the population.

References

AARDES (1975) *Association Algérienne pour la Recherche Démographique, Économique, et Sociale: étude socio-économique sur les attributaires de la première phase de la Révolution Agraire*, Algiers: Secrétariat d'État au Plan.

Abun-Nasr, J. (1987) *A History of the Maghrib in the Islamic Period*, Cambridge: Cambridge University Press.

Adair, P. (1982) 'Économie politique de l'habitat rural: les "villages socialistes" algériens', *Espaces et Sociétés*, 41, pp. 39–49.

Ageron, C.-R. (1979) *Histoire de l'Algérie contemporaine II: de l'insurrection de 1871 au déclenchement de la guerre de libération*, Paris: Presses Universitaires de France.

Ageron, C.-R. (1980) *'L'Algérie algérienne' de Napoléon III à De Gaulle*, Paris: Sindbad.

Alleg, H., de Bouis, J., Douzon, H.-J., Freire, J., and Haudiquet, P. (1981) *La Guerre d'Algérie*, 3 vols, Paris: Temps Actuels.

Bernard, A. (1930) *Histoire des colonies françaises et l'expansion de la France dans le monde. Tome II: Algérie*, Paris: Plon.

Berque, J. (1967) *French North Africa: The Maghreb between the Two Wars*, London: Faber & Faber.

Berque, J. (1978) *L'Intérieur du Maghreb, XVe–XIXe siècles*, Paris: Éditions du Seuil.

Bouhouche, A. (1978) 'The French in Algeria: the politics of expropriation and assimilation', *Revue d'Histoire Maghrébine*, 12, pp. 238–60.

Bourdieu, P., and Sayad, A. (1964) *Le déracinement: la crise de l'agriculture traditionnel en Algérie*, Paris: Éditions de Minuit.

Brûlé, J.-C. (1976) 'Transformations récentes de l'espace rural algérien', *Bulletin de la Société Languedocienne de Géographie*, 10 (1), pp. 115–35.

Brûlé, J.-C. (1985) 'Géographie régional de la Révolution Agraire algérienne', *Bulletin de l'Association des Géographes Français*, 62 (1), pp. 5–20.

Brûlé, J.-C., and Fontaine, J. (1986) *L'Algérie: volontarisme étatique et aménagement du territoire*, Tours: URBAMA.

Brunschwig, H. (1966) *French Colonialism, 1871–1914: Myths and Realities*, London: Pall Mall.

Burgat, F. (1982) 'Des villages pas comme les autres?' *Autrement*, 38, pp. 187–94.

Cornaton, M. (1967) *Les regroupements de la décolonisation en Algérie*, Paris: Éditions Ouvrières.

Côte, M. (1981) *Mutations rurales en Algérie: le cas des Hautes Plaines de l'Est*, Paris/Algiers: Éditions du CNRS/Office des Publications Universitaires.

Côte, M. (1988a) 'L'habitat rural en Algérie: formes et mutations', in P.-R. Baduel (ed.) *Habitat, état et société au Maghreb*, Paris: Éditions du CNRS, pp. 299–315.

Côte, M. (1988b) *L'Algérie ou l'espace retourné*, Paris: Flammarion.

Danziger, R. (1977) *Abd-al-Qadir and the Algerians: Resistance to the French and Internal Consolidation*, New York: Holmes & Meier.

Dominelli, L. (1986) *Love and Wages: The Impact of Imperialism, State Intervention and Women's Domestic Labour on Workers' Control in Algeria, 1962–1972*, Norwich: Novata.

Émerit, M. (1941) *Les Saint-Simoniens en Algérie*, Paris: Belles Lettres.

Enfantin, B.-P. (1842) *Colonisation de l'Algérie*, Paris: Bertrand.

Exploration scientifique de l'Algérie pendant les années 1840, 1841, 1842, publié par ordre du gouvernement et avec le concours d'une commission académique (1844–67), 23 vols., Paris: Imprimerie Royale/Nationale/Impériale.

Fontaine, J. (1983) *Villages kabyles et nouveau réseau urbain en Algérie: le cas de la région de Bejaïa*, Fascicule 12, Tours: URBAMA.

Franc, J. (1928) *La colonisation de la Mitidja*, Paris: Honoré Campion.

GGA (1867–1903) *Gouvernement Général de l'Algérie: Statistique Générale de l'Algérie*, Paris: Imprimerie Algérienne.

GGACC (1922) *Gouvernement Général de l'Algérie: direction de l'agriculture, du commerce et de la colonisation – La colonisation en Algérie, 1830–1921*, Algiers: Imprimerie Algérienne.

GGACC (1927) *Gouvernement Général de l'Algérie: direction de l'agriculture, du commerce et de la colonisation – Tableau général des communes de l'Algérie: situation au 7 mars 1926*, Algiers: Imprimerie Algérienne.

GGASE (1936) *Gouvernement Général de l'Algérie: direction des services économiques – service central de statistique: répertoire statistique des communes de l'Algérie, 1936*, Algiers: Imprimerie Algérienne.

GGASE (1937) *Gouvernement Général de l'Algérie: direction des services économiques – service central de statistique: annuaire statistique de l'Algérie, 1937*, Algiers: Imprimerie Algérienne.

Gallissot, R. (1975) 'Precolonial Algeria', *Economy and Society*, 4, pp. 418–45.

Haider, F. (1982) 'Effets et limites de la politique d'habitat en milieu rural', in INEAP, *Développement rural et catégories intellectuelles: le cas de la Révolution Agraire en Algérie*, Algiers: Ministère de la Planification et de l'Aménagement du Territoire, pp. 77–92.

Halvorsen, K.H, (1978) 'Colonial transformation of agrarian society in Algeria', *Journal of Peace Research*, 15 (4), pp. 323–43.

Hamdani, A. (1985) *La verité sur l'expédition d'Alger*, Paris: Balland.

Heffernan, M.J. (1989) 'The Parisian poor and the colonization of Algeria during the Second Republic', *French History*, 3 (4), pp. 377–403.

Holsinger, D.C. (1980) 'Trade routes of the Algerian Sahara in the nineteenth century', *Revue de l'Occident musulman et de la Méditerranée*, 30 (2), pp. 57–70.

Horne, A. (1987) *A Savage War of Peace: Algeria 1954–1962*, 2nd edn, London: Macmillan.

Isnard, H. (1950) *La réorganisation de la propriété rurale dans la Mitidja: ses conséquences sur la vie indigène*, Algiers: A. Joyeux.

Isnard, H. (1951–4) *La vigne en Algérie*, 2 vols, Ophrys: L. Jean.

Julien, C.-A. (1970) *History of North Africa: Tunisia, Algeria, Morocco from the Arab conquest to 1830*, London: Routledge & Kegan Paul.

Julien, C.-A. (1972) *L'Afrique du Nord en marche: nationalismes musulmans et souveraineté française*, Paris: Julliard.

Julien, C.-A. (1979) *Histoire de l'Algérie contemporaine I: la conquête et les débuts de la colonisation 1827–1871*, Paris: Presses Universitaires de France.

Kaddache, M. (1980) *Histoire du nationalisme algérien*, 2 vols, Algiers: SNED.

Kielstra, N. (1976) 'The beginnings of social life in an Algerian socialist village', *Maghreb Review*, 3 (10), pp. 14–19.

Lacoste, Y. (1984) *Ibn-Khaldun: The Birth of History and the Past of the Third World*, London: Verso.

Lacoste-Dujardin, C. (1986) 'L'Invention d'une ethnopolitique: Kabylie – 1844', *Hérodote*, 42, pp. 109–25.

Laroui, A. (1977) *The History of the Maghrib: An Interpretative Essay*, Princeton, NJ: Princeton University Press.

Lesbet, D. (1983) *Les 1,000 villages socialistes en Algérie*, Paris/Algiers: Éditions du CNRS/Office des Publications Universitaires.

Lesne, M. (1962) 'Une expérience de déplacement de population: les centres de regroupement en Algérie', *Annales de Géographie*, 71, pp. 567–603.

Leveau, P. (1975) 'Le Chénoua: de la décolonisation au village de regroupement', *Revue de l'Occident musulman et de la Méditerranée*, 19, pp. 101–12.

Lucas, P., and Vatin, C. (1975) *L'Algérie des anthropologues*, Paris: Maspero.

MG (1838–68) *Ministère de la Guerre. Tableau de la situation des établissements français dans l'Algérie*, 18 vols, Paris: Imprimérie Royale/Nationale/Impériale.

MHU (1982) *Ministère de l'Habitat et de l'Urbanisme. Habitat rural: bilan physique arrêté au 31.12.1981*, Algiers: MHU.

Meynier, G. (1981) *L'Algérie révélée: la guerre de 1914–1918 et le premier quart du XXe siècle*, Geneva: Droz.

Miège, J.-L. (1981) 'Le commerce trans-saharien au XIXe siècle: essai de quantification', *Revue de l'Occident musulman et de la Méditerranée*, 32 (2), pp. 93–119.

Mutin, G. (1977) *La Mitidja: décolonisation et espace géographique*, Paris: Éditions du CNRS.

Mutin, G. (1979) 'Un nouveau village socialiste en Mitidja: Beni Chougrane-Tamesguida', in Équipe de Recherche Associée No. 706, *Urbanisation et nouvelle organisation des campagnes au Maghreb*, Fascicule de Recherche No. 5, Poitiers: Centre Universitaire d'Études Méditerranéenes, pp. 117–42.

Mutin, G. (1980) 'Implantations industrielles et aménagement du territoire en Algérie', *Revue de Géographie de Lyon*, 55 (1), pp. 5–37.

Mutin, G. and Rebbouh, H. (1978) 'Aménagement du territoire ou déstructuration de l'espace en Mitidja orientale', *Cahiers de l'Aménagement de l'Espace*, 1, pp. 12–49.

Nora, P. (1961) *Les français d'Algérie*, Paris: Juillard.

Nordman, D., and Raison, J.-P. (eds) (1980) *Sciences de l'homme et conquête coloniale: constitution et usages des humanités en Afrique (XIXe et XXe siècles)*, Paris: Presses de l'École Normale Supérieure.

Nouschi, A. (1961) *Enquête sur le niveau de vie des populations rurales constantinoises de la conquête jusqu'en 1919: essai d'histoire économique et sociale*, Paris: Presses Universitaires de France.

ONS (1979–81) *Office National des Statistiques: Annuaire Statistique de l'Algérie 1979*, Algiers: ONS.

Peillon, P. (1970) 'L'occupation humaine en Basse-Kabylie', Doctorat du Troisième Cycle, University of Lyon II.

Perkins, K. J. (1980) *Quaids, Captains, and Colons: French Military Administration in the Colonial Maghrib, 1844–1934*, New York: Africana.

Peyerimhoff, M. de (1906) *Gouvernement Général de l'Algérie – direction de l'agriculture, du commerce et de la colonisation: enquête sur les résultats de la colonisation officielle de 1871 à 1895 – rapport à Monsieur Jonnart, Gouverneur Général de l'Algérie*, 2 vols, Algiers: Imprimerie Torrent.

Pierre, C. (1966) 'L'Évolution des centres de regroupement de la Mitidja occidentale', *Annales Algériennes de Géographie*, 1(2), pp. 120–46.

Pouyanne, H. (1895) *La propriété foncière en Algérie*, Algiers: Jourdan.

Powers, D. S. (1989) 'Orientalism, colonialism, and legal history: the attack on Muslim family endowments in Algeria and India', *Comparative Studies in Society and History*, 31 (3), pp. 535–71.

Prévost-Paradol, A. (1868) *La France nouvelle*, Paris: Lévy.

RGPH (1989) *Recensement Général de la Population et de l'Habitat, 1987: Résultats par Agglomérations – Collections Statistiques 13*, Algiers: ONS.

Ruedy, J. (1967) *Land Policy in Colonial Algeria: The Origins of the Rural Public Domain*, Berkeley: University of California Press.

Sahli, M. C. (1965) *Décoloniser l'histoire: introduction à l'histoire du Maghreb*, Paris: Maspero.

Said, E.W. (1978) *Orientalism*, London: Routledge & Kegan Paul.

Sari, D. (1970) *Les villes précoloniales de l'Algérie occidentale*, Algiers: SNED.

Sari, D. (1972) *L'Insurrection de 1871*, Algiers: SNED.

Sari, D. (1977) *La dépossession des Fellahs, 1830–1962*, 2nd edn, Algiers: SNED.

Shaw, B.D. (1981) 'Climate, environment, and history: the case of Roman North Africa', in T.M.L. Wigley, M.J. Ingram and G. Farmer (eds) *Climate and History: Studies in Past Climates and Their Impact on Man*, Cambridge: Cambridge University Press, pp. 379–403.

Smith, T. (1974) 'Muslim impoverishment in colonial Algeria', *Revue de L'Occident musulman et de la Méditerranée*, 17 (1), pp. 139–62.

Stambouli, F., and Zghal, A. (1976) 'Urban life in pre-colonial North Africa', *British Journal of Sociology*, 27 (1), pp. 1–20.

Steele, H.M. (1965) 'European settlement versus Muslim property: the foundation of colonial Algeria, 1830–1850', unpublished Ph.D. thesis, Columbia University, New York.

Stora, B. (1989) *Les sources du nationalisme algérien: parcours idéologiques, origines des acteurs*, Paris: L'Harmattan.

Sullivan, A.T. (1983) *Thomas-Robert Bugeaud, France and Algeria, 1784–1849: Power and the Good Society*, New Haven, Conn.: Archon.

Sutton, K. (1972) 'Algeria: changes in population distribution, 1954–66', in J.I. Clarke and W.B. Fisher (eds) *Populations of the Middle East and North Africa*, London: University of London Press, pp. 373–94.

Sutton, K. (1981) 'The influence of military policy on Algerian rural settlement', *Geographical Review*, 71 (1), pp. 379–94.

Sutton, K. (1984) 'Algeria's socialist villages – a reassessment', *Journal of Modern African Studies*, 22, pp. 223–48.

Sutton, K. (1987) 'The socialist villages of Algeria', in R.I. Law less (ed.) *The Middle Eastern Village*, London: Croom Helm, pp. 77–114.

Sutton, K., and Lawless, R.I. (1978) 'Population regrouping in Algeria: traumatic change and the rural settlement pattern', *Transactions of the Institute of British Geographers*, 3 (3), pp. 331–50.

Thompson, A. (1987) *Barbary and Enlightenment: European Attitudes towards the Maghreb in the Eighteenth Century*, Leiden: E.J. Brill.

Tinthoin, R. (1947) *Colonisation et évolution des genres de vie dans l'ouest d'Oran de 1830 à 1885*, Oran: Fouque.

Tomas, F. (1977) *Annaba et sa région: organisation de l'espace dans l'extrème-est algérien*, St Étienne: Guichard.

Trautmann, W. (1989) 'The nomads of Algeria under French rule: a study of social and economic change', *Journal of Historical Geography*, 15 (2), pp. 126–38.

Turin, Y. (1976) 'La crise des campagnes algériennes en 1868, d'après l'enquête agricole de la même année', *Revue d'Histoire et de Civilisation du Maghreb*, 13, pp. 79–86.

Valensi, L. (1977) *On the Eve of Colonialism: North Africa before the French Conquest*, New York: Africana.

Vatin, J.-C. (ed.) (1984) *Connaissances du Maghreb: sciences sociales et colonisation*, Paris: Éditions du CNRS.

Wansbrough, J. (1968) 'The decolonisation of North African history', *Journal of African History*, 9 (4), pp. 643–50.

Wolf, J. B. (1979) *The Barbary Coast: Algeria under the Turks, 1500–1830*, New York: Norton.

Yacono, X. (1953) *Les bureaux arabes et l'évolution des genres de vie indigènes dans l'ouest du tell algérien*, Paris: Larose.

Yacono, X. (1954) 'Peut-on évaluer la population de l'Algérie vers 1830?', *Revue Africaine*, 3–4, pp. 277–307.

Yacono, X. (1955) *La colonisation des plaines de Chélif (de Lavigérie au confluent de la Mina)*, 2 vols, Algiers: Imprimerie Imbert.

Yacono, X. (1966) 'La Régence d'Alger en 1830 d'après l'enquête des commissions de 1833–1834', *Revue de l'Occident musulman et de la Méditerranée*, 1 (1), pp. 229–44 and 2 (2), pp. 227–47.

CHAPTER 8

Ousting Singbonga:
The Struggle for India's Jharkhand

Stuart Corbridge

On 4 September 1980 the police in south-west Singhbhum District, Bihar, India, moved at the behest of local politicians, mine owners and timber contractors to arrest 4,100 tribals and non-tribals for 'unlawfully cutting trees'. The arrests took place close to Gua township, an iron-ore mining settlement buried deep in the degraded forests of the Jharkhand. The Jharkhand, or the 'land of the forests', was once ruled by and for an indigenous 'tribal' population.

The next day saw a counter-move by the Jharkhand Mukti Morcha, a radical political movement committed to the (re)-formation of a Jharkhand state in Chota Nagpur, Santal Parganas and surrounding districts (see Figure 8.1). The Morcha called a demonstration against 'police terror and state employment policies' to be held at Gua on 8 September. According to an observer for the Adelaide-based Bihar Tribal Action Group, the purpose of this demonstration was entirely peaceful and consisted of an organised march from the local airstrip to Gua market place. Had the demonstrators been of violent intent they would have marched towards the forests on the outskirts of Gua and not into a 'vulnerable position' in the town. On arrival, the police, acting on orders, detained two of the meeting's leading speakers. This prompted an 'inevitable ruction' in the ranks of the demonstrators, at which point the police opened fire. In the ensuing mêlée eight marchers were shot dead and three policemen were killed.

According to the Chief Minister of Bihar this whole episode had its origins in a terrible provocation of the forces of law and order. For its part, the Bihar Tribal Action Group cites the Gua incident as a prelude to three days and nights of police terror and rapine in the surrounding villages. Whatever the truth – and my own researches suggest that the Action Group is nearest the mark – it is important to note that these bloody events form part of a continuing struggle for the territory and the environment of Jharkhand. It is an unequal struggle waged by disparate groups of tribal and non-tribal citizens inspired by some notion or another of a past golden age – a local 'natural economy' – and an intrusive modernisation fashioned by industrial capital and its allies in the state.

The purpose of this chapter is to document this struggle. The first section describes the space-economy of the Jharkhand as it might have looked in the eighteenth century. Although far from a pristine, communal society, the

153

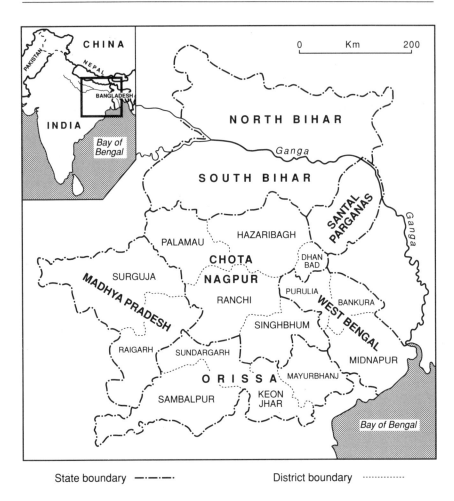

8:1   The state of Bihar and the Jharkhand.

Jharkhand was then home to numerous tribal communities, each of which was engaged in a private and collective agro-forestry, and each of which drew from the landscape a mythology of tribal economy and society which emphasised a very particular communion of god and nature. The forests then, as now, were more than just providers of food and shelter; they were also mythical places, governed and haunted by various benign deities and evil spirits. The forests were central to most of the events and processes by which tribal solidarities were constructed and reaffirmed.

The second section examines the incorporation of these quasi-natural economies into the widening circuits of commodity production and exchange over which the British Raj presided. Central to this examination is an account of the contradictory policies by which the Raj sought to discipline its tribal periphery. On the one hand, the Raj (especially through its Home Departments and in alliance with local collectors, missionaries and anthropologists) sought to empathise with its tribal subjects. The noble savage was praised for *his* innocence and for *his* vigour, and was to be protected by a paternalist Raj against the unscrupulous attentions of Hindu *mahajans* (moneylenders) and *zamindars* (landlords). On the other hand, this attitude of 'isolationism' (or divide and rule) was undone in those areas where the tribal populations happened to live on top of vast reserves of tin and mica, coal and iron ore (not to mention amidst sal trees which could be used as railway sleepers). In India's 'resource triangle' (the Jharkhand: see Figure 8.2), an instinct for mummification was consistently set aside in favour of the desire of the colonial state, and its favoured magnates, to seek the economic transformation of peninsular India. The violence implicit in this challenge is documented here with particular reference to Singhbhum District. Also emphasised is the early and continued resistance by local populations to this reshaping of their environment.[1]

The third and final section continues the narrative beyond independence in 1947. The expulsion of the British from India was of particular benefit to those tribal communities designated as Scheduled Tribes in the Constitution of 1950 (Galanter, 1984). The Scheduled Tribes of India are guaranteed representation in the Lok Sabha, have certain jobs in the public sector reserved for them, and have not been the victims of state terror or genocide in the way that indigenous populations elsewhere in Asia have been. Nevertheless, the post-colonial state has sought the integration of the Jharkhand into mainstream Hindustan and to this end has continued to sponsor a destruction of diverse local economies in the name of a supposed national interest. The coalmines are now larger, the iron and steel industry has boomed, and the trees have continued to fall (and to be cut in forests arrogated to the state and its clients). The paradox is that this process is made much easier by virtue of the greater reach of the post-colonial state. Although resistance continues (and changes in form: witness Gua, witness the Mukti Morcha), the organs and agencies of state power are now so efficient, in terms of presence, surveillance and punishment, that resistance is localised and often ineffective. The fragile dominion of an often brutal Raj has been replaced by the more secure reign of a nation-state and a national interest. This theme is taken up in the conclusion to the chapter.

The Lords of the Forest

Prior to the Aryan invasions of South Asia, India was occupied by various autochthonous communities of which the Kolarian aborigines (including the Mundas and the Hos) were among the most significant. Although problems of historical reconstruction remain, it seems likely that these 'tribes' once colonised an area of north India extending from Punjab to Assam. Each tribe would periodically migrate to escape local conflicts.

In the sixth century BC the main Kolarian communities moved south-eastwards from present-day south Bihar into the Jharkhand region (Roy, 1970). The Santals then turned eastwards, toward present-day Bhagalpur, Birbhum

8:2 India's iron and steel belt.

and Santal Parganas (Allanson, 1912). The Munda tribe, meanwhile, engaged in an extensive process of forest clearing in what today is Ranchi District – in the process displacing the smaller Asur community deeper into the surrounding jungles (Prasad, 1961). The Mundas and the Hos, and various smaller tribes, were later joined in Chota Nagpur by the Oraons. This last major tribe had moved northwards into Bihar from south India (Roy, 1984). The Oraon language is related to the Dravidian family of languages dominant in south India and found throughout South-East Asia. Together, the Mundas, Hos, Oraons and Santals, with perhaps another eighty aboriginal and semi-aboriginal communities, remained the main occupants of the Jharkhand until the end of the nineteenth century. Even the Constitution of 1950, which is more restrictive in its designation of Scheduled communities than was the Raj (with its aborigines and semi-aborigines), recognises thirty tribes in contemporary Bihar. These communities comprise the easternmost extension of a tribal belt which cuts across central India and which links the Mundas and the Santals to the Bhils and the Gonds of Madhya Pradesh and Gujarat. India's Scheduled Tribes comprise 7 per cent of the total population of the Republic.

The designation of particular communities as tribals or as caste Indians is not unproblematic (Ghurye, 1980), and the narrowing boundaries of 'tribalness' announced in the 1950 Constitution reflect still pressing political debates and considerations (Corbridge, 1988). The state in independent India is concerned with national integration; the Raj was more concerned with difference and division. Nevertheless, if it is often difficult to distinguish a tribal from a non-tribal in contemporary Chota Nagpur (despite the extraordinary claims to the contrary made by Myron Weiner (1978, pp. 155–6), it is the case that the Scheduled tribal communities can trace back an ancestry to the short, dark-skinned and despised Dasas of the Rig Veda (Roy, 1970). From the earliest times, the tribals of central India have been marginalised communities, at least in the sense that these communities were considered to lie beyond the march of development and of Hinduism. Most tribal communities in turn consider themselves to be India's true sons (and daughters) of the soil – the true lords of the forest, as the Mundas proclaim themselves to be in Chota Nagpur.

The bases for such claims are not much disputed. Having migrated to the Jharkhand it was the Mundas and the Hos, the Santals and the Kharias, who set to clear the forests. In parts of south-east Ranchi District there remain villages where households can trace a line of descent to the original clearers of the village. These are the *khuntkattidar* households, which still enjoy certain privileges of rank and tenure. When local pressures upon land became too great, several households would move away from the village to clear another part of the forest (in the process becoming *khuntkattidars* themselves). Marriage links between villages, but within *killis* or lineages, would be formed according to local customs of endogamy and patrilocality. At some point, too, the tribal communities would attract various service castes, including smiths, weavers and cowherds. These local outsiders – the *eta-haturenko*, or men of other villages – 'had no right to the village-lands but could only enjoy the crops of such specific plots of land as might have been allotted to them by the *khuntkattidars* for their maintenance' (Roy, 1970, p. 64).

The political and economic organisation of the Kolarian and Dravidian communities survived reasonably intact until British times, and, in certain respects, until the present. The headman of a Munda village is the *munda*; the spiritual leader, the *pahan*. (The Santal equivalents are the *manjhi* and the *naike*.) The main duties of the *munda* relate to questions of land management and to issues of crime and punishment. In return for his efforts the *munda* is rewarded by various small gifts from the other households in his village. It should be noted that these gifts were not intended as fixed taxes or rents in kind. The position of the *munda*, although hereditary, is that of *primus inter pares*. His position and status is not supposed to signal an incipient form of kingship. The same holds true in the case of the *manki*, the dominant headman of each group of twelve or so Munda villages bound together in a *patti*, or inter-village council.

The economic bases of the tribal communities of the Jharkhand have always been diverse. Some smaller tribes, such as the Birhors, are nomadic groups which survive by collecting various fauna and flora, and by making ropes for exchange in local markets (Sinha, 1968). Others, such as the Asur and the Lohars, have specialised in iron smelting and working (Leuva, 1963). The larger tribes, by contrast, have for centuries practised forms of settled plough agriculture, in combination with slash-and-burn cultivation and a collective management of local forest resources. The ecology and climate of the Jharkhand is such that a single rain-fed rice crop is usually sown, with several vegetables and pulses also. When the rice crop fails, the local community is thrown back on to the collection of minor forest products. O'Malley (1910, p. 120) caught the importance of the forests very well in his *District Gazetteer of Singhbhum, Seraikela and Kharsawan*: 'There has not been a famine here since 1866', he says, 'chiefly because the majority of the population are aboriginals and a considerable part of their food supply consists of edible forest products.'

The management of the forests in turn reflects upon the nature of the tribal communities. Despite a common assumption that slash-and-burn agriculture is ecologically destructive, and that ill-educated tribals are not the best guardians of a forest environment – roughly the assumptions of the 'scientific forestry' of the late nineteenth and twentieth centuries (Forsyth, 1919) – the available evidence suggests that this was far from being the case. As Sarat Chandra Roy explains:

> Generally, it is in the months of *Chait* or *Baisik* (March to May) before the rains set in, that in many villages the Munda and Pahan on a day appointed beforehand lead the villagers into the village-jungles and the necessary fuel and timber for the year is cut down by the villagers from a specified part of the jungle, leaving the other part or parts to be similarly dealt with by rotation in successive years. And the wood thus cut down is then taken home by the villagers according to their respective needs. By this prudent procedure, the village jungles can never be devastated. (Roy, 1970, p. 63)

The forests are also treated with respect for religious and cultural reasons. Just as all the land in a Munda village belongs finally to the village-family (despite *de facto* private tenancies), so also 'bits of the jungle [are] specifically reserved for the village gods (*hatu bongako*) and are called the Sarnas' (Roy, 1970, p. 63). Roy continues: 'These Sarnas are the only temples the Mundas know. Here the village gods reside, and are periodically worshipped and propitiated with sacrifices' (Roy, 1970, p. 222). The forests are also home to various evil spirits and demons who daily do battle under the watchful eye of the benign great spirit of the Mundas, *Singbonga*. The forests, in short, are the local landscapes of an Indian magical realism (Bardhan, 1990; Tutuola, 1954). Besides being a source of nourishment and shelter – of work and exchange value – the forests are central to the processes by which tribal identities and solidarities are constructed. An *adivasi* (tribal) is known to outsiders, derisively, as a *Junglee*; to the tribals themselves, an *adivasi* is characterized by an extraordinary knowledge of the forest environment (Chapman, 1983). A tribal is also known to himself by his participation in the great hunt – a time when wild animals are stuck or shot, and when local solidarities are widened spatially and reinforced in opposition to the world of the *dikus* (or non-tribal outsiders).

Of Rajas and the Raj: The Jharkhand Undermined

The concept of a *diku* is central to notions of tribal identity and solidarity in the Jharkhand. Even today, the flag of the Jharkhand Party is green in colour (to emphasise the common cultural and ecological heritage of all Jharkhandi tribals) and its election symbol is a *sismandi* (a particular kind of fowl sacrificed to a *bonga*: Hembram, 1983). *Diku* culture shows little respect for either of these icons. Nevertheless, it would be wrong to suppose that the Jharkhand was precisely as we have described it, even in the eighteenth century. Although the institutions of *munda* and *manki* were not intended to be the instruments of a local state-building, it was already the practice to deliver *abwabs* and other fixed taxes (including unpaid labour) to local tribal chieftains, or *rajas*, who had converted to Hinduism (Sinha, 1962). In spite of fierce opposition, the various *rajas* of Chotanagpur – including the Nagbansi *maharaja* – were able to convert large tracts of *khuntkatti* land into *rajhas* lands, or lands where rents were payable to a *raja* or one of his *thiccadars*. As court life became more lavish, the *rajas* sought to reward their various gurus and *goondas*, hangers-on and financiers, with rights to revenues to be drawn from tribal villages. By the time the British arrived in Chota Nagpur, in 1770, a widespread alienation of tribal lands was evident, as also was a growing presence in the Jharkhand of powerful and exploitative *dikus*.

Colonial tribal policy: the 'official' version

The British occupation did little to restore tribal fortunes. In the late eighteenth century the main interest of the British in the Jharkhand was twofold: first, to make the then Maharajah of Chotanagpur a vassal of the East India Company and to collect from him a sizeable annual tribute; and, second, to pacify the region in order that trade between the Gangetic plains and coastal

Bengal could be secured. An assault upon the property rights of titled individuals was not central to British thinking. It was only in the nineteenth century that the British began seriously to think about a tribal policy for central India. Following the Kol rebellion of 1831–2, and the Santal *hul* (rebellion) of 1855 – both well-organised affairs, despite official protestations to the contrary (Guha, 1988) – the British began slowly to put in place a tribal policy which built upon three sets of aims and assumptions.

As ever, the main plank of British policy in India was a commitment to the use of force. Although some British officials proved sympathetic to the claims of the Kols and the Santals – and some even to the grievances of the Birsaites at the time of the Mundari *Ungulam* (1895–1900) – the official policy of the Raj was that violence and disorder were not to be tolerated. The British were consistent in their refusal to see in the great tribal rebellions of the nineteenth century a rejection of the Raj itself; this, despite an intention on the part of the Santal leaders to 'slay the rajas of Pakur and Maheshpur as well as all other landlords, mahajans, policemen and white planters, railway engineers and officials they could lay their hands on' (Guha, 1983, p. 111). The British instead preferred to represent such actions as misguided responses to the rapacious intrusions of Hindu moneylenders and *zamindars* (Hunter, 1975). In so far as such actions were prompted by criminal elements within the tribes themselves, it followed that a criminal action must be punished. In the aftermath of the Santal *hul*, the British burned Santal villages in revenge. In the case of the earlier Kol rebellion, the British moved first to restrain 'local criminals' before seizing fifteen peers from the Porahat king and placing the Kolhan Estate under direct British rule (Jha, 1964). To ensure that the Kols did not again turn to 'violent affray', 'the Government thought that strong measures, such as subjecting the rebels to capital punishment by blowing them from the mouth of a gun, combined with conciliation after an impression had been made, were absolutely necessary' (Basu, 1957, p. 18; see also Bhadra, 1988).

A second element of colonial tribal policy concerned itself with patterns of administration and governance in the tribal areas. British rule in India was, at best, paternalist, and its dominant imagery was that of the adult caring for and chastising an innocent yet naughty child (Nandy, 1988). In tribal India this paternalism was taken to extremes. Having decided that the Kol and Santal rebellions were rebellions against the non-British *dikus* – against those who confiscated tribal lands and those who entrapped the garrulous tribals in relations of usury and bondage – the British opted for a form of executive rule in tribal India. The pattern was first worked out in 1833 with the formation of a South West Frontier Agency in lower Bengal. The agency consisted of Chota Nagpur and Pargana Dhalbhum, and within its boundaries the

> administration of Civil and Criminal Justice and the collection of the revenue was suspended, and authority in these and all other matters was vested in an officer, denominated Agent to the Governor-General. Power was taken to prescribe rules for the guidance and control of the Agent and the officers subordinate to him. (Reid, 1912, p. 27)

After the Santal *hul* this pattern of rule grew more sophisticated and it was allied to a concern to enact land tenancy legislation in the Jharkhand which would begin to curb a continuing alienation of tribal lands. (In this vein, note the enactment of the Chota Nagpur Tenancy Act of 1908.) Nevertheless, the logic behind these changing structures of rule remained the same. The British undertook to rule India's tribals in protected geographical areas. Within the boundaries of these non-regulation districts, or Scheduled Districts as they became known after 1874, the British were content to leave matters of day-to-day government to those *mundas* and *manjhis* whom they considered loyal to the Raj. If and when local systems of justice broke down, law and order was dispensed directly by the governor and/or one of his agents. In his person goodness and right was singularly embodied. When the rest of India moved slowly in the direction of part-elective legislatures (after 1919), tribal India remained locked into a framework of executive rule (Figure 8.3). The government argued that *because* tribal Indians were gullible, and *given* that non-tribal Indians were their chief exploiters, it was not reasonable to place the latter in charge of the former. Responsibility must instead fall on the British. As a Colonel Wedgewood put it in a House of Commons debate in 1935:

> The only chance for these people [the tribals] is to protect them from a civilisation which will destroy them and for that reason, I believe, direct British control is the best . . . Unless you have our experience of the last fifty or even one hundred and fifty years in dealing with this problem, it is impossible to say that any other race on earth can look after them as well as we can. (Government of the United Kingdom, 1935)

A third component of 'official' tribal policy in British India was the doctrine of isolationism. This doctrine is associated especially with British anthropologists and missionaries working in tribal India in the early twentieth century. Men like Elwin and Archer, Grigson and Hutton, believed passionately that the tribals of central and north-eastern India had to be protected against the pleasures and pains of modernisation (Elwin, 1964; Archer, 1984; Grigson, 1949; Hutton, 1922). According to Elwin, the tribes of India shared certain qualities of innocence and honesty, not to mention happiness, which spoke to their closeness to nature (or Eden), and which belied only the faintest of touches with original sin. To safeguard these qualities, and to guard against the loss of nerve which Elwin believed would mark a 'tribe in transition' (Elwin, 1944), Elwin and others proposed in the 1930s that certain tribes should be protected in a national park, or ethnological zoo.[2]

The colonial government was happy to seize upon this suggestion. Whereas Elwin and Archer were prepared to float the doctrine of isolationism for the best of reasons (and neither was a dupe of empire), the government found in this ideology a cloak for its reluctance to spend heavily in tribal areas which were not considered to be major contributors to the imperial fisc. London and Delhi also saw in the doctrine of isolationism a convenient banner under which the Indian National Congress could be kept out of the tribal areas

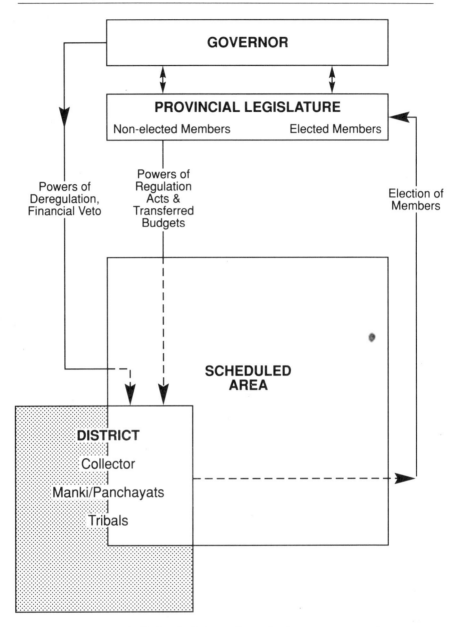

8:3 **Government/tribal administrative relations 1919–1935 (partially excluded areas).**

of central and north-eastern India (Grigson, 1946). If divide and rule was not a mainspring of 'official' tribal policy in colonial India, it was a fateful partner for a system of governance born of paternalism, force and a need to respond to local rebellions.

The 'official' tribal policy betrayed

The doctrine of isolationism became a particular target of attack for Indian National Congress politicians in the 1930s and 1940s. Even at the time of the Constituent Assembly debates (1947–50), a discourse which opposed isolationism to assimilationism was central to Indian debates on the 'tribal problem'. Representative B. Das from Orissa was moved to complain that:

> Though it has been thought wisdom for over a hundred years or more by British imperialists to keep these tribal people and these Scheduled Areas as museums for purposes of demonstration and exhibition before the world to justify their existence in India, what is the purpose today to perpetuate this evil?. . . I must frankly state that I am not at all happy for the way in which we have been proceeding, copying in most cases important portions of the Act of 1935. (Government of India, 1949)

The Act of 1935 confirmed the provisions for Excluded and Partially Excluded Areas made in the Act of 1919.

Das was right to fear that the governments of independent India would continue with tribal policies worked out in most respects by the British (see also Kanekar, 1942). But there is further irony in the suggestion that colonial tribal policies were ever isolationist. Although various departments of the Raj were committed to an 'official' tribal policy of isolationism, other agencies of the colonial state were working in the Jharkhand to make isolationism an impossibility. For all their rhetoric of protecting endangered communities and areas, the colonial governors of the Jharkhand were driven increasingly to undermine their own policies by encouraging the exploitation of the forest and mineral resources of Chota Nagpur.

The forests

The erosion of popular forestry rights in India can be traced back to 1865. In that year the first Forest Act was passed, to be replaced later by the more elaborate provisions of Act VII of 1878 and Act XVI of 1927. More important than either of these Acts, however, was a Resolution on Forest Policy in India (Resolution No. 22-F) issued by the Government of India on 19 October 1894. It was this resolution – the so-called Voelcker Resolution – which first defined the rights of the state and local groups in the forests. The resolution of 1894 states that:

> The sole object with which forests are administered is the public benefit. In some areas the public to be benefited are the whole body of tax payers, in others the people of the tract within which the forest is constituted, but in almost all cases the constitution and preservation of forests involves, in greater or lesser degree, the recognition of rights and restrictions of privileges of use in the forest area, which may previously have been enjoyed by the inhibitants of its immediate neighbourhood. (Government of India, 1967, p. 12)

Voelcker argued that the preservation of forests in India was a *sine qua non* of continued agricultural prosperity. Without adequate forest cover, runoff would increase, soil erosion would ensue and cultivable land would be lost. The British also detected in tribal forestry practices – and in shifting cultivation especially – a primitive, irrational and damaging relationship with India's flora.

Acting upon Voelcker's advice, the British divided India's forests into four groups: reserved forests, protected forests, private forests and village forests and wastes. In the latter two groups tribal and non-tribal rights of access continued much as before. In the village forests there were no statutory restrictions on grazing or felling, while in the private forests any restrictions were imposed by local *zamindars* and often took the form of forced labour days. In the protected forests, by contrast, and more especially in the reserved forests, the rights of local peasants to graze their animals, to cultivate crops, to fell trees, and to collect honey, mahua flowers, tendu leaves and so on, now came under the strict control of the state.

The main victims of this process of reservation were the tribals of central India. In Bihar, large forest tracts in Singhbhum, Palamau, Ranchi and Santal Parganas were brought under the guidelines of 1894, and in these districts the tribal peasant was brought face to face with a new commodification of time and space. Measurement replaced mythology as the forests fell to management practices designed to maximise the production of commercial timber. In place of the mixed forest, with its delicate balance of major and minor forest products, the tendency now was to replace trees such as mahua and kusum with sal and teak plantations. In place of open access to the forests there now appeared wire fences and forest guards. In place of a complex landscape of irregular jungles and symbolic centres, there now appeared a management plan which emphasised regular coppicing and which introduced straight-line planting. In place of rights there now emerged privileges and offences. Finally, in place of customary use based on local need, there emerged a set of restrictions based upon a minute regulation of time and space. Grazing, henceforth, would be for specific types of animals, on particular days of the week, in particular parts of a forest. The felling of trees, meanwhile, was policed such that (for example): '*sakhua* trees could not be felled if they were of a girth of twenty-seven inches or more at a height three feet from the ground' (Reid, 1912, p. 126).

It is hard to exaggerate the impact that these changes had upon the tribal communities of the Jharkhand.[3] Hunts were disrupted and deities offended. Emigration to the tea plantations of Assam increased dramatically as the region fell victim to famines which previously might have been avoided (Table 8.1). Meanwhile, the village forests themselves fell into disrepair as a desperate peasantry sought to exploit those forest resources still available to it. None of this sits comfortably with the paternalist assumptions and claims of isolationism. Nor, too, were the political goals of government best served by the resurgence in tribal unrest which followed the promulgation of the new forest policies. The *Annual Progress Reports on Forest Administration in Bihar (and Orissa)* record a high and rising level of 'forest offences' in Chota Nagpur and

Santal Parganas between 1911–12 and 1938–9 (Table 8.2). These offences incurred certain penalties and tribals were regularly fined for unauthorised felling and grazing. By the 1930s and 1940s, however, there is a suggestion that the colonial authorities were prepared to see such offences for what they were – a traditional form of peasant resistance (Guha, 1989) – and that they acted to commute most of the punishments accordingly. Having stoked up tribal malcontent, the state was, finally, unwilling to risk a further round of tribal insurgency in the Jharkhand. In this respect, the colonial state knew its limitations.

Mining and manufacturing

In Singhbhum district, the loss of tribal lands to the state forests was compounded by a loss of land to the Bengal Iron and Steel Company (BISCO) and to the Tata Iron and Steel Company (TISCO). Land was also lost to the mica mines in Hazaribagh and to the coal industry in Manbhum (Dhanbad). The BISCO and the TISCO were each incorporated at the turn of the present century following the discovery of extensive iron-ore reserves at Gorumahisini Hill in Mayurbhanj State, and at Gua and Noamundi in Singhbhum.[4] Prior to 1900 there was little incentive to prospect for minerals, owing to a strict prohibition on the issuing of prospecting licences to companies and syndicates (Government of India, 1899).

The iron and steel industry first made a mark on Singhbhum District in terms of land being acquired for its mines. The land markets of Chota Nagpur and Santal Parganas were protected from the middle part of the nineteenth century by legislation designed to prohibit the transfer of lands from tribals to non-tribals (except with the consent of the local Collector). This legislation was far from robust, however, in the face of a demand for tribal lands from the BISCO and the TISCO. By virtue of the Land Acquisition Act of 1894, the state was able to secure for the mining companies almost limitless access to tribal lands on the grounds that industrial development would serve 'a public purpose'. Between 1915 and 1925 up to 100,000 acres of tribal lands in southwest Singhbhum passed into the 'public domain' for the quarries themselves, for housing compounds, for service roads and railways and so on. A similar loss of land would befall Ranchi District in the 1950s and 1960s as the state acquired land from Munda and Oraon communities for the development of the heavy engineering complex at Hatia (S.P. Sinha, 1968).

The terms of these land transfers were far from equitable (even assuming that some tribals were willing to accept monetary compensation). Data from the *Annual Reports on the Land Revenue Administration in the Province of Bihar (and Orissa)* allow us to construct a diagram which compares the scale of land acquisition in Chota Nagpur with that in the rest of Bihar (Figure 8.4), and another which compares the prices at which lands were acquired in different parts of the state (Figure 8.5). Even allowing for the fact that land is less valuable in Chota Nagpur than in the more fertile plains of north and south Bihar, it is hard to accept that the average price of an acre of land acquired in Singhbhum District should be, on several occasions, less than 5 per cent of the price paid elsewhere in Bihar.

Table 8.1 *Labour Importations into Assam by Source, 1878–1930*

	Total Importations	Importations from Chota Nagpur and Santal Parganas	
		Number	%
1878	32,189	16,932	52.60
1879	18,286	10,824	59.19
1880		no data	
1881			
1882	18,952	8,980	47.38
1883	26,390	11,577	43.87
1884	32,747	16,795	51.29
1885	21,144	9,790	46.30
1886	22,715	12,160	53.53
1887	29,090	16,385	56.33
1888	33,317	20,252	60.79
1889	37,548	22,877	60.93
1890	26,205	13,162	50.23
1891	37,939	16,557	43.64
1892	41,802	17,910	42.84
1893	37,143	17,837	48.02
1894	35,706	17,833	49.94
1895	56,501	18,369	32.51
1896	61,301	16,122	26.30
1897	66,328	28,078	42.33
1898	33,516	18,594	55.48
1899	25,872	11,192	43.26
1900	45,044	17,605	39.08
1901	19,887	7,558	38.00
1902/3	20,199	6,661	32.98
1903/4	17,769	6,513	36.65
1904/5	19,050	7,048	37.00
1905/6–1911		no data	
1911/12	45,905	10,670	23.24
1912/13	46,239	14,205	30.72
1913/14	45,849	9,314	20.31
1914/15	46,212	16,058	34.75
1915/16	72,608	26,506	36.51
1916/17	33,998	14,871	43.74
1917/18	15,084	6,385	42.33
1918/19[1]	135,610	57,703	42.55
1919/20	65,463	27,455	41.95
1920/21[2]	571,526	217,856	38.12
1922		no data	
1923	372,131	162,575	43.69
1924		no data	
1925	382,743	152,261	39.78

Table 8.1   *contd.*

	Total Importations	Importations from Chota Nagpur and Santal Parganas	
		Number	%
1926	179,518	38,855	21.64
1927	394,735	145,618	36.89
1928	400,710	147,563	36.83
1929	424,980	156,944	36.93
1930	433,349	159,655	36.84

Notes: 1. *'The number of immigrants was the highest on record for many years. The increase was chiefly due to the existence of scarcity in recruiting districts and to the stoppage of the abnormal demand for labour caused by the war' (Report on Labour Immigration, 1918/19, p. 1).*
2. *From 1920/21 no statistics on immigration are provided. The data thereafter refers to the labour force and includes past labour and new importations.*
Source: *Government of India, 1878–1930.*

The development of an iron and steel industry in Singhbhum also had conse-quences for local patterns of employment, remuneration and capital forma-tion. Although it is often argued that the development of India's resource triangle turned the Jharkhand into an internal colony (Minz, 1968; Sinha, 1973; Rothermund and Wadhwa, 1978), the historical record suggests a more nuanced set of causes and effects (Corbridge, 1987). It is true that the tribals of Chota Nagpur were excluded from those jobs in mining and manufacturing which offered the highest rewards. Anglo-Europeans, Madrasis, Punjabis and others long dominated the managerial ranks of such enterprises, and face workers and drillers were often recruited on contract from the caste Hindu populations of north Bihar and Gorakhpur (Simmons, 1976). On the other hand, in the iron-ore mines of Singhbhum District, local tribals were put to work in great numbers between 1920 and the late 1960s (Figure 8.6). It was common, indeed, for tribal families to work together within a mining com-pound. The males would work as skilled and unskilled miners, and the females as loaders and carriers (Goverment of India, 1945; see also Keenan, 1950; Majumdar, 1937; Ghosh, 1973). Further, while the wages earned by these households were not as high as some wages on offer in the coal mines, they were, in the 1940s, 1950s and 1960s especially, well in excess of the wages which could be earned in local non-industrial employment (Figure 8.7). Many families were able to earn sufficient rewards from mining and manufacturing to purchase land from other tribal households. It is partly for this reason that a tribal middle class began to emerge in the Jharkhand in the middle part of this century.

A third effect of the industrial development of Chota Nagpur concerns demography and ethnicity. The reservation of forest lands in the Jharkhand worked to expel large numbers of tribals to Calcutta and Assam. Between 1890 and 1930 up to a million Jharkhandis made their way to Assam, often

Table 8.2 *Forestry Offences in Reserved and Protected Forests of Chota*
Nagpur and Santal Parganas, 1911/12 to 1934/5

| YEAR | Singhbhum | | Chaibassa/Kolhan | | Santal Parganas | | Palamau | |
	Felling	Grazing	Felling	Grazing	Felling	Grazing	Felling	Grazing
1911/12	108	12	32	19	167	11	87	14
1912/13	33	5	105	28	127	10	62	15
1913/14	30	2	104	24	112	5	52	20
1914/15	77	5	114	34	118	5	87	13
1915/16	49	1	136	31	68	7	70	14
1916/17	119	2	83	12	129	–	62	6
1917/18	98	12	97	4	77	–	62	12
1918/19	97	12	52	2	104	–	107	33
1919/20	86	13	31	3	113	8	64	11
1920/1	42	6	35	–	92	1	86	17
1921/2	94	11	51	1	158	21	113	51
1922/3	66	6	92	11	220	50	71	17
1923/4	70	8	77	14	166	43	55	14
1924/5	69	8	64	17	185	41	87	15
1925/6	54	17	68	13	192	35	96	19
1926/7	30	–	70	11	152	37	101	22
1927/8	82	2	77	1	94	45	110	12
1928/9	75	6	121	2	112	22	64	7
1929/30	116	5	125	–	217	23	78	4
1930/1	92	7	82	6	234	10	82	9
1931/2	104	11	89	6	224	19	36	8
1933/4	126	8	124	10	156	26	102	12
1934/5	101	7	106	12	172	13	82	10

Note: *After 1934/5 the reserved and protected forests of Jaharkhand were regrouped into the Saranda,
Kolhan, Chaibassa and Santal Parganas forests. The data collected thereafter are not truly comparable.
Source: Government of Bihar and Orissa (1911/12–1934/5).*

under duress.[5] With the development of a mining and manufacturing capacity in Chota Nagpur, the picture changed dramatically (Table 8.3). Large numbers of migrant labourers now flocked to Chota Nagpur, in the process changing the recognised ethnic composition of the region. Whereas, in 1872, 51.38 per cent of Chota Nagpuris were classified by the British as aboriginals and semi-aboriginals, by 1971 only 30.94 per cent of the region's population belonged to the scheduled tribes of Bihar. For all that the colonial state spoke of its desire to protect *its* aborigines in Scheduled Districts and Areas, its overriding commitment to the industrial development of the Jharkhand ensured that such a desire would be unfulfilled. The state, in Chota Nagpur and Santal Parganas, was the main catalyst of a process of 'detribalisation' which it claimed to abhor.

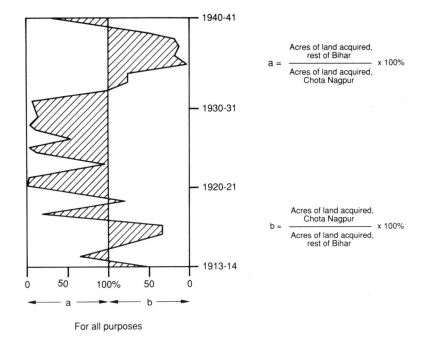

$$a = \frac{\text{Acres of land acquired,}}{\text{rest of Bihar}} \times 100\%$$
$$\frac{}{\text{Acres of land acquired,}}{\text{Chota Nagpur}}$$

$$b = \frac{\text{Acres of land acquired,}}{\text{Chota Nagpur}} \times 100\%$$
$$\frac{}{\text{Acres of land acquired,}}{\text{rest of Bihar}}$$

For all purposes

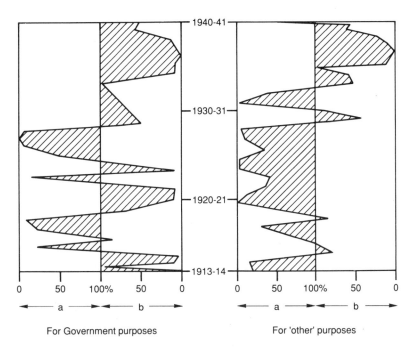

For Government purposes   For 'other' purposes

8:4 Comparisons of the scale of acquisition of land for public purposes: Chota Nagpur v. the rest of Bihar, 1913–14 to 1940–41. *Source: Reports of the Land Revenue Administration for Bihar and Orissa 1913–1914 to 1935–36, and for Bihar 1936–37 to 1940–41*

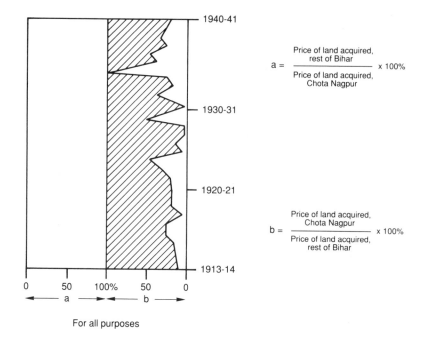

$$a = \frac{\text{Price of land acquired, rest of Bihar}}{\text{Price of land acquired, Chota Nagpur}} \times 100\%$$

$$b = \frac{\text{Price of land acquired, Chota Nagpur}}{\text{Price of land acquired, rest of Bihar}} \times 100\%$$

For all purposes

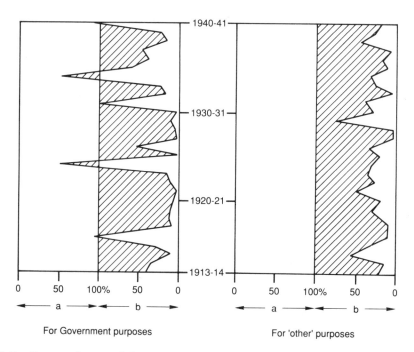

For Government purposes

For 'other' purposes

8:5 **Comparisons of the prices paid as compensation for lands taken up for public purposes: Chota Nagpur v. the rest of Bihar, 1913–14 to 1940–41.** *Source: Reports of the Land Revenue Administration for Bihar and Orissa 1913–14 to 1935–36, and for Bihar 1936–37 to 1940–41*

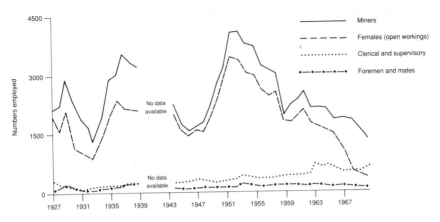

8:6 Trends in employment: Singhbhum iron mines. *Source: Chief Inspector of Mines, Annual Reports, 1927–77*

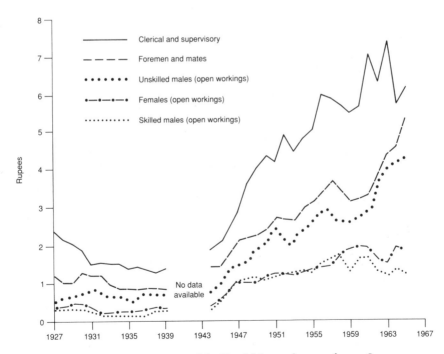

8:7 Trends in daily wages paid: Singhbhum iron mines. *Source: Chief Inspector of Mines, Annual Reports, 1927–77*

171

Table 8.3 *Immigration and Emigration: Santal Parganas and Chota Nagpur, 1891–1971*

	Immigration	Emigration
1891	96,000	333,000
1901	179,000	NA
1911	293,000	707,000
1921	307,000	947,000
1931	307,000	NA
1941	NA	NA
1951	480,000	NA
1961	1,073,920	NA
1971	1,429,805	NA

Source: K.S. Singh (1978), Statement VII, p. 69.

Integration and Disintegration: The Jharkhand after Independence

The intentions of the colonial state in the Jharkhand were always contested by the local populations. In the nineteenth century, the great tribal rebellions shook the Raj, as did the forest *satyagrahas* (non-violent protests) of the 1920s and 1930s. By the 1940s, the inhabitants of the Jharkhand were also beginning to make their voices heard in what was to become the parliamentary arena. A number of mission-educated, mainly urban tribals, centred in Ranchi, joined together in 1937 to create the Chota Nagpur Adivasi Mahasabha. In 1950 this became the Jharkhand Party, a political organisation committed to the formation of a tribal state in the Jharkhand. The leader of the Jharkhand Party until its near collapse in 1963 was Jaipal Singh, an Oxford-educated Munda of great charismatic appeal. In the national and state elections of 1952 and 1957, the Jharkhand Party proved itself to be the main vote-winner in Singhbhum, Ranchi and Santal Parganas Districts, and the main opposition to the Congress Party in the State of Bihar. However, the Jharkhand Party did less well in the border areas of Orissa and West Bengal (Panchbhai, 1983).

It was in this local context that power was transferred from a colonial administration to a post-colonial state. Not surprisingly, it is a context (of a persistent tribal 'threat') which encouraged the new rulers to continue to treat their tribal populations in a contradictory manner. In the Jharkhand, especially, the Government of Bihar has pushed ahead with a massive exploitation of the forest and mineral wealth of the region, while maintaining, in its 'official' tribal policies, a belief that 'the tribals should be allowed to develop along the lines of their own genius' (Government of India, 1955; see also Government of India, 1967, 1975, 1978).

Turning first to the official tribal policies of the post-colonial state, one can point to three sets of interventions, each of which is supposed to secure an equitable integration of tribal and non-tribal India. There is, first, a commitment to continue to schedule certain populations as 'tribal' (usually in Scheduled Areas), while promising that these schedules will periodically be revised and will always be tightly drawn. In practice, the tendency has been to sanction a slow drift to detribalisation, with communities such as the Bauris becoming descheduled *on account of* their 'development' (as coal miners). A Catch 22 of this sort has pressing implications for Jharkhandi politics. It means that the various Jharkhand parties face increasing difficulties in sustaining a political appeal based on ethnicity alone. The Government of Bihar is well aware of this paradox and is not slow to exploit it (Sengupta, 1982).

A second strand of 'official' tribal policy in modern India – that is, the policy of the Ministry of Home Affairs, the Commissioner for Scheduled Castes and Tribes and several Hindu 'mission' organisations – is a commitment to positive discrimination. Seats are reserved for Scheduled tribals in the Lok Sabha and State Legislative Assemblies, and jobs are reserved for some tribals in public-sector corporations. Notwithstanding a lack of funding for such policies (Corbridge, 1989), positive discrimination has secured many benefits for the tribal populations of independent India. Ironically, too, it has served to fortify an emerging tribal middle class, for it is this group which monopolises most of the benefits on offer. Again, this tends to undermine the ideology of undifferentiated tribal communities upon which tribal policy is based, and from which a traditional tribal politics derives. (The emergence of a tribal middle class is somewhat discouraged by the protective land legislation still in place in the Jharkhand.)

A final aspect of modern tribal policy is less well advertised in the brochures of State Tribal Welfare Departments. Put bluntly, it is an inducement to co-optation, and/or a willingness to resort to the carrot and the stick. In Bihar, successive Congress and Janata administrations have sought to dampen opposition to their initiatives in the Jharkhand by making available to local tribal leaders certain offices within the state machine. This was especially apparent at the time of Jaipal Singh's defection to the Congress Party in 1963. No doubt impressed by the goverment's claim that the Jharkhand could not be granted statehood (and had missed the boat in the 1956 States Reorganization Act), Jaipal Singh decided that he could serve the tribal cause best as Minister for Tribal Affairs in a Congress-dominated Bihar. Others have been treated less well. Several activists of the Mukti Morcha have been targeted as Naxalites[6] and still languish in the jails of Chaibasa, Ranchi and Jamshedpur.

The treatment meted out to some *Morcha* activists should make us wary of accepting at face value all of the claims of the official tribal policies of the post-colonial state. These policies clearly have done much to improve the lot of most tribals, and money is now being poured into the Scheduled Areas in a manner which must shame the mean efforts of the British. Nevertheless, there is a dark side to state–tribal relationships in the Jharkhand and it is growing darker still.

The reasons for this take us back to the gap which exists between the rhetoric and reality of state interventions in Chota Nagpur and Santal Parganas. Bluntly stated, various Governments of Bihar have contrived to sponsor the rapid industrial development of the Jharkhand more or less regardless of the offence that this does to the local communities that they are obliged to protect.

This is especially obvious in the case of the forests, where, by virtue of the National Forest Policy of 1952, 'what in 1894 became rights and privileges, in 1952 became rights and concessions and then concessions' (Bhowmick, 1981, p. 35). Bhowmick is right to maintain of this Act (and still more of the provisions of the Draft Forest Bill of 1980: see Srivastava, 1987) that its strictures on grazing and gleaning turned 'the tribals, who formerly regarded themselves as lords of the forests . . . into subjects of the Forest Department' (Bhowmick, 1981, p. 35). Offence is also apparent in the linked arenas of mining and manufacturing. Since 1950, hundreds of thousands of acres of tribal land in the Jharkhand has been lost to new industries, and some half a million jobs have been created in the region. In itself, this is no bad thing, but in the 1970s the representation of the Scheduled Tribes in the industrial labour force of Bihar was sharply reduced. In the iron-ore mines this was mainly a result of mechanisation. In the coal industry, however, it is widely believed that the Government of Bihar, in alliance with the so-called Dhanbad Mafia, connived to expel thousands of Jharkhandis from the pits and to replace them with 'client workers' from north Bihar. The Jharkhandis – mainly tribals, but also Mahatos and others – were then obliged to return to their villages, adding to a local pressure of people upon the land. Their fate has not been a happy one. Meanwhile, the cities of Ranchi, Dhanbad and Jamshedpur continue to grow rapidly and to provide homes for an ever-rising number of non-tribal *dikus*. Talk of an internal colony (of tribals) no longer seems so misplaced.

Conclusion

To write thus of the post-colonial state is unsatisfactory because so much is left unsaid. We still await detailed accounts of the lives of tribal ex-miners who returned to their villages. We also need more information on contemporary patterns of labour-force participation in the Jharkhand, on regional reinvestment rates, on areas of environmental degradation and so on (although see Das, 1983; Maharaj, 1980; Pathak, 1982). Nevertheless, we can venture some tentative conclusions regarding the changing relationships between the state and the local populations of the Jharkhand. Two conclusions, in particular, deserve elaboration.

There is, first, the question of 'the tribal problem'. It is symptomatic both of the colonial state and its post-colonial successors that tribal India is considered as a problem for government. Although different administrations have made efforts to relate to their tribal citizens in different ways, a common point of reference has been that of social and spatial control. Various agencies of the state have come to fear their tribal subjects, both as a threat to 'development' and to the territorial control of the state. In the Jharkhand such fears are not without foundation. Most tribals are sceptical of the official tribal policies of the state, and most are deeply opposed to the project of modernisation which these policies seek to occlude. A local desire to recreate a local 'natural economy' is by no means vanquished.

A second conclusion concerns the mechanisms and capacities of state control in tribal India. In the Jharkhand, the territorial reach of the colonial state was often very fragile. This was demonstrated by the tribal rebellions of the nineteenth century and by the decision of the Raj to commute certain fines for forest offences committed in the 1920s, 1930s and 1940s. It is also consistent with what we know about the physical presence of the British in Chota Nagpur and Santal Parganas. Even allowing for indirect patterns of rule, the comparative absence of police and army personnel, forest guards and local courts, made it difficult for the British to enforce a day-to-day oppression of the peoples of the Jharkhand (as opposed to a wider, and periodically more brutal, political and economic hegemony). The fiscal and geopolitical concerns of the Raj also cautioned the colonial state against an ideology of developmentalism. Although a doctrine of isolationism was set aside in Chota Nagpur, the colonial state was not prepared to sponsor a full and rapid capitalist development of central India (Kumar and Desai, 1982).

The post-colonial state, by contrast, suffers from few such restrictions and inhibitions. Although the modern state still clings to an ideology of 'benign integration' for its tribals (and to continuing policies of protection, exclusion and positive discrimination), its overriding ambition is to 'develop' the resources of the Jharkhand as rapidly as it can. To this end, it has poured foreign aid moneys, and state revenues, into new steel mills at Rourkela and Bokaro, and into the heavy industries of Hatia and Jamshedpur. State housing schemes have prospered, new transport lines have been built, and even the timber industry has been befriended by the state. Moreover – and more sinisterly – the modern state is well equipped to survey and to persecute those Jharkhandis who contest its developmental ambitions. Forest guards, in particular, are now present in great numbers in the Jharkhand and are loathed more than ever. Christoph von fürer-Haimendorf (1982, pp. 96–7) captures their role very well in his account of state/tribal relations in contemporary Andhra Pradesh:

> Anyone who refuses to pay the illegal fines is certain to be harassed by the forest guard, who can prevent those in his bad books from collecting even legally permitted forest produce and may charge the defaulter with forest offences which have never been committed. Today, the tyranny of forest guards is certainly as bad as it was in 1940 and there is no indication of any action on the part of the higher forest officers to curb the illegal activities of their subordinates.

This rings true also of Bihar (Shiva, 1989).

A similar capacity to survey and to punish is evident in the state's policing of Jharkhandi politics. Although political opposition is tolerated in independent India, such opposition is expected to know its place. In the 1950s and early 1960s this caused few problems in Chota Nagpur and Santal Parganas, where the Jharkhand Party was committed to the parliamentary road, and where its local successes posed few problems for the Governments of Bihar and India. In the late 1960s and 1970s, however, the Birsa Seva Dal, Bihar

Prant Hul Jharkhand Party and Jharkhand Mukti Morcha were each set up to contest the 'tyranny of developmentalism' both within and outside the parliamentary arena. Elections were contested by these organisations, but so too were their activists involved in the forcible cropping of *diku* lands (Duyker, 1987), in sabotaging local transport lines and in organising new forest *satyagrahas*.

The problems facing such groups, however, were amply illustrated by the Gua incident of September 1980. Instead of this bloody confrontation sparking a fresh wave of Jharkhandi rebellions, it prompted only a massive police and army presence and a widespread resort to the criminalisation and imprisonment of political activists. The Morcha, in the 1980s, was driven underground, only to emerge again in new guises and locations (Munda, 1988). The state, for its part, has been vigilant in monitoring local opposition to its policies and in continuing a large-scale destruction of tribal environments. Although a committed local opposition still exists, the Jharkhand is becoming a land of dams and mines, of timber plantations, factories and army units. Given the power of the modern state, the land of the forests may soon be no more.

Acknowledgements

The research project on which this chapter draws has been kindly supported by grants from the British Academy, the Central Research Fund of the University of London, and the Smuts Memorial Fund of Cambridge University. My thanks are also due to Sarah Jewitt, who commented on a first draft of the chapter, and to Ram Dayal Munda for his hospitality and guidance.

Notes

1. For the purposes of this chapter, the Jharkhand is taken to refer to the Bihar Jharkhand, or Chota Nagpur and Santal Parganas (unless otherwise stated). In part, this is for pedagogic reasons; in part, it is because an organised Jharkhand Movement has been most successful as a movement in and against the State of Bihar. It should be noted that the proposed Jharkhand State is not confined to Chota Nagpur and Santal Parganas, and that Jharkhandi activists are still seeking to build bridges to Jharkhandi communities in West Bengal, Orissa and Madhya Pradesh. In August 1989, Ram Dayal Munda led thousands of activists on a march across the Bihar–Orissa border. The march was intended to draw media attention to the movement and to challenge both the Government of Orissa and the validity of the boundary line itself.

2. Elwin's career was both fascinating and exemplary. An Oxford-educated Christian missionary before he landed in India, Verrier Elwin quickly became a disciple of M. K. Gandhi. His remarks on a possible national park for tribals were made in the context of his studies and service among (and on behalf of) the Muria, the Baiga and the Agaria (Elwin, 1942). Although rebuked by Indian nationalists for his 'isolationism', Elwin later became

an adviser to the governments of Pandit Nehru on matters to do with tribal welfare. In this latter role he came to reflect, poignantly, on his earlier apologia for an ethnological zoo (Elwin, 1955). Elwin's life and career are well documented in his autobiography (Elwin, 1964) and in the biography written by his close friend, Shamrao Hivale (Hivale, 1958). Elwin's passion for 'his' tribals (two of whom he married) is well attested to in his correspondence with Edward Hyde, the Collector of Mandla District (now in Madhya Pradesh) in the 1940s (Hyde, 1978).

3. If the absurdities of Empire knew few bounds (cf. the sakhua trees), the best imperial officers knew full well what offence was being done to the aboriginal populations of central India. The settlement officer for Ranchi District, John Reid, wrote thus of the new forest policy: 'It is usual now-a-days to talk of the encroachments of the raiyats in jungle areas. Europeans and Indians alike ... sometimes fail to perceive that it is in reality themselves who have encroached, and by degrees deprived the village communities of their ancient proprietary rights' (Reid, 1912, p. 126).

4. The Tata Iron and Steel Company Limited was incorporated in Bombay in 1907 at a value of £1,630,000. From the outset, the company was promised cheap land at Kalimati (Jamshedpur) and cheap freight rates on the Bengal–Nagpur railway line. The company's main iron-ore mine is at Noamundi. The Bengal Iron and Steel Company Limited was incorporated in England, in 1889, at a value of £150,000. It was acquired, in 1936, by the Indian Iron and Steel Company Limited (IISCO), a firm incorporated in Calcutta, in 1918, by British interests. The IISCO was nationalised by the post-colonial state. Its main iron-ore mines are at Gua. On the history of the iron and steel industry in India, see Mather, 1927; Parkinson, 1950; Bagchi, 1972.

5. The figure of 1 million is an estimate based on known labour importations and probable associated movements of close family members. The migration was not always permanent. On the cruelty of the Assam trade, note the remarks made by the Deputy Commissioner of Santal Parganas in 1892: 'I have no reason to change my opinion as to the so-called free emigration system. It is nothing but coolie-hunting, eight free coolies selling for the price that is fetched by one newly caught eight foot elephant, while the risk and the expense of the sport are not nearly so great ... A man who can catch two or three coolies in a month makes as large an income as a Deputy Magistrate of eight years service and the small men are met occasionally personally conducting their captures to Raniganj or Calcutta. I call them captures, for a man that is sold for Rs. 100 is not free in fact, whatever he may be in theory ... I am certain that this unchecked "free recruiting" system is politically dangerous and is disturbing and demoralising the population' (quoted in Government of India, 1892, p. 8). The tribals, for their part, referred to the tea-garden contractors as *horoakirinko*, or sellers of men. It should be noted that not all officials were disturbed by the Assam trade. Dr V. Richards, the Officiating Superintendant of Inland Emigration in 1878, wrote that: 'Regarding the food, I think the scale now in force is far too liberal for the jungle coolies (*adivasis*) on

board the steamers, as they are apt to gorge themselves' (Government of India, 1877–8, p. 17).

6. The Naxalites (CPI–ML) emerged in the late 1960s in the Naxalbari area of West Bengal. Having split from the Communist Party of India (Marxist), the Communist Party of India (Marxist–Leninist) was led by Charu Mazumdar as a Maoist party, committed to an armed class struggle in the countryside. Naxalite groups later emerged in Bihar and Andhra Pradesh, amongst other states. Scheduled tribals, especially Santals, were strongly involved in these movements. On the Naxalite movement, see Dasgupta, 1974.

References

Allanson, H.L.L. (1912) *Final Report on the Survey and Settlement Operations in the District of Sonthal Parganas, 1898–1910*, Calcutta: Bengal Secretariat.

Archer, W.G. (1984) *Tribal Law and Justice: A Report on the Santal*, New Delhi: Concept.

Bagchi, A.K. (1972) *Private Investment in India, 1900–1939*, Cambridge: Cambridge University Press.

Bardhan, K. (ed.) (1990) *Of Women, Outcastes, Peasants and Rebels: A Selection of Bengali Short Stories*, Berkeley: University of California Press.

Basu, K.K. (1957) 'Early administration of the Kol Peers in Singhbhum Bamangati', *Journal of Bihar Research Society*, 42, pp. 357–76.

Bhadra, G. (1988) 'Four rebels of eighteen fifty seven', in R. Guha and G.C. Spivak (eds) *Selected Subaltern Studies*, Oxford: Oxford University Press, pp. 129–75.

Bhowmick, P. (1981) 'Forestry, tribe and forest policy in India', In L.P. Vidyarthi (ed.) *Tribal Development and Its Administration*, New Delhi: Concept, pp. 29–38.

Chapman, G.P. (1983) 'The folklore of the perceived environment in Bihar', *Environment and Planning A*, 15, pp. 945–68.

Corbridge, S. (1987) 'Industrialisation, internal colonialism and ethnoregionalism: the Jharkhand, India, 1880–1980', *Journal of Historical Geography*, 13, pp. 249–66.

Corbridge, S. (1988) 'The ideology of tribal economy and society: politics in the Jharkhand, 1950–1980', *Modern Asian Studies*, 22, pp. 1–42.

Corbridge, S. (1989) 'Tribal politics, finance and the state: the Jharkhand, India, 1900–1980', *Ethnic and Racial Studies*, 12, pp. 174–207.

Das, A.N. (1983) *Agrarian Unrest and Socio-Economic Change in Bihar, 1900–1980*, New Delhi: Manohar.

Dasgupta, B. (1974) *The Naxalite Movement*, New Delhi: Allied.

Duyker, E. (1987) *Tribal Guerrillas: The Santhals of West Bengal and the Naxalite Movement*, New Delhi: Oxford University Press.

Elwin, V. (1942) *The Agaria*, Oxford: Oxford University Press.

Elwin, V. (1944) *Loss of Nerve: A Comparative Study of the Contact of Peoples in the Aboriginal Areas of Bastar State and the Central Provinces*, Bombay: Oxford University Press.

Elwin, V. (1955) 'Do we really want to keep them in a zoo? In Government of India (ed.) *The Adivasis*, New Delhi: Ministry of Information and Broadcasting, ch. 2.

Elwin, V. (1964) *The Tribal World of Verrier Elwin: An Autobiography*, Oxford: Oxford University Press.

Forsyth, J. (1919) *The Highlands of Central India*, London: Chapman & Hall.

Fürer-Haimendorf, C. von. (1982) *The Tribes of India: The Struggle for Survival*, Berkeley: University of California Press.

Galanter, M. (1984) *Competing Equalities: Law and the Backward Classes in India*, New Delhi: Oxford University Press.

Ghosh, M. (1973) *Our Struggle*, Calcutta: Mukhodpadhyay.

Ghurye, G. S. (1980) *The Scheduled Tribes*, New Brunswick: Transaction.

Government of Bihar (and Orissa) (1911/12–1940/1) *Annual Reports of the Land Revenue Administration in the Province of Bihar and Orissa (and Bihar)*, Patna: Bihar and Orissa (and Bihar) Secretariat.

Government of Bihar and Orissa (1911/12–1934/5) *Annual Progress Reports on Forest Administration in the Province of Bihar and Orissa*, Patna: Bihar and Orissa Secretariat.

Government of India (1927–77) *Annual Reports of the Chief Inspector of Mines (and Series)*, Delhi: Government of India Secretariat.

Government of India (1878–1930) *Annual Reports on Labour Immigration into Assam*, Shillong: Assam Secretariat.

Government of India (1875/6–1898) *Annual Reports on Inland Emigration*, Calcutta: Bengal Secretariat.

Government of India (1899) *Report upon the Manufacture of Iron and Steel in India* (R. H. Mahon), Delhi: Government of India Secretariat. Commerce Department: Coal and Industry.

Government of India (1945) *Report on Labour Conditions in the Iron Ore Mining Industry* (B. P. Adarkar), Simla: Government of India Secretariat.

Government of India (1946–9) *Debates of the Constituent Assembly of India*, 9 vols, New Delhi: Government of India Secretariat.

Government of India (1955) *The Adivasis*, New Delhi: Ministry of Information and Broadcasting.

179

Government of India (1967) *Report of the Committee on Tribal Economy in the Forest Areas* (Chairman: H. Singh), New Delhi: Government of India, Department of Social Welfare.

Government of India (1975) *Report of the Task Force on the Development of Tribal Areas* (Chairman: L.P. Vidyarthi), New Delhi: Government of India, Ministry of Home Affairs.

Government of India (1978) *Report of the Study Team on Social Services in Tribal Areas during the Medium Term Plan, 1978–1983*, New Delhi: Government of India, Ministry of Home Affairs.

Government of the United Kingdom (1935) *Parliamentary Debates: Official Report, 5th Series*, vols 299–301. London: Hansard.

Grigson, W.V. (1946) 'The aboriginal in future India', *Man in India*, 26, pp. 81–95.

Grigson, W.V. (1949) *The Maria Gonds of Bastar*, London: Oxford University Press.

Guha, Ramachandra (1989) *The Unquiet Woods: Ecological Change and Peasant Resistance*, Delhi: Oxford University Press.

Guha, Ranajit (1983) *Elementary Aspects of Peasant Insurgency in Colonial India*, New Delhi: Oxford University Press.

Guha, Ranajit (1988) 'The prose of counter-insurgency', in R. Guha and G.C. Spivak (eds) *Selected Subaltern Studies*, Oxford: Oxford University Press, pp. 45–86.

Hembram, P. (1983) 'Return to the sacred grove', in K.S. Singh (ed.) *Tribal Movements in India,* vol. 2, New Delhi: Manohar, pp. 87–92.

Hivale, S. (1958) *Scholar Gypsy: Verrier Elwin*, Delhi: Oxford University Press.

Hunter, W.W. (1975) *Annals of Rural Bengal* (first published 1868), Delhi: Cosmo.

Hutton, J. (1922) 'Depopulation of primitive communities', *Man in India*, 2, pp. 220–6.

Hyde, E. (1978) *Private Papers*, Box 1, Cambridge: Centre of South Asian Studies.

Jha, J.C. (1964) *The Kol Insurrection of Chota Nagpur*, Calcutta: Thakur, Spink & Co.

Kanekar, P. (1942) 'Isolation or assimilation?', *Social Science Quarterly*, 28, pp. 97–115.

Keenan, V. (1950) *A Steel Man in India*, London: Chapman & Hall.

Kumar, D. and Desai, M. (eds.) (1982) *A New Cambridge Economic History of India*, vol. 2, Cambridge: Cambridge University Press.

Leuva, K.K. (1963) *The Asur*, New Delhi: Bharatiya Adimjati Sevak Sangh.

Maharaj, R. (1980) The impact of state policy on agriculture in Dhanbad, in D. Rothermund (ed.) *Urban Growth and Rural Stagnation*, New Delhi: Manohar, pp. 178–260.

Majumdar, D. (1937) *A Tribe in Transition*, Calcutta: Longmans, Green.

Mather, R. (1927) 'The iron and steel industry in India', *Journal of the Royal Society of Arts*, 75, pp. 600–16.

Minz, N. (1968) *A Memorandum on the Adivasi Problems in the Central Tribal Belt of India and Their Permanent Solutions*, Ranchi: Mimeo.

Munda, R.D. (1988) 'The Jharkhand movement: retrospect and prospect', *Social Change*, 18, pp. 28–58.

Nandy, A. (1988) *The Intimate Enemy: Loss and Recovery of Self Under Colonialism*, Delhi: Oxford University Press.

O'Malley, L.S.S. (1910) *District Gazetteer of Singhbhum, Seraikela and Kharsawan*, Calcutta: Bengal Secretariat.

Panchbhai, S. (1983) 'The Jharkhand movement among the Santals', in K.S. Singh (ed.) *Tribal Movements in India*, vol. 2, New Delhi: Manohar, pp. 31–52.

Parkinson, E.V. (1950) 'The development of the iron and steel industry in India', *Journal of the Royal Society of Arts*, 98, pp. 668–85.

Pathak, M. (1982) 'Death of a worker', in N. Sengupta (ed.) *Fourth World Dynamics: Jharkhand*, Delhi: Authors Guild, pp. 65–73.

Prasad, N. (1961) *Land and People of Tribal Bihar*, Ranchi: Government of Bihar.

Reid, J. (1912) *Final Report on the Survey and Settlement Operations in the District of Ranchi, 1902–1910*, Calcutta: Bengal Secretariat.

Rothermund, D. and Wadhwa, D. (eds.) (1978) *Zamindars, Mines and Peasants: Studies in the History of an Indian Coalfield*, New Delhi: Manohar.

Roy, S.C. (1970) *The Mundas and Their Country*, New York: Asia (first published in 1912).

Roy, S.C. (1984) *The Oraons of Chotanagpur*, Ranchi: Catholic Press (first published in 1915).

Sengupta, N. (ed.) (1982) *Fourth World Dynamics: Jharkhand*, Delhi: Authors Guild.

Shiva, V. (1989) *Staying Alive: Women, Ecology and Development*, London: Zed.

Simmons, C. (1976) 'Recruiting and organising an industrial labour force in colonial India: the case of the coal mining industry, c. 1880–1939', *Indian Economic and Social History Review*, 13, pp. 455–85.

Singh, K.S. (1978) 'Tribal ethnicity in a multi-ethnic society', Mimeo.

Sinha, D.P. (1962) *Culture Change in an Inter-Tribal Market*, New York: Asia.

Sinha, S. (1973) *The Internal Colony: A Study in Regional Exploitation*, New Delhi: Sindhu.

Sinha, S.P. (1962) 'State formation and Rajput myth in tribal central India', *Man in India*, 42, pp. 35–80.

Sinha, S.P. (1968) *The Problem of Land Alienation in and around Ranchi (1955–1965)*, Ranchi: Bihar Tribal Research Institute.

Srivastava, R. (1987) 'The Forest Bill of 1980 and crises facing tribals of Madhya Pradesh, India', in S.P. Sinha (ed.) *Tribals and Forests*, Ranchi: Government of Bihar, pp. 41–54.

Tutuola, A. (1954) *My Life in the Bush of Ghosts*, London: Faber & Faber.

Weiner, M. (1978) *Sons of the Soil: Migration and Ethnic Conflict in India*, Princeton, NJ: Princeton University Press.

CHAPTER 9

The Last Colonies:
Failures of Decolonisation?

John Connell and Robert Aldrich

The period of decolonisation, like the era of colonialism which preceded it, would now seem to be over. The independence of Namibia in 1990 and the cession of Hong Kong and Macao to China in the late 1990s appear to be postscripts to the process by which European and other imperial powers have given up their overseas possessions. From giant countries like India and Indonesia in the 1940s to micro-states such as Tuvalu and Kiribati in the 1970s, most colonies have acceded to independence. Yet, on closer examination, the process has not been, and never will be, completed. Secession and independence movements, which often charge that sovereign states maintain a form of colonialism, are numerous and active. On the Papua New Guinean island of Bougainville, in the Ethiopian territories of Eritrea and Tigre, in the Baltic republics of the Soviet Union, as in many other places, organised political parties, rebels or guerrilla warriors press for the creation of separate states. Furthermore, the theory of 'internal colonialism' posits the existence of economically and politically 'colonised' groups or regions inside various states, while the idea of 'neo-colonialism' stresses the maintenance of colonial ties between metropoles and their former imperial outposts, in similar even refined forms. Finally, there remain in every ocean and on every continent a large number of dependent territories which have not gained (and, in some instances, have not sought) independence from their 'mother countries'. These 'colonies', as demonstrated by events ranging from the Falklands War to the violence which troubled New Caledonia through the 1980s, constitute significant stakes for their administrating powers and can often be flashpoints for geopolitical disputes. They represent apparent anomalies in the history of decolonisation and, therefore, pose interesting questions about the theory and practice of decolonisation, the definition and limitations of the nation-state, and notions about both relations between the centre and periphery and strategies of development.

Overseas territories with constitutional links to metropolitan states include those only loosely connected, as 'freely associated states', as well as those almost totally assimilated into the administering countries, such as the American states of Alaska and Hawaii and the French *départements d'outre-mer*. Although some are populous (such as Hong Kong) or geographically vast (for example, French Guiana), most are small island territories. Their populations are often ethnically or culturally different from those of the metropole, even if some are peopled largely by European settlers. (Others, however, have no permanent population.) These territories are, in general, vestiges of the expansionism of the seventeenth century or the 'new imperialism' of the nineteenth; many have thus been colonial possessions for centuries; Bermuda is Britain's oldest colony, and France's West Indian islands are its oldest overseas domains. Yet in Antarctica, European powers remain engaged in a process of expansion. In short, these territories vary by location, resources and constitutional status; what unites them is the continuation, and even the enhancement, of legal and political ties with a distant source of economic and political power. This chapter is a broadly comparative analysis of the French, American and, to a lesser extent, New Zealand experience, each relatively poorly documented in comparison with the British example.

The Case of France

France provides perhaps the best contemporary example of the phenomenon of overseas possessions in the sense that the populations are large and there has been a vociferous, and intermittently violent, struggle for independence, notably in New Caledonia. Early in the twentieth century, France possessed the world's second largest colonial empire. Decolonisation brought early independence to Indo-China and the French colonies in Africa, and more recently to Djibouti, the Comoros and Vanuatu. However France retains a group of ten *départements et territoires d'outre-mer* (DOM-TOMs): Saint-Pierre and Miquelon off the coast of Canada, Martinique and Guadeloupe in the Antilles, Guiana (Guyane) in South America, the islands of Réunion and Mayotte in the Indian Ocean, New Caledonia, the archipelagos of French Polynesia and Wallis and Futuna in the South Pacific, and the French portion of Antarctica and various sub-Antarctic islands, grouped together as the Austral and Antarctic Territories. Together, these ten DOM-TOMs account for some 1.5 million French citizens (Aldrich and Connell, 1991).

Four of the DOM-TOMs, the *départements d'outre-mer*, have since 1946 been legally as much a part of France as Paris or Provence. Their law codes, institutions and political systems almost entirely replicate those of metropolitan France. The five *territoires d'outre-mer* have a more devolved administration and greater legalistic particularities. For both, however, the French Parliament holds ultimate law-making authority, and the French ministries, including the Ministry of the DOM-TOMs, are responsible for administration. The French residents of both DOMs and TOMs are full French citizens with total right of abode in the metropole; there is no French equivalent of a British overseas passport. The French in the DOM-TOMs elect representatives to the French Chamber of Deputies and Senate, as well as their own local assemblies. Local governments are headed by the president of the elected *conseil général* (in the DOMs) or a similar official, and the French state is represented by a prefect or high commissioner.

In addition to being politically linked with France, the DOM-TOMs are also economic dependencies of the metropole. None produces enough agricultural, industrial or tertiary income to be self-supporting. In fact, only the nickel mines of New Caledonia provide a major source of export earnings. Elsewhere, agricultural products such as sugar, rum and ylang-ylang, maritime products like fish and pearls, and tourism account for other small portions of the gross domestic product. France itself, through direct transfers, subsidies and the salaries paid to a large civil service, provides most of the finance on which the DOM-TOMs have become dependent. In French Polynesia, for instance, less than one-fifth of imports are covered by exports and in Wallis and Futuna a mere one-hundredth of imports are covered by exports. The large sums that France appropriates to the DOM-TOMs have local advantages: the standards of living, in terms of educational and health status and per capita incomes, are significantly higher than those of most of their neighbours and, in some cases, comparable with those of France itself. In the Caribbean, for example, Martinique and Guadeloupe enjoy the highest standard of living in the region, while the old French colony of Haiti, which became independent in the 1790s, is the poorest country in the Western Hemisphere. A similar situation occurs in the Pacific, in the contrast between Vanuatu (once the Anglo-French Condominium of the New Hebrides) and New Caledonia, as well as in the Indian Ocean, between the Comoros and Mayotte. Such contrasts are actively promoted by opponents of independence. The level of French funding, for all its benefits, has been criticised, however, as setting up 'artificial', 'transfer' or 'consumer' economies lacking an indigenous base or the capacity for diversification, in which most of the profits accrue to a small local elite or make their way back to France in bureaucrats' repatriated salaries or orders to French companies. In each of the DOM-TOMs, the employment structure is increasingly characterised by a large and growing service sector and a small and declining agricultural sector. Were any of the DOM-TOMs to gain independence, French funding would not be maintained at such high levels, as France has threatened in the case of New Caledonia, and equivalent funding through more diversified aid could not be obtained elsewhere.

Several particular projects in the French DOM-TOMs are firmly linked to the basic structure of political and economic dependence and also help to explain France's resolve to retain the overseas regions. The French space station in Guyane (the Centre spatial guyanais), in a location near the equator which is technically ideal, makes France one of a select group of countries with a space programme. From Kourou, the launch site, France puts into orbit telecommunications and other satellites which serve national interests as well as those of France's European partners. (The European Space Agency, a consortium of European nations interested in space activities, uses the French base.) France also earns revenue from the launching of private satellites. In the Pacific, France carries out testing of nuclear weapons in French Polynesia (at the Centre d'expérimention du Pacifique). The isolated and unpopulated atolls of Mururoa, Hao and Fangataufa provide the sites for the underground tests of explosive devices and back-up bases for technicians and troops. Despite ardent protests against nuclear testing from French Polynesia's neighbours in Oceania, Paris maintains that the testing is necessary to ensure the efficacy and continued modernisation of France's nuclear force; nuclear weapons are the pivot of France's defence policies and its claims to be a world power.

Space exploration and nuclear testing both took place in Algeria before that French colony became independent. They could both conceivably be transferred to other French territories and (less plausibly) to the metropole itself. The DOM-TOMs, however, allow France to pursue these efforts in areas over which it has legal sovereignty, which are easy to secure against outside menaces, and which provide a labour force. Both the space station and nuclear testing enterprise are the single most important economic activities in Guyane and French Polynesia in their provision of employment and their generation of ancillary service activities. They provide a powerful rationale for France to maintain control over these external territories. Several of the other DOM-TOMs also have strategic significance. Martinique and Guadeloupe are integrated into the French defence network which centres on Guyane, while New Caledonia serves as a support base for the testing in Polynesia. Fears of a 'domino effect' if, for example, New Caledonia became independent and French Polynesia were in line for the same 'fate', preoccupy policy-makers in Paris.

Not only are there specific strategic reasons for France's presence in each of the three oceans, but these regions give France a firm physical stake in global affairs. Moreover, the DOM-TOMs complement each other: nuclear testing in French Polynesia and the space station in Guyane, which may monitor global military activity, benefit from back-up provided by the Pacific and Caribbean territories respectively, and Réunion and Mayotte provide facilities in the Indian Ocean for French fleets and shore bases. Unoccupied islands, such as Kerguelen in the Antarctic Ocean, or Clipperton, far from the Mexican coastline, could provide airstrips and bases for French activity should they be needed. A former French prime minister has noted that even 'Wallis and Futuna are in a strategic position in the centre of the South Pacific and this will become increasingly important in the future' (Connell and Aldrich, 1989, p. 169). It is the Pacific, described by the prestigious Institut du Pacifique as the 'new centre of the world', that is the jewel in the contemporary colonial crown and where some geopoliticians have anticipated that France could play a substantial future role, holding the balance of power between the USA and the Soviet Union, to create amicable relations and encourage a sense of 'co-responsibility' in the region. With the increasing importance of the Pacific, France argued in the 1980s that security and prosperity can be best assured by continued control over the foreign policy and defence of the islands, an independent nuclear deterrent and strong conventional defence forces. Moreover, the interests of the superpowers in the region, with the Soviet Union's being increasingly apparent, made a French presence seem even more vital (Institut du Pacifique, 1986; Aldrich, 1988). Thus France, in this strategic arena so distant from the Hexagon, and through its global physical presence, is performing as a superpower.

Over time, the structure of this global presence may change as different strategic issues become important. France may eventually abandon its nuclear testing site at Mururoa in French Polynesia, perhaps in favour of an Indian Ocean island. This may precipitate a very slow and reluctant disengagement from the South Pacific. However, France now resolutely pursues a global vision in its intentions to retain an independent nuclear strike force and to hold a global balance of power. This vision is sealed together through the 'confetti of empire' that give France a presence in every ocean (Guillebaud, 1976). After the 'loss' of Vanuatu in 1980, France has dug in against any 'domino effect. In France the DOM-TOMs are thus not perceived as separate entities but as components of an important global arena.

Strategic interests, therefore, are a large part of the explanation for France's presence in *outre-mer*. But France also derives, or hopes to procure, economic benefits from the DOM-TOMs. Nickel is at present the only commodity the DOM-TOMs produce in significant quantities. Hope resides with the potential riches of the sea, maritime resources and the minerals which may lie on the continental shelf or on the ocean floor. The Law of the Sea convention gives France exclusive economic zones (EEZs) of 200 miles around each of its territories. As the far-flung islands of the French *outre-mer* total some 10 million square kilometres of EEZ, the DOM-TOMs provide France with the third largest maritime zone (in terms of EEZ) in the world. Even uninhabited islands, such as Clipperton in the Pacific and the Austral Islands off the coast of Antarctica, assume importance in this sense. Projects for exploitation of underwater resources may never materialise, yet in retaining the DOM-TOMs France guards its rights to whatever resources may eventuate. Classic economic arguments for retaining the DOM-TOMs are minimal. The economic benefits from the DOM-TOMs are, as they have almost always been, a hope for the future rather than an economic reality.

A variety of other reasons present arguments for French control of the DOM-TOMs, either in the present or in the future. Kerguelen Island in the Antarctic Ocean could conceivably provide an alternative site for nuclear testing, should this continue into the more distant future. The French have also registered ships in Kerguelen's 'capital', the uninhabited Port-aux-Français, to circumvent requirements for French-registered vessels to hire a certain proportion of highly paid nationals for their crew. The rights to fish the waters around Clipperton and the sub-Antarctic islands can be rented to tuna trawlers or other vessels. Each of the DOM-TOMs serves as a showplace of French goods and culture to the surrounding nations; for instance, the French universities in the Antilles, Réunion and the Pacific enrol students from neighbouring states. The DOM-TOMs give France what are described as 'windows on the world' in their respective region. Holiday resorts in the tropics allow tourists to experience exoticism and the familiarity of French life simultaneously. In the 1960s, though less so today, Martinique, Guadeloupe and Réunion provided a large force of Francophone labour officially recruited and brought to France, generally to work in subaltern white-collar positions in the post office, health-care activities and bureaucracy. Conversely the DOM-TOMs provide places for a certain number of senior French public servants to work, and these overseas *fonctionnaires* reap high rewards in salary loadings and other benefits. The votes of the DOM-TOM electorate assume a great importance in close elections; each political party in France has allies, which it assiduously courts, in the *outre-mer*, a situation which further accounts for financial generosity.

Beyond these strategic, notional economic and other reasons for the continuing French presence, there exist links of culture and sentiment that have tied the four overseas *départements*, the *vieilles colonies*, to France, but perhaps above all, there is the lack of real pressure for independence. Consequently France has more reasons to retain the DOM-TOMs than to give them up. International opinion, domestic opposition or sheer cost could provide arguments for granting independence to the DOM-TOMs. International organisations, such as the Non-Aligned Movement and the United Nations Decolonisation Committee (as well as certain statesmen and lobby groups) have taxed France with continued colonialism, but France can safely ignore such criticism, as it has ignored such agreements as the South Pacific Nuclear Free Zone Treaty (the treaty of Rarotonga) which called for the denuclearisation of the South Pacific. Those countries that have most actively called for French decolonisation have been the South Pacific island states of Papua New Guinea, Vanuatu and the Solomon Islands. In the Caribbean and Indian Oceans there has been little direct regional opposition, hence the countries that have opposed France have been states of slight international significance. By contrast the metropolitan powers, including France's fellow members of the EC and the United States, as well as most of France's client states (many of them former French colonies in Africa) seem content with the *status quo* (Connell, 1988a). Within the DOM-TOMs, there is significant domestic opposition only in New Caledonia, where clashes between the pro-independence coalition, the Front de Libération Nationale Kanake et Socialiste (FLNKS), a mainly Melanesian (Kanak) organisation, and largely European 'loyalists' led to considerable violence in the 1980s. The Matignon Accord, negotiated between the French government and both supporters and opponents of independence in 1988, provides for a ten-year moratorium before a further referendum on independence; demographic trends, political attitudes and tension within the FLNKS suggest that it is unlikely that the pro-independence groups will then achieve a majority. Elsewhere in the DOM-TOMs, only in French Polynesia have *indépendantistes* gained as much as one-fifth of the votes in elections; pro-independence movements, marked by internecine quarrels, have achieved little political success and are on the wane.

Inside France itself, the demand for 'decolonisation' is similarly muted and the absence of a significant peace movement has defused any debate on the future of nuclear testing. In terms of cost, the DOM-TOMs are indeed a burden on the French budget, necessitating subsidies, social security payments, defence costs and other expenses. The cost of maintaining the DOM-TOMs has been variously estimated at between 0.2 and 2.3 per cent of the total French budget. Although a substantial sum, this is minimal for a country with France's resources. By falling below the global aid levels of some other comparable world powers, France can finance the DOM-TOMs and concentrate its overseas assistance on territories from which the 'leakage' to the private sector in France is very high. A substantial proportion of the public money spent in the DOM-TOMs, perhaps as high as 90 per cent in the smallest states like French Guiana and Wallis and Futuna, returns to France through the private sector. The real costs of maintaining the DOM-TOMs are thus very small. In the early 1970s there was some feeling that 'Cartierism' – named after Raymond Cartier, who suggested that France give not only autonomy but independence to the overseas *départements* since they were a drain on resources that could better be used in the Hexagon – would grow as financial difficulties imposed austerity on France. In reality the French economy has grown and the DOM-TOMs have absorbed substantially more resources, without significant comment in France. In strategic terms, too, there has been no economic pressure on French military and nuclear strategy though the dramatic political restructuring of the European political economy in 1989 may contribute to France constructing a different vision of the necessity for a global presence. However, advocates of the DOM-TOMs argue that, in any case, it is as illogical to calculate the cost of Martinique or Wallis and Futuna as trying to figure the cost of Corsica, Brittany or central Paris. Moreover, the DOM-TOMs are little known in France and few are interested in such arcane considerations. In short, there is little reason for France to withdraw from the DOM-TOMs, and the real or potential benefits of maintaining them work in favour of continued ties. Through parliamentary politics, education, the media, migration and marriage, the DOM-TOMs are now tied more closely, and more profoundly, to France than ever before.

Ultimately the simplest argument for a continued French presence is a legalistic one: residents of the DOM-TOMs are fully fledged French citizens. Until and unless a majority of voters in any particular DOM or TOM decides to withdraw from the Republic, Paris cannot grant independence. In fact, the Constitution of France does allow for the TOMs to accede to independence and would also permit greater autonomy, even the sort of 'independence-association' envisaged in 1985 for New Caledonia (Connell, 1987a). However, the Constitution also charges the president with maintaining the integrity of the Republic, and international law recognises France's sovereignty in the DOM-TOMs.

Other Overseas Territories

European metropoles

France is the best example of the retention of links with overseas dependencies, but it is by no means the only one. European states provide several other cases. Britain, for instance, administers over a dozen 'dependent territories', in addition to the 'crown colony' of Hong Kong. Many are remote, small and unproductive islands, such as St Helena in the Indian Ocean or Pitcairn in the South Pacific. But some provide benefits to Britain and its allies. For instance, Diego Garcia, the rump of the British Indian Ocean Territory, is leased to the United States as a major military base; so too is Ascension, and American troops are stationed in the British Atlantic colony of Bermuda. The Turks and Caicos Islands – like Bermuda, the Virgin Islands and Montserrat – are a centre for offshore banking and financial transactions (and the former has been a centre for drug-trafficking). Gibraltar guards the entry to the Mediterranean, where Britain has long had interests, and London considered the Falkland Islands so important that it went to war to defend them against Argentina. There are satellite tracking stations on Tristan da Cunha, as well as on other British islands. As is true with the French DOM-TOMs, the British territories provide substantial exclusive economic zones.

Unlike the situation of the DOM-TOMs, British colonies are recognised as having a colonial political status; they have no representation at Westminster and have their own political assemblies, with variable but restricted powers. With the exception of Bermuda and Hong Kong, which have strong economies, they are dependent on significant financial support from the United Kingdom; their exports are minimal though their invisible earnings (from tourism and as tax havens) are sometimes significant, at least in the Caribbean. Their standards of living are also often superior to those of nearby independent states. In the exceptional case of the Falkland Islands, the costs of the war with Argentina, subsequent rehabilitation and attempts to establish a more viable economy have been extremely high, thus placing a heavy financial burden on the British economy. Unwillingness to accede to Argentinian claims to sovereignty placed additional political burdens on the United Kingdom, through widespread condemnation of what was seen, in some quarters, to be a colonial war. At the very least, the war emphasised Britain's continued global situation as a perhaps somewhat reluctant colonial power. Britain has also been criticised within the colonies (notably in Bermuda, Montserrat and, above all, Hong Kong) for its unwillingness to grant resident rights to its colonial citizens. The absence of viable economic activities in the British colonies has contributed to the rapid growth of a tertiary economy and increased emigration. Except in the particular case of the Falkland Islands, because of the irredentist claims of Argentina, there has been neither regional pressure on the United Kingdom to withdraw as a colonial power nor concerted demands from pro-independence parties (largely conspicuous by their absence) in the colonies themselves. Indeed, as the albeit exceptional case of Hong Kong demonstrates, there is much support for a continued British presence.

Despite the Falklands War, fought in support of an island whose inhabitants are entirely European, there is little obvious advantage to the United Kingdom in the retention of its colonial possessions. Unlike France, Britain no longer claims to be a global power (having only minimal military presence outside Europe) and has largely transferred the strategic advantages of its colonies to the United States. The advantages championed by France are not therefore claimed by Britain, and Britain has encouraged independence, especially during the 1970s, even pushing colonies that were reluctant to become independent to sever their ties with the United Kingdom. However, in the unusual case of the Turks and Caicos Islands, where the islands' government promoted independence in 1980, it was soundly defeated in elections and all consideration of independence ceased (Thorndike, 1989). Elsewhere, there are some pressures for independence only in Bermuda and Montserrat, but no concerted or majority demands. British policy has favoured greater economic self-reliance in the Caribbean territories, if not in the isolated South

Atlantic colonies; but even in the larger Caribbean colonies, greater self-reliance has proved difficult to achieve and has engendered local opposition. Achieving economic growth, as the examples of the Turks and Caicos Islands and Montserrat demonstrate, has led to island governments crossing the bounds of legality, and the British government reclaiming more direct political control. In the most recent case of Montserrat, this has been resented as 'a retrograde step which may be designed to facilitate a recolonisation of the island' (*Guardian Weekly*, 1989; Anon, 1989a). Despite the costs of the remaining colonies, and the minimal advantages received by Britain, the fragments of empire remain intact and (with the exception of Hong Kong) show little sign of taking on a new political status.

The overseas 'empires' of other European states are smaller than those of Britain and France, today as in the heyday of colonialism. The Netherlands, however, possesses six islands in the Caribbean. Although one of them, Aruba, is being prepared for independence, they form an integral though autonomous part of the Dutch kingdom. Denmark controls the vast expanses of Greenland as well as the tiny North Atlantic Faeroe Islands. Greenland provides fish for Denmark, as well as serving as a joint Danish–American military base. Greenlanders, like the Faeroe Islanders, have full rights as Danish citizens, although both territories enjoy self-government. Spain administers the offshore Balearic Islands, as well as the Canary Islands near the west coast of Africa. In addition, Spain has two enclaves in Morocco, the *presidios* of Ceuta and Melilla. Municipalities attached directly to the Spanish province of Cadiz, these north African cities have been Spanish outposts since the 1500s; despite perennial (if not very determined) remonstrances from Rabat, Madrid shows no signs of ceding them to Morocco. Finally, Portugal administers the Azores and Madeira as well as, until 1999, Macao. For each of these European states, the colonial territories provide only minimal economic or strategic benefits (few claiming to be even regional military powers) and the Netherlands especially would prefer to divest itself of those that remain (Aldrich and Connell, in preparation). Yet, as with the British colonies, colonisation has proved to be more straightforward than decolonisation.

The United States

The phenomenon of overseas territories is not confined to Europe. The United States incorporated distant, and once culturally distinct, Alaska and Hawaii into the Union as the forty-ninth and fiftieth states. Puerto Rico is a largely self-governing 'commonwealth' of the United States, although there exist political parties there which campaign variously for full independence or full American statehood. The Virgin Islands in the Caribbean, like American Samoa and Guam in the Pacific, are 'unincorporated territories' of the United States. In addition, Washington controls various small islands in the north Pacific (such as Johnston and Wake). Two Micronesian states, the Marshall Islands and the Federated States of Micronesia (FSM), formerly part of United Nations Trust Territory of the Pacific Islands (TTPI) administered by American authorities, have signed treaties of 'free association' with the United States, and a third, Palau, permanently hovers on the brink of a similar relationship. In return for American rights to maintain their defence and enjoy a tutelary role over their foreign relations, the Micronesian states receive large amounts of American aid, preferential access to American markets and migration rights to the United States. The American territories of the Caribbean and Pacific are home to 3.5 million American citizens and nationals (mainly in Puerto Rico) and the economic, political and demographic ties between the American metropole and its overseas possessions are strong.

Apart from the Micronesian states in 'free association' with the United States, and the tiny North Pacific islands, the overseas possessions have some political representation in Washington. Because of their relative population size this is of minimal significance compared with that of the DOM-TOMs. None of the overseas territories has a significant export economy. Puerto Rico, however, does have a diversified agricultural base and substantial industrialisation, and though poor by American standards, is relatively affluent in the Caribbean. American Samoa, by virtue of its cannery, is a major exporter of tuna; second-grade tuna is exported as petfood, some 2 per cent by value of the territory's exports but greater than the total value of exports from neighbouring Western Samoa. Though the Virgin Islands, Guam and the Northern Marianas have thriving economies, they are heavily dependent on American capital expenditure. Even where there are significant exclusive economic zones, it is the case, certainly in the Pacific, that they are of little actual or potential value.

The basis of the economy of the three emerging Micronesian states is public-sector employment, whilst the contemporary productive sector is conspicuous by its absence. In 1980, only 9 per cent of the funds for the whole region was derived from tax revenues, whilst the annual US grant and US Federal Program grants represented 87 per cent of the budget. Micronesia has had a forty-year history of living off US government subsidies and is heavily dependent on government salaries. For tiny, remote islands, the prospects of reversing a structure of development planning that was in some respects established in interwar Japanese colonial times, emphasised under the US administration and only rarely questioned even in the past decade (as other Pacific states gained their independence), are extremely poor. The rhetoric of self-reliance has become no more than the attempt to establish a guaranteed income from any possible source: 'Micronesia's meal ticket has become its rights, not its resources, and economic development has lately become a superfluity' (Hezel, 1975, p. 7). Service economies, fuelled by government salaries, cannot become productive economies.

America's overseas territories have enormous strategic value. Guam, above all, has been a major military base, notably during the Vietnam War, and is perceived (with Palau) as a key fallback position for American forces in the western Pacific, in the event of difficulties in the Philippines. The chain of islands from Palau and Guam eastwards through Micronesia and Johnston to Hawaii constitutes a *cordon militaire* across the northern Pacific, a region perceived in the United States to be of considerable strategic significance. Kwajalein in the Marshall Islands is a crucial centre in the 'Star Wars' programme. American Samoa, of historic naval value, is the sole outpost in the South Pacific. The Caribbean territories are valuable in a sea where the Cuban presence and possible political turbulence of the kind that prompted the invasion of Grenada are perceived as threats to regional stability.

In the postwar years the American overseas territories have become more closely integrated into the United States. In the 1970s, when Palau, the Marshall Islands and the FSM began talks on the dissolution of the TTPI, the other component of the TTPI, the Marianas, chose instead to become a commonwealth under permanent US sovereignty. The commonwealth status negotiated by Covenant for Puerto Rico in 1952 was a loose model, though the Northern Marianas sought greater control of local government and more limitations on federal authority. Commonwealth status was achieved in 1975, with the USA having authority over defence and foreign affairs although its status in other areas remained ambiguous. Massive economic growth followed extensive US-funded capital improvements alongside duty-free status and exemptions from US import quotas, resulting in extensive migration, mainly from the Philippines. Recent stresses in the relationship over the extent of self-government (especially in terms of control of the exclusive economic zones, citizenship of alien migrant workers and control over immigration) have prompted the President of the Northern Marianas Senate to petition the United Nations Trusteeship Council for assistance and to declare that 'under the cover of an unprecedented economic boom, the United States has been deliberately chipping away Commonwealth sovereignty' (*Pacific News Bulletin*, 1989). As elsewhere, political and economic integration with the metropole has not been without costs.

A decade after the Northern Marianas achieved commonwealth status the Marshall Islands and the FSM negotiated a Compact of Free Association (CFA) with the United States, along somewhat similar lines, with the United States retaining control of foreign affairs and defence and providing substantial budget funding over a fifteen-year period (Connell, 1991). In both states there was only minority support for the alternative of independence. Palau remains a trust territory, since seven referenda (the last in February 1990) have failed to secure the necessary 75 per cent support that would override the anti-nuclear provisions of the 1979 Constitution and grant Palau 'free association'; this would provide a large thirty-year aid package in exchange for potential US military use of land and water. Opposition centres on military use, not on the extent of economic aid, and support for the alternative of independence has always been small. For the Marshall Islands and the FSM, American aid has been 'front-loaded': it is intended to decline until budgetary self-reliance is achieved after fifteen years. This situation is unlikely to occur and there are already pressures in the FSM (where, unlike the Marshall Islands, military expenditure is minimal) for a renegotiation of the compact in favour of continuous economic aid into the indefinite future.

Assured prosperity in Guam blunted political discontent over limited local power until the 1970s, when political negotiations over the future of the TTPI fuelled debate on the future of Guam. The political and economic gains of the commonwealth of the Northern Marianas were perceived to be inequitable and a number of commissions examined new forms of political status. A plebiscite in 1976 found that 57 per cent of the population sought an 'improved status quo', 21 per cent sought statehood and 5 per cent preferred independence; there was also a growing demand for indigenous Chamorro rights (Souder-Jaffery, 1987). A dramatic increase in tourism (and thus greater financial self-reliance) and the strengthened strategic significance of Guam because of pressures to renegotiate America's military presence in the Philippines have, more recently, created renewed pressure for commonwealth status for Guam.

In Puerto Rico there have also been recent demands for a plebiscite on the future political status of the commonwealth. Support is growing for Puerto Rico to become the fifty-first state of the United States, but underlying doubts in Puerto Rico remain about the virtues of such a new status, a debate which 'comes down to national dignity versus economics'. Both proponents of statehood and the socialist Independence Party (which attracts barely 10 per cent of local support) argue that Puerto Rico should 'shake off the remaining shackles of colonialism' but disagree over how this should be done (Anon, 1989b). Puerto Ricans pay no federal income tax and there are substantial incentives to local industry; with either independence or statehood such incentives would decline or be removed. Statehood might also encourage the present radical minority to seek independence through terrorist means. Thus, in both Guam and Puerto Rico, where political ties with the metropole have been most enduring, debates over the future political and economic status are intense.

Australia and New Zealand

In the Southern Hemisphere, Australia and New Zealand also have overseas territories. Australia administers Norfolk Island, populated by residents of European stock, in the South Pacific; the Torres Strait Islands, a group lying between Australia and New Guinea populated by Melanesians; and the Cocos (Keeling) Islands and Christmas Islands, whose inhabitants are largely of Malay origin, in the Indian Ocean, as well as several uninhabited islands off Antarctica. These islands extend Australia's defence perimeter beyond its continental borders; the most influential report on Australian defence in the 1980s spoke of Australia's defensive perimeter arching from the Cocos to Norfolk Island (Dibb, 1986). Norfolk Island is a popular tourist resort, and the Cocos-Keeling Islands and Christmas Island respectively export copra and phosphate. Islanders enjoy the right of abode in Australia. Demands for changing political status have rarely sought independence, and a referendum on political status in the Cocos-Keeling Islands in 1983 brought an overwhelming vote in favour of greater integration with Australia, and no support for independence (Freeman, 1984). In the Torres Strait, however, there has been some recent symbolic pressure for independence, in response to perceived neglect of the economic interests of islanders, though the Torres Strait is one area where the transition from 'subsistence to subsidy' was first achieved in the region.

New Zealand controls the outlying Chatham Islands, where a European

population has now replaced the remnants of a Maoriori (Polynesian) population. More significantly, Niue and Tokelau are dependent territories; New
Zealand provides almost all their budgetary support and is responsible for
defence and foreign affairs. The rather larger Cook Islands have a status of
'association' with New Zealand, with similar rights exercised by Wellington;
this status resembles that negotiated by the Micronesian states with the United
States. The smallest territory, Tokelau, remains satisfied with its colonial
status, preferring this 'to the looseness of free association', whereas both Niue
and the Cook Islands have preferred a greater degree of autonomy (Bertram,
1987, p. 21). New Zealand has consistently opposed political integration, but
has also avoided pressing reluctant island states to seek full independence
(though pressing for self-government). It provides substantial financial support
in a region of increased strategic significance where New Zealand has security
interests. Both the Cook Islands and Niue may terminate the political relationship unilaterally, simply by amending their own constitutions: 'Free association
for them can be seen as genuinely free', a quite different situation from that
of the Micronesian states, which cannot act unilaterally (Firth, 1989, p. 78).
None of these three island groups has an independence movement. However,
the Chatham Islands has recently sought greater autonomy, in exactly the same
manner as the Torres Strait Islands, out of frustration over economic development issues (Connell, 1988b).

Throughout the world, European powers, the United States, Australia and
New Zealand retain overseas territories. For some, like the United States,
decolonisation has been minimal, though for other small powers, without
pretensions to a global military economic or cultural presence, usually tiny
territories have remained dependent despite the encouragement for decolonisation from the centre. Those dependent territories, where 'colonial' ties are
most sought after and independence movements wholly absent, are either
extremely small, remote (and hence without much semblance of a self-reliant
local economy), with a population of European origin or threatened by
neighbouring irredentist claims. Where all of these occur simultaneously, as
in the Falkland Islands, any hint of decolonisation is threatening. Dependent
political status conveys significant rights, usually those of some degree of
participation in democratic government (often both locally and in the metropole), security, migration opportunities, employment options and extensive
subsidies. Living standards are invariably superior to those of neighbouring
independent states though there are disadvantages in terms of limited
(sometimes diminished) sovereignty, racial conflicts, inequality and minimal
recognition of distinctive cultures. Such disadvantages, however, are often also
present in independent island states.

Other 'Colonies'?

Even this diverse group of dependent territories does not come close to
exhausting the number of what in broad terms might be considered 'colonies'.
Most countries have regions or islands which have at various times objected
to rule from the centre. For instance, when Mauritius became independent,

in 1968, the island of Rodrigues, occupied almost entirely by a Creole population, expressed reservations at independence in fear of the domination of Mauritian politics by the Indian majority. In 1987, after military *coups d'état* in Fiji, in which native Melanesians overthrew a government dominated by ethnic Indians, the Polynesian island of Rotuma, an outlying part of Fiji, objected and unsuccessfully called for independence (Bryant, 1989). Elsewhere in the Third World, ethnic disputes with colonial connotations have spilled over into civil war, as in the Katanga uprising in Zaire in 1960, the Biafran revolt in Nigeria, the war of independence by Bangladesh against Pakistan and Melanesian demands for independence in Irian Jaya (Indonesia). Such disturbances have been widespread, and opposition to central control has been either quietened through negotiation (as in the Indian outlying states of Kashmir and Sikkim) or more commonly repressed (as in China's treatment of Tibet).

Territorial contiguity does not lessen nationalist claims or charges of colonialism. The term 'internal colonialism' was specifically applied to the economic and political position of the 'Celtic fringe' of Scotland, Wales and Cornwall in the United Kingdom, for example (Hechter, 1975). Violent opposition by Basques to Madrid's centralisation (and discontent with post-Francoist decentralisation) finds parallels in nationalist movements inside the Breton and Corsican areas of France. The Baltic republics of Latvia, Lithuania and Estonia have long claimed that the Soviet annexation of their territories in 1940 was illegal, and Lithuania has recently declared itself independent. In fact, recent years have seen a resurgence of nationalism in the Soviet Union, from the Baltic to Uzbekistan, the Armenian regions of the south and elsewhere. Other East European countries have also seen ethnic disputes, such as the treatment of ethnic Hungarians by Romania and of ethnic Turks by Bulgaria. Other outlying regions have also often exhibited traits of colonial status. For example Canada's northern lands, the Yukon and Northwest Territories, have been characterised as colonies (Coates, 1985).

To regard all such cases as 'colonialism' is unhelpful, yet nowhere is free from situations of dependent development, and the combination of ethnicity, nationalism, remoteness and political activism is a global phenomenon. The overseas territories of imperial powers are simply the most evident examples of this phenomenon. Yet, ironically, their residents are sometimes more a part of the metropole, despite their distance, than those residents of contiguous territories; Martiniquais and Réunionnais have been French subjects since the mid-1600s and citizens since 1848, while the Balts have been under the control of Moscow only since 1940 and the Palestinians have been controlled by the Jewish state of Israel only since 1948 or, in the occupied territories, since 1967. Deciding which are the most 'dependent' or which are the more 'exploited' is difficult and ultimately impossible. Certainly, movements of opposition, ranging from the *intifada* in the occupied Palestinian territories to the decisions made by the Lithuanian Parliament, the terrorism of the Basques and the wars of post-colonial Africa, are more dramatic than any similar actions (with the partial exception of New Caledonia) in either the French DOM-TOMs or in other 'colonial' territories. In fact, in many of the 'colonies' of European states, from the Falklands to Gibraltar, from Wallis and Futuna to Mayotte, and from the Marianas to the Cocos-Keeling Islands, the trend has been, with the approval of the local population, towards greater integration rather than to the severing of ties.

Failures of Decolonisation?

Contemporary discussions of the prospects for future global decolonisation have largely focused on the French DOM-TOMs for two principal reasons. First, intermittent violent struggles for independence, especially in New Caledonia, have drawn attention to a 'colonised' and ethnically distinct people seeking independence, a struggle that has led to the reinscription of New Caledonia with the United Nations Committee on Decolonisation. (Conversely, independence movements have sometimes been repressed by a French state that emphasises the integrity of the French Republic and does not recognise the 'colonial' status of the DOM-TOMs, especially not that of the *départements*.) Secondly, unlike most other dependent territories, several of the DOM-TOMs are large in area and population, and thus appear to have some potential for an independent future. With certain exceptions neither situation is true of other dependent territories. France's ambitions have ensured that the DOM-TOMs remain firmly in place, an apparent anomaly that strengthens France's global presence. Yet their existence may not be so anomalous. Most small territories, even where politically independent, have invariably been partly integrated into the economies of metropolitan states through aid, trade or migration. Only in France, however, have current overseas territories been invested with such ideological and political significance.

Overseas dependent territories are no longer the classic colonies that once led to a wealth of literature on the evils of unequal exchange, dependency, exploitation and uneven development. By contrast, they are now the recipients of considerable largesse from the centre, most apparent for the smallest territories where exports are minimal and dwarfed by imports (though significant income also flows through the invisible earnings of tourism and tax havens). Partly in consequence, demands for greater incorporation into the centre have become stronger than pressures for independence. Indeed it has been argued that *départementalisation* represents a form of decolonisation without independence; Albert Ramassamy, a French senator for Réunion, has suggested that 'for the old colonies that have become *départements* integration is a form of decolonisation just as much as independence for those who have chosen that' (Ramassamy, 1987, p. 8). Yet this version of 'decolonisation' is not without its problems; within the DOMs (and TOMs) there is an inequitable distribution of resources, an unemployment rate much higher than in France and ethnic tensions that overlie cultural and economic differences. This particular definition of 'decolonisation' has scarcely been formulated or considered outside France.

With the principal exception of New Caledonia, independence movements are absent, and, in a number of the DOM-TOMs even the tiny independence movements have noted that although independence would provide the

197

psychological boost of political autonomy it could also lead to some decline in the physical quality of life. In French Polynesia the late John Teariki, a prominent supporter of autonomy, commented on the prospects for independence: 'It would be difficult now as the people are not ready for independence. The Tahitians live an unnatural life now. They live off imported goods, tinned food and other things. There would be struggles, unemployment, all possible things.' In Guadeloupe the principal pro-independence party has stated: 'One must choose freedom and its difficulties' or even 'dignity and deprivation'. Not surprisingly ideological austerity and minimal resultant support have tended to prevail (Aldrich and Connell, 1991; Blaut, 1987). More generally, as in Bermuda, there is a general concern that fractional politics in a small island-state would be disruptive and that dependent political status is preferable, as it appears to guarantee the continued success of business activity (especially tourism and tax havens) and security (Connell, 1987b).

In the DOM-TOMs especially, incorporation has led to the construction of a welfare state, the diverse financial advantages of which have diminished the rate of emigration (though this remains significant in the Caribbean). Elsewhere, less generous financial provisions, and even less viable domestic economies, have ensured that the ability to migrate to the metropole is a right that is zealously guarded. In the Cook Islands and American Samoa, the right to migrate to New Zealand and the United States respectively has been a critical factor discouraging demand for political independence. For the Micronesian states, the movement in 1986 from trusteeship to a looser association with the United States was accompanied by a formal Compact of Free Association in which the two states sought the provision that any of its citizens 'may enter into, lawfully engage in occupations and establish residence as a non-immigrant in the United States and its territories and possessions', to ensure that a 'safety-valve' was put in place. Since then there has been considerable migration to Guam and the Northern Marianas, and the start of onward migration to the United States (Hezel and Levin, 1990).

Underlying all debates on changing political and economic status, and hence relationships with the metropole (and with other regional and metropolitan states), are two conflicting issues, well summarised in the case of Guam:

> There is in Guam's quest for political identity a fundamental contradiction in what Guam is trying to accomplish. The Chamorro activists belatedly seized upon self-determination as the major principle behind commonwealth. But self-determination marches under the flag of freedom, whereas commonwealth marches under the banner of equality. Although they may seem to go arm in arm, Alexis de Tocqueville noted long ago that freedom and equality will always be at odds with each other. (Rogers, 1988, pp. 25–6)

Political integration, as in the French *départements*, provides no hope of more self-reliant economic development, or the recognition of local cultural issues and rights. Movement towards more self-reliant economic and political development reduces external financial support and causes local concern over both the quality of life and security. In small, often remote territories where prospects for economic development based on local resource exploitation are inherently poor and dependent on overseas links (tourism, tax havens, trade concessions or direct budgetary support) and where there is significant ethnic and cultural diversity, tensions over the direction of future economic and political status are certain to persist. In the tiniest and most remote territories – Pitcairn, Wallis and Futuna or Tristan da Cunha – challenges to metropolitan dominance are implausible, but in situations of substantial ethnic inequality where prospects of some degree of greater self-reliant development are not impossible – as in New Caledonia – contradictions and conflicts in aspirations are inevitable. In New Caledonia, where ethnic nationalism and the quest for identity emphasise decolonisation, the late leader of the pro-independence FLNKS, Jean-Marie Tjibaou, once claimed: 'As long as one Kanak survives a problem for France remains' (Connell, 1987a, p. 445).

Independent island states have (not surprisingly) rarely sought any diminution of political autonomy. However, in Dominica, situated between the French *départements* of Martinique and Guadeloupe, there has been intermittent (and almost certainly minority) interest in becoming a French overseas *département*, whilst in the much larger state of Jamaica, the Prime Minister, Michael Manley, has recently observed: 'In the Caribbean we are accelerating the integration process because we will not survive as a set of disparate mini-states, unless we want to become a department of France' (Gauhar, 1989, p. 11). More generally in island micro-states political autonomy has rarely met the economic aspirations of islanders. There has been significant (often illegal) migration into the French Caribbean *départements*, notably from Haiti to Guadeloupe, from Dominica and St Lucia to Martinique and from Brazil and Suriname to French Guiana. Other Caribbean island territories, notably Puerto Rico and the American and British Virgin Islands have also experienced significant immigration from nearby independent states. In the Indian Ocean, there has similarly been a massive recent migration from the Comoros to Mayotte. In the Pacific, approximately half the population of American Samoa has migrated from Western Samoa, and many people have gone from Tonga to Niue. In some cases this represents the first stage of migration to the metropole.

Though most island states have development plans, and even policies, which emphasise the need to achieve greater self-reliance, such statements are rhetorical rather than realistic, a legacy of the post-independence optimism of the 1970s. In a similar manner to the situation in the DOM-TOMs, for such small island states as Kiribati greater self-reliance is only possible 'at a price. It will not be achieved without further sacrifice in terms of forgone consumption and restricted aspirations. Many more sacrifices will be required in the future if a true commitment to self-reliance is to be maintained' (Pollard, 1987). Such sacrifices in tandem with ideological purity are rare. By contrast, the decline or stagnation of the productive sector (especially agriculture) and the absence of industrialisation, accompanied by aid flows, remittances and tourist revenue (in more accessible states) have led to the expansion of employment in the service sector and the consolidation of what have been described as MIRAB (migration, remittances and bureaucracy) states. Indeed, since it is government employment that dominates the bureaucracy of island micro-states, a better acronym might be MIRAGE, a state where the traditional concept of economic development is increasingly elusive (Bertram and Watters, 1985).

Where aid and remittances have been substantial, the structure of the economy has been transformed from subsistence to subsidy; small states have moved from productive to rentier status. Exactly the same structural transformation is occurring amongst many minority peoples on the periphery of larger states, for example in the Arctic and amongst Aboriginal populations in Australia. Flexible structures of dependence, co-operation and interdependence are nothing new; autarchy was probably little more welcome in the past that it is now. Political independence has not always been a significant variable in the quest for development. In the DOM-TOMs, the American and New Zealand island dependencies and elsewhere, the central economic problem is to preserve and enhance their status as rentier economies. Moreover, practices once regarded in a largely negative light, such as tourism and emigration, have widely become enshrined as policies after conventional development strategies have proved disappointing. Industrialisation occurs by imitation and invitation; tax havens are created and territorial waters leased out as dependence is increasingly negotiated. Rising expectations, ecological degradation on land and sea and population growth reduce historically valid economic options. For the moment rentier economies have been able to diversify into new arenas as governments contemplate a variety of options and, where territories (especially island territories) occupy strategic locations, real prospects for maintaining and enhancing rentier status exist.

Although island states have officially sought greater self-reliance, and also regional economic co-operation, in the post-independence era, they have invariably been integrated into the economies of metropolitan states. Regional co-operation has largely been a failure and small states have maintained and even increased their ties with distant metropolitan powers. Moreover, micro-states and colonies that have a 'special relationship' with a metropolitan power may be better off than those which do not. Dommen (1980, p. 195) has bluntly stated that 'the particularly poor island countries are those which have failed to establish sufficiently intimate relations with a prosperous protector'. In the same vein, it has been suggested that the remaining British colonies might be better off by strengthening their ties with the United Kingdom in the same manner that French 'colonies' have become overseas territories and *départements* (Winchester, 1985). Early in 1987, when it was feared in the Turks and Caicos Islands that the United Kingdom might relinquish its sovereignty, there were moves there to make the colony a ward or territory of Canada. In the Pacific, as one prominent Member of Parliament in the Australian Labor Party government, Gordon Bilney, has recently pointed out, despite its being 'an unfortunate fact for those who believe in independence and freedom of determination', standards of living, including health levels, were higher in associated territories. 'Perhaps the best thing that countries like Australia should be doing in the South Pacific is encouraging moves towards closer satrapy – towards closer association and, indeed, even eventual incorporation of these polities into the major powers such as Australia' (Connell, 1988c, p. 83). At much the same time, it was noted that 'the question of closer political integration with metropolitan countries has received little serious attention to date, but it is a possibility that Pacific leaders may wish to address' (Fairnbairn, 1987, p. 51). Because of the structure of development, the smallest states are inexorably moving towards a situation where their autonomy is severely constrained, yet none is likely to relinquish what was sometimes a hard-won independent political status.

The states that are the greatest per capita recipients of global aid are primarily colonies and territories. This has discouraged independence sentiments. Moreover, as Tuvalu and Mayotte have shown in quite different ways, secession from an independent island state substantially increases material rewards. The smaller Caribbean states, such as Grenada, 'particularly sought independence ultimately to gain access to multilateral aid funds and to participate in international forums primarily concerned with economic development, rather than from an appreciation of its intrinsic worth' (Thorndike, 1985, p. 8). The combination of a degree of isolation (and hence strategic significance) and a measure of political 'independence', through either sovereign status or recognition in some manner as a separate political entity, has granted superior access not only to aid but to new areas of policy formation and concessions of other kinds. In these respects colonies have definite advantages. The reality of closer incorporation underlies most development practice and widespread high levels of migration are the reality and metaphor of development. Small is no longer beautiful; remote islands are 'beautiful but no place to live' (Bedford, 1980, p. 57). By freely choosing strategies that enable the manipulation of metropolitan national policies, the structure of development of island states and dependent territories will continue to converge. As they do so, the global era of decolonisation draws to a close. The ties that bind are likely to endure, though the conflict between freedom and equality is sure to persist.

References

Aldrich, R. (1988) 'Rediscovering the Pacific', *Journal de la Société des Océanistes*, 87, pp. 57–71.

Aldrich, R., and Connell, J. (1991) *France's Overseas Frontier: the départements et territoires d'Outre-Mer*, Cambridge: Cambridge University Press.

Aldrich, R., and Connell, J. (in preparation) *The Last Colonies*, Cambridge: Cambridge University Press.

Anon. (1989a) 'Montserrat: stormy weather', *Economist*, 313, 7632, p. 47.

Anon. (1989b) 'Puerto Rico: still star gazing', *Economist*, 313, 7632, p. 40.

Bedford, R.D. (1980) 'Demographic processes in small islands: the case of internal migration', in H.C. Brookfield (ed.) *Population–Environment Relations in Tropical Islands: The Case of Eastern Fiji*, Paris: UNESCO, pp. 27–59.

Bertram, G. (1987) 'The political economy of decolonisation and nationhood in small Pacific societies', in A. Hooper (ed.) *Class and Culture in the South Pacific*, Suva: Institute of Pacific Studies, pp. 16–29.

Bertram, G., and Watters, R. (1985) 'The MIRAB economy in the South Pacific', *Pacific Viewpoint*, 26, pp. 497–519.

Blaut, J.M. (1987) *The National Question: Decolonising the Theory of Nationalism*, London: Zed.

Bryant, J. (1989) 'Rotuman response to uneven development: independence or migration?', *Publications de l'Université Française du Pacifique*, 1, pp. 65–70.

Coates, K. (1985) *Canada's Colonies: A History of the Yukon and Northwest Territories*, Toronto: Lorimer.

Connell, J. (1987a) *New Caledonia or Kanaky? The Political History of a French Colony*, Pacific Research Monograph No. 16, Canberra: National Centre for Development Studies.

Connell, J. (1987b) *Bermuda: A Failure of Decolonisation*, Working Paper No. 492, Leeds: School of Geography, University of Leeds.

Connell, J. (1988a) *New Caledonia: The Matignon Accord and the Colonial Future*, Occasional Paper No. 5, Sydney: Research Institute for Asia and the Pacific, University of Sydney.

Connell, J. (1988b) 'Chatham wants better deal from New Zealand', *Pacific*, 13, p. 60.

Connell, J. (1988c) *Sovereignty and Survival: Island Microstates in the Third World*, Monograph No. 3, Sydney: Department of Geography, University of Sydney.

Connell, J. (1991) 'The new Micronesia: pitfalls and problems of dependent development', *Pacific Studies*, 15, forthcoming.

Connell, J., and Aldrich, R. (1989) 'Remnants of Empire: France's overseas departments and territories', in R. Aldrich and J. Connell (eds) *France in World Politics*, London: Routledge, pp. 148–69.

Dibb, P. (1986) *Review of Australia's Defence Capabilities*, Canberra: Australian Government Publication Service.

Dommen, E. (1980) 'External trade problems of small island states in the Pacific and Indian Oceans', in R.T. Shand (ed.) *The Island States of the Pacific and Indian Oceans*, Canberra: Development Studies Centre, Australian National University, pp. 179–99.

Fairnbairn, T.J. (1987) 'Pacific states and development options', *Islands Business*, 13 (4), p. 46.

Firth, S. (1989) 'Sovereignty and independence in the contemporary Pacific', *The Contemporary Pacific*, 1, pp. 75–96.

Freeman, C. (1984) 'Cocos islanders did not vote for independence', *Australia Today*, 11, pp. 20–4.

Guardian Weekly (1989) Letter of 31 December, p. 2.

Gauhar, A. (1989) 'Manley rides the New Wave', *South*, 105, pp. 10–11.

Guillebaud, J.-C. (1976) *Les Confettis de l'Empire*, Paris: Seuil.

Hechter, M. (1975) *Internal Colonialism: the Celtic Fringe in British National Development, 1536–1966*, London: Routledge & Kegan Paul.

Hezel, F.X. (1975) 'The new formula for self-reliance', *Marianas Variety*, p. 5.

Hezel, F.X., and Levin, M.J. (1990) 'Micronesian emigration: beyond the brain drain', in J. Connell (ed.) *Migration and Development in the Southern Pacific*, Canberra: National Centre for Development Studies, pp. 42–60. (Pacific Research Monograph No. 24).

Institut du Pacifique (1986) *Le Pacifique, 'nouveau centre du monde'*, Paris: Berger-Lavrault.

Pacific News Bulletin (1989) 4 September, p. 10.

Pollard, S. (1987) *The Viability and Vulnerability of a Small Island State: The Case of Kiribati*, Islands/ Australia Working Paper No. 87/4, Canberra: National Centre for Development Studies.

Ramassamy, A. (1987) *La Réunion: décolonisation et intégration*, Saint Denis: AGM.

Rogers, R.F. (1988) *Guam's Commonwealth Effort, 1987–1988*, Guam: Micronesian Area Research Center.

Souder-Jaffery, L. (1987) 'A not so perfect union: federal territorial relations between the United States and Guam', in L. Souder-Jaffery and R. Underwood (eds) *Chamorro Self-Determination*, Guam: Micronesia Area Research Center, pp. 7–31.

Thorndike, T. (1985) *Grenada: Politics, Economics and Society*, London: Pinter.

Thorndike, T. (1989) 'The future of the British Caribbean dependencies', *Journal of Interamerican Studies*, 31, pp. 117–40.

Winchester, S. (1985) *Outposts*, London: Hodder & Stoughton.

CHAPTER 10

Thailand:
The Legacy of Non-Colonial Development in South-East Asia

Chris Dixon and Michael J.G. Parnwell

Introduction

The chapters in this volume have focused on the impact of Western colonial control and influence on various aspects of economic, social and environmental change in Africa, Asia and the Pacific. Discussion has also touched on the ways in which the experience of these countries under the auspices of colonial control has influenced the pattern and process of development in the post-colonial era. In many cases the legacy of colonialism has been wide, and enduring internal spatial disparities and continuing links with the West in general and with the former colonial powers in particular.

A small number of African and Asian states managed to avoid direct Western rule during the nineteenth and twentieth centuries[1] as did the 'informal British Empire' in Latin America (see Chapter 1). These countries were, however, generally incorporated into a variety of informal structures which linked them to the international economy through formal imperial economies and, in some cases, adjacent colonial states. How distinctive was the development of these non-colonial economies? Here the example of Thailand, which alone of the South-East Asian states retained independence, is used to argue that such countries developed similar economic structures, conspicuous internal spatial disparities and relations to the international market similar to those of the formal colonies.

The similarities between the processes of economic transformation which occurred in Siam[2] and those which took place in neighbouring British Burma and French Indo-China during the late nineteenth and early twentieth centuries are particularly striking (Brown, 1988; Dixon, 1991). In all these countries there was a massive expansion in rice cultivation, mainly in the deltas and flood plains of the Chao Phraya, Irrawaddy, Mekong and Red rivers, primarily for the export market. As international markets developed, so the demand for other primary commodities expanded, particularly tin, timber and rubber. With the expansion of trade and primary processing came the growing involvement in these sectors of immigrant Asians, who gradually came to dominate the commercial and industrial sectors of these countries. Another corollary of the development of international markets and burgeoning trade was a substantial rise in imports, particularly of capital and consumer goods.

This in turn had a devastating impact on cottage and handicraft industries (Brown, 1988, pp. 2–3; Resnick, 1970). Another similarity was the focusing of administrative and economic activity in key urban centres, the primacy of which was further enhanced by their pivotal position in steadily expanding communications networks.

The changes which took place in mainland South-East Asia during the late nineteenth and early twentieth centuries laid the foundation for the emergence of a number of the contemporary development problems of the sub-region, notably a heavy reliance on primary commodity production and trade, a very weak indigenous industrial base, and (before socialist revolutions in Burma and Vietnam) the domination of local economies by foreign capital.

Given these broad historical similarities in the emerging economic structures of these countries, but also the striking contrasts in their respective political development, it is pertinent to question the oft-stated view[3] that it was formal Western colonialism which was primarily responsible for introducing disequilibrium and dependency to the Third World. The fact that Thailand managed to maintain independence, and yet depicts many of the characteristics of the 'typical' colonial territory, begs questions about this contention.

The aim of this chapter is to examine why Thailand is 'differently similar' to neighbouring South-East Asian countries in respect of the emergence of internal economic disparities and the development of linkages with the international economy. Attention will focus on two inter-related lines of inquiry. First, that it was not colonialism *per se* but the economic transformations and changes which were associated with imperialism which had the most profound impact on South-East Asian territories in this respect. Second, that Thailand was a colony in everything but name, and that the country's pattern of development and change were very much influenced by external powers.

Because of constraints of space, discussion will focus on the spatial aspects of economic and structural change which have taken place since the mid-nineteenth century. Of course, there were also a number of non-spatial effects of European annexation of South-East Asian territories and their intervention in the internal affairs of these states: contradictions between wealth and poverty; selective and discrimination improvements in social welfare facilities; the discouragement of industrialisation; and the devastating impact of imported manufactures on domestic cottage industries.

Colonialism and Uneven Development in South-East Asia

We have described in more detail elsewhere the influence of Western imperialism on the emerging spatial structure of the economies of South-East Asia (Dixon, 1991; Parnwell, 1991). There, we have emphasised the importance of both endogenous factors (such as physical structure and location), and changes which have taken place both prior to and following the colonial period, in influencing the pattern and process of development and change. Nonetheless, there is little doubt that it was during the period of European intervention in the internal affairs of South-East Asian states from the beginning of the sixteenth century, but particularly during the latter half of the nineteenth century, that some of the most profound changes in the spatial structure of these territories took place.

European influence was restricted in its spatial extent and, until the mid-nineteenth century, was somewhat superficial in terms of its penetration and impact on established economic and social structures. During the period from the early sixteenth to mid-nineteenth centuries, the Europeans' main preoccupation was with the extraction of a surplus of various forms of tropical produce for trade in European markets. Thus, they were content to operate in association with, rather than in place of, indigenous ruling and trading groups. The European traders inserted themselves between the established production and trading systems and the international economy. Indeed, until the nineteenth century it is debatable whether the European powers had the military or technological power to do more, particularly with respect to the South-East Asian mainland states.

In the main, the Europeans were initially attracted to existing centres of production and development ('core areas') which they proceeded to develop further, initially by the expansion of trade and later by discriminatory investment in physical and institutional infrastructure. In some instances, several centuries of European presence served only to entrench existing spatial patterns (Kirk, 1990, pp. 24–42). However, during the course of their intervention some new foci were also established, as in the case of the British in Burma and the French in Indo-China.

The extension of control over the wider territory was typically a protracted process which in some cases was not completed by the time of decolonisation. Often it was the more remote, environmentally marginal and less hospitable areas which were the last to be incorporated. The selective opening up of the interiors thus tended to reinforce pre-existing contrasts between ecologically advantaged and disadvantaged regions. Early European activity focused on the coastal and riverine areas, linked to the importance of ports, and served to concentrate economic activity in key areas, whilst at the same time heightening the peripherality of interior regions.

The selective opening up of the interiors, associated especially with the extraction of minerals and other key natural resources, took the form of restricted enclave development. On the other hand, infrastructural investment in support of this process created opportunities for the partial extension of market-centred activity into the interior regions, which in turn served to emphasise the duality of economic activity under the auspices of European intervention. New crops were introduced, and with them came new systems of production, together with new levels of vulnerability, linked to the vagaries of world market conditions. Sharp differentials emerged both within communities and between the urban and rural areas. Population growth and land shortage, the latter exacerbated by the large-scale removal of land from the traditional sector, resulted in increased migration to urban areas.

The Europeans had a profound impact on the urban structure of South-East Asia; in many cases the national economy became dominated by a single primate city. Urban systems became reoriented as new or selected centres were expanded to cope with changing structures of commodity exploitation (Drakakis-Smith, 1991). The major urban centres established during the colonial period formed the focus for the development of capitalist relations of production. It was through the major port cities that the region became firmly locked into the international division of labour as a major supplier of raw materials.

In the Netherlands East Indies, for example, the focus of Dutch trading activity for almost two centuries was on a relatively restricted part of the archipelago. Initially this was associated with the expropriation of spices from the Moluccas islands, and later was built around the production of export crops such as sugar, coffee and indigo on Java. Thus, from the beginning of the seventeenth century until well into the nineteenth century, large sections of present-day Indonesia remained outside the sphere of Dutch influence. Furthermore, even where the Dutch were most closely involved in surplus extraction, they did little to change prevailing relations of production, 'merely superimposing themselves upon an existing system of peasant production in which surplus was extracted by means of political coercion' (Robison, 1986, p. 5).

Significant changes began to occur from the early nineteenth century. Because of increasing pressure in the homeland for the colonies to 'pay their way', the process of surplus extraction was intensified through the 'forced delivery' of crops such as coffee, sugar and rice. From 1830 the Javanese peasantry was introduced to an intensified, monopolistic system of commercial crop exploitation known as the Culture System. This brought cultivators under the direct control of the agents of Dutch colonialism, who coerced them into producing export crops, or working on government estates and projects, in return for the remission of taxes which the Dutch themselves introduced (Geertz, 1963, pp. 52–3). The Culture System tended to accentuate the dual nature of the Javanese economy, introducing a sharp contrast between the capital-intensive export sector and the labour-intensive subsistence sector.

Nonetheless, in terms of the spatial pattern of economic activity, the focus continued to be mainly on Java, with some extensions into neighbouring islands, including southern Sumatra (Chin Yoon Fong, 1977, p. 131). Thus the contrast between 'inner' and 'outer' Indonesia[4] was further heightened by this system. On the other hand, the infrastructural improvements which accompanied the intensification of export-oriented agriculture on Java at least served to integrate more fully the island as a whole. The extension of the island's irrigation and transportation networks supported a massive expansion in the cultivated area. New agricultural systems were introduced, including rubber, coffee and tea estates in the upland areas, and the commercial cultivation of sugar and tobacco in the lowlands. The relative political stability which accompanied these developments resulted in a dramatic increase in the population of Java.[5] However, because the Dutch did little to encourage industrialisation, and as urbanisation did not involve the native population to any great extent, the island's rapidly increasing population had to be absorbed within the rural sector.

207

Only with the introduction of large-scale corporate production, following the 1870 Agrarian Land Law, did the pattern of economic activity, and with it European colonial control, spread more widely in the archipelago. The Agrarian Land Law decreed that all uncultivated land was the inalienable property of the state. This land could be leased to private plantation companies, a number of which rapidly established themselves in parts of the outer islands. This development was supported by considerable infrastructural investment financed by large banking corporations, and considerable movement of labour from Java.

By the 1870s the phenomenal growth of population on Java, and associated problems of land hunger and poverty, determined that a growing burden was placed on the outer territories to maintain levels of export trade. In the last decades of Dutch rule the whole balance of the East Indies was changed. From being the richest island in the chain Java became impoverished and congested. In 1944 Furnivall (p. 56) described Java as an 'economic millstone round the country's neck'. By 1940, the outer islands were producing some two-thirds of the country's total agricultural exports and, in addition, a substantial proportion of the country's petroleum, tin and other minerals production (Geertz, 1963, p. 104; Furnivall, 1944, p. 337). However, the spread of economic activity to the outer islands was highly localised and capital-intensive and as a result the local populations derived only limited benefits. As activity was also mainly focused on a single agricultural product or mineral, the outer territories were also left at the mercy of the vagaries of world market conditions. Elsewhere, very little change took place, and even by the end of Dutch colonial rule there were vast areas in the interiors of Kalimantan (Borneo), Irian Jaya (New Guinea) and Nusatenggara (Lesser Sunda Islands) that were truly extra-periphery (Kirk, 1990).

Thus in the case of the Netherlands East Indies, European annexation aggravated pre-existing regional disparities, emphasising a basic core–periphery pattern of development. With the consolidation of Dutch political and economic control, which was linked to the shift from mercantile to industrial capitalism, came a gradual extension in the pattern of economic activity, both nationally and within established core areas. By the end of the colonial era, Indonesia was characterised by a distinctive pattern of uneven development which, although partly determined by pre-colonial political and economic patterns as well as environmental and locational factors, was largely a result of the characteristics and purpose of Dutch colonial policy.

Elsewhere in South-East Asia we can identify similar patterns. In the Philippines, for example, Spanish activity focused on central Luzon and the northern islands, with the more remote northern uplands and most of the southern islands remaining outside their control until the late nineteenth century. Where their presence was most keenly felt, the Spaniards had a profound impact on the system of access to cultivable land. In order to support the Spanish government in the Philippines, and in the face of competition from rival European powers, the Spaniards instituted a system of forced labour and the expropriation of peasant products (Cushner, 1971, p. 101). The *encomienda* system developed as a means of facilitating this process. Large tracts of land were granted to the *conquistadores* and Christian missionaries. Although they did not own this land, the process of removing land from peasant producers made possible the gradual commutation of *encomienderos* into *de facto* landowners by the end of the eighteenth century. The native Filipino aristocrats rose to prominence through their role as agents for absentee *encomienderos*.

Following the declaration of Manila as a free port in 1834, the country was rapidly opened up to foreign trade and capital. As we saw in the case of the Dutch East Indies, the resultant shift to corporate production brought about a rapid expansion of the economy and an extension in the spatial pattern of economic activity. With trade falling increasingly into non-Spanish hands, the Spaniards shifted their attention towards the production of export crops. The *hacienda* plantation system expanded rapidly to produce sugar, abaca, tobacco, indigo and coconuts for the export market (Constantino and Constantino, 1978, pp. 124–6). Large numbers of smallholdings were expropriated and local manufacturing, notably of textiles, collapsed in the face of cheap British imports (Canlas *et al.*, 1988, p. 18). In contrast to these essentially disequilibrating processes, the Spaniards also helped to integrate those parts of the archipelago over which they were able to establish direct control. They were responsible for moulding a 'nation' out of a scattered collection of small, self-sufficient communities. The Christian missionaries also introduced an embryonic urban system to the archipelago, a communications system which linked these towns and villages and also irrigation and public-works schemes (Tate, 1971, p. 345).

The unbalanced pattern of development which emerged during the Spanish colonial period was further emphasised by the Americans who, from the beginning of the twentieth century, accelerated economic activity in the core regions which had been developed under Spanish rule. For instance, a great deal of the manufacturing and processing activity which was associated with the improvements in productivity and the greater range of crops which were introduced during the American period was centred on Manila (Kirk, 1990, pp. 27–8). A further corollary of American involvement in the Philippines archipelago was a growing dependence on the United States as both a market for primary commodity exports from the Philippines and a source of imported manufactures which, in both cases, amounted to about four-fifths of the country's total import and export trade.

However, the Americans also sought to ease growing congestion in the core area by facilitating the development of the periphery. This they attempted by means of infrastructural improvements (especially in inter-island shipping) and through agricultural colonisation schemes in the Cagayan valley of northeast Luzon. In the southern islands of Mindanao and Bohol this policy involved the movement of substantial numbers of people in assisted or part-assisted resettlement programmes.

In the Malay peninsula, the Europeans were once again first attracted to a strategically important core region focused around the Straits of Malacca. With maritime trade again providing the *raison d'être* for their initial presence, the Straits Settlements (Malacca, Penang and Singapore) were very much oriented towards Europe and other parts of Asia, rather than inwards towards the interior of the peninsula. Over time, however, these settlements became the nuclei of a broader territorial realm which incorporated most of the western lowlands of the Malay peninsula.

From the middle of the nineteenth century, tin provided the main impetus for the landward extension of economic activity and settlement. Although initially restricted by water transport to coastal and riverine areas, once external capital became available considerable improvements in transportation infrastructure, particularly the construction of railways, greatly extended the range of tin mining. Improvements in transportation also served to open parts of the interior for commercial agriculture, particularly the production of rubber and oil palm. However, such transformations were almost exclusively restricted to the strategically advantaged western side of the peninsula. Thus, by the early twentieth century, there had developed a sharp contrast between the advanced, modern, urbanised and industrialised west coast and the more traditional, agricultural and economically backward east coast. Prior to these developments the contrasts between the east and west coasts were slight and indeed in certain periods the east had been the more significant (Khoo Kay Kim, 1977).

In Burma we can identify a rather different situation. Following the establishment of British control (Figure 10.1) the focus of economic activity shifted from the central dry belt to the Irrawaddy delta. The British transformed the delta region from a sparsely settled area into a major rice-producing region. Rangoon replaced Mandalay as the capital city, and it was radically transformed from a small river port to the primate capital centre of this new colonial core. Rapidly developing transportation networks converged on the capital city, further emphasising its centrality. It developed into the country's main commercial, industrial and service centre.

With the annexation of Upper Burma in 1886, British capital also moved into the dry zone, where the commercial cultivation of cotton and groundnuts was actively encouraged. Foreign capital also facilitated the exploitation of Burma's vast teak resources, although forestry largely took the form of enclave development in the country's upland areas. Foreign investment was also important in the development of the dry zone's oil fields. These developments slightly redressed the imbalances which had resulted from the earlier colonial preoccupation with the delta region, which, however, continued to dominate the space-economy of colonial Burma. Furthermore, the concentration of colonial activity in the delta region and the dry belt greatly emphasised the inequality which existed between these areas and the rest of the country, particularly the peripheral uplands.

Finally, we find in French Indo-China an essentially similar pattern of development and transformation. Although the French had had a much earlier presence in South-East Asia, it was not until the middle of the nineteenth century that France entered the colonial fray. Seeking to open a back door into southern China, a French force captured Saigon in 1859 and established the colony of Cochin China. Towards the end of the nineteenth century, Hanoi was occupied and Tonkin and Annam became French protectorates. Together

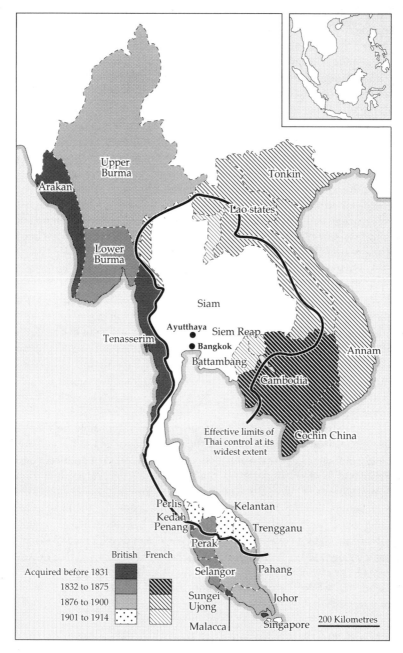

10:1 The establishment of European control over mainland South-East Asia. *Source: Tate (1971, p. 507)*

with Cambodia and various Lao states, these territories made up the French Indo-Chinese Union.

After 1902, the main focus of the French colonial economy was on the densely populated Tonkin region. The capital of the Indo-Chinese Union was moved to Hanoi, and foreign capital was used extensively in developing the city and in improving communications in its hinterland areas. Its focal position in this regard further emphasised the city's role as a commercial and industrial centre. Existing high population densities in this fertile region were further increased by rapid population growth which followed from the relative political stability and prosperity the French brought to the region. However, population growth led to the subdivision of landholdings, and growing levels of rural poverty and indebtedness. These pressures were reinforced by large-scale expropriation of land by the colonial state and the granting of estates to French citizens and collaborators (Marr, 1971). Despite the development of irrigation systems the North came to rely increasingly heavily on rice imports from the South.

The French were also responsible, by means of irrigation and drainage schemes, for colonising the Mekong delta region (Murray, 1980, p. 179), thus resurrecting its ancient status as one of the ricebowls of Asia (Kirk, 1990). The development of infrastructure in the southern region also facilitated the introduction of coffee and tea estates, and a rapid expansion of mainly French-owned rubber plantations. The subsequent development of Saigon-Cholon as a processing and marketing centre served to restrict the sharpness of regional disparities in Vietnam. Away from these two key areas, however, development was extremely limited, save for isolated pockets of commercial agriculture and resource exploitation.

Thus, in virtually all cases, the Europeans were responsible for emphasising internal spatial disparities through their focusing of economic activity on a limited number of key areas. Only with the consolidation of political control, and faced with both the imperatives and facilities of capitalist production, was the spatial pattern of colonial economic activity extended to other parts of the space economy. Even so, large areas remained outside the realm of colonial influence until the period of decolonisation and independence.

Before we go on to examine the spatial pattern of development in Thailand during the height of Western colonialism in South-East Asia, it is first necessary to highlight briefly how, and to what extent, Thailand managed to retain her independence while in the surrounding territories European expansionism seemed irresistible.

Thailand: The Maintenance of Political Integrity

Before 1855 the various European powers had, at different times, been quite closely involved in trade with Siam, but because of the power of the Thai state and the shrewd and perceptive leadership of the monarchy, which had effectively played one off against the other, none had succeeded in attaining the upper hand. For instance, King Narai (1656–88) developed close relations with the French in order to offset the growing influence of the British and

Dutch. However, Siam also experienced the trickery, military might and economic power of the Europeans, to such an extent that, upon the death of King Narai in 1688, Siam greatly restricted European involvement in the economy (Wyatt, 1982, pp. 107–17).

Following the recovery from the Burmese invasion of 1767 and the removal of the capital to Bangkok-Thonburi in 1782, Thailand underwent a period of remarkable growth and territorial expansion. These developments were closely related to the expansion of trade (Hong Lysa, 1984, pp. 38–72; Evers, 1987, pp. 762–3; Viraphol, 1977, p. 177). During the early nineteenth century Bangkok emerged as major collection centre for South-East Asian produce destined for the China trade (Sar Desai, 1977, p. 20). There were also sharp increases in the production of a wide range of primary produce, as well as refined sugar, metal goods and textiles (Hong Lysa, 1984, pp. 38–74). Most striking was the development of the shipbuilding industry, which by the 1820s was the most sophisticated in the region (Viraphol, 1977, p. 180). Overall, as Wyatt (1984, p. 180) has concluded, the Siamese Empire (Figure 10.1) 'was more powerful and extensive than at any previous time. It dwarfed all its mainland neighbours and set an example for them by its ability to act constructively and forcefully in a dangerous world.'

During the early nineteenth century Western agents again unsuccessfully sought to develop closer commercial ties with Siam. British interest was reinforced by the need either to control the Bangkok-based entrepôt trade between South-East Asia and the China entrepôt or divert it to Singapore (Sar Desai, 1977, p. 20), the need to secure the border with the Burmese territory seized in 1826 (Figure 10.1), and the need to reach some understanding with Bangkok concerning control over the Malay peninsula. Siamese influence extended over most of the peninsula (Figure 10.1) and this was considered to be a major barrier to the expansion of British trade based at Penang and Singapore.

The Siamese felt no need for trade with the West, and were reluctant to sign treaties with Western powers because of the possible dangers involved. They were also unwilling to open their markets to competition from Western merchants (Likhit Dhiravegin, 1977, p. 9). Thus the Crawfurd Mission of 1821 failed to achieve any concession beyond the formal recognition of the British occupation of Penang (which had taken place in 1786). In 1826 following the seizure of Arakan (Figure 10.1), the Burney Treaty was signed. This reduced and simplified taxation on British trade, eased some of the restrictions on trade, and went some way towards clarifying the extent of Siamese control over the Malay states. Following this treaty there was a marked increase in trade, particularly with Singapore. However, from the late 1830s the Siamese began to restrict European involvement in their international trade. Duties on shipping were increased in 1839 and the royal monopolies were used to reduce European trade (Sar Desai, 1977, p. 84).

It was only in 1851, with the accession to the throne of the European-educated King Mongkut, that Thailand once again became open to Western European trade and influence. Realising that the Europeans were becoming immensely powerful in South-East Asia, King Mongkut decided that the only

213

way to counter the potential threat of colonialism was to accommodate Siam to the outside world, seeking, wherever possible, to introduce Western ideas, methods and institutions. Trade restrictions were eased, and in 1855 the Bowring Treaty of Friendship and Commerce with Britain was signed, establishing extra-territoriality, free trade and fixed import and export duties. During the 1860s King Mongkut aptly summarised the situation facing his country:

> Since we are now being constantly abused by the French because we will not allow ourselves to be placed under their domination like the Cambodians, it is for us to decide what to do; whether to swim up-river to make friends with the crocodile [the French] or to swim out to sea and hang on to the whale [the British] . . . It is sufficient for us to keep ourselves within our house and home; it may be necessary for us to forgo some of our former power and influence. (Cited in Moffat, 1961, p. 124)

In addition to making concessions to the West in respect of trade, Siam also had to concede substantial amounts of the kingdom's territory to the French and British (Figure 10.1). The former obtained territory in Cambodia (1867), the Lao states (1893) and Siem Reap and Battambang (1907), whilst the latter received the northern Malay states of Kelantan, Terengganu, Kedah and Perlis (1909). The kingdom also came to rely very heavily on a large corps of European advisers and administrators, and upon European trade and investment.

An Anglo-Siamese Convention was agreed in April 1897 in which Siam undertook to consult Britain on any future territorial concessions, in return for a promise of British backing against aggression. Siam also agreed to seek British approval before making commercial concessions (Likhit Dhiravegin, 1977, pp. 24–5). Mounting Anglo-French tension over Thailand was resolved in treaties of 1896 and 1904 which 'guaranteed' the kingdom's independence. Siam was to form a buffer state between the two competing European powers. Through such concessions and arrangements, Siam was able to preserve its independence, but at a cost to its political and commercial integrity. As Tate (1979, p. 497) has noted:

> The rulers of the Chakri dynasty succeeded in their primary object, that of preserving the political sovereignty of Thailand, but this did not prevent − in fact was largely achieved by − the country becoming to all intents and purposes an economic 'satellite' of Great Britain in particular and an extension of the colonial imperiums of the West in general.

Thus Siam became an informal part of the British imperial economy and, in many respects, an extension of the colonial economic structure established in the Malay states. However, the significant issue in the context of this chapter is the impact that Thailand's unique (in South-East Asia) process of incorporation into the international economy had on the pattern and process of its future development.

The Bowring Treaty, and the profusion of subsequent treaties with other Western countries, thrust Siam onto centre stage in the international trade of certain commodities, particularly teak, rubber, tin and rice, and heralded a rapid influx of Western enterprise. Foreign trade, which before 1855 was almost exclusively in the hands of Chinese operating within the protective framework of the Royal Trade Monopoly, passed into the hands of Western, mainly British, firms. By 1890, 70 per cent of the foreign trade (by value) was handled in this way (Holm, 1977, p. 134).

There also occurred a significant change in the make-up of Siamese trade. In 1850 Thailand exported a wide range of products, including rice, sugar, metal goods and textiles (Ingram, 1955, p. 22). With the exception of rice, all of these declined rapidly in importance between 1855 and 1870. Domestic industries also foundered in the face of growing competition from superior-quality imported manufactures (Akira, 1989, pp. 33–8). Textile production was particularly badly affected. Between 1870 and 1913 the value of cotton-textile imports, mainly from Britain, increased sevenfold (Caldwell, 1978, p. 8). By the late nineteenth century Thailand had become almost entirely dependent on rice exports (Feeney, 1979, p. 133). From the early years of the twentieth century the range of export commodities increased, with tin, teak and rubber rising in prominence. However, up until the Second World War more than four-fifths of Thailand's export earnings were derived from just four primary commodities: rice, rubber, teak and tin.

Economic and Spatial Transformations in Thailand Post-1855

In spite of her tenuous independence, Thailand mirrored a great many of the changes in the spatial pattern of development which elsewhere in South-East Asia were closely associated with Western colonial rule.

As we have seen, 1855 represents a watershed in Thailand's economic history. In terms of the spatial impact of the changes wrought in the late nineteenth and early twentieth centuries, these were manifold. For example, the country's growing involvement in international trade had a profound impact on the country's urban structure, placing particular importance on the capital city.[6] With a huge proportion of the country's trade focused on the Chao Phrya river, and a significant proportion of economic surplus emanating from the adjoining Central Plain, the location of first Ayutthaya and later Bangkok/Thon Buri assured for the capital city a central and pivotal position in the country's emerging space-economy.

More significantly, the Bowring Treaty removed all restrictions to Thailand's export trade which had hitherto been limited by the government's virtual monopoly over trade. One corollary of the growth of this trade was the heightening of interregional disparities (Dixon, 1977). Opening the country up to the world food market led to a massive increase in the demand for rice. The area planted to *padi* increased from less than 1 million hectares in 1850 to

3.4 million hectares in 1939, and the volume of exports increased from 59,400 tonnes in 1857 to more than 1.52 million tonnes in 1939 (Ingram, 1955, pp. 44 and 39).

The crucial point is that the changes resulting from the growth of Siam's export economy did not affect all areas of the country equally. The massive expansion of the rice industry was, in the early period at least, largely confined to the Central Plain: the flood plain of the Chao Phrya river, one of the country's most fertile and productive regions (Takaya, 1987). A number of factors determined its prominent position in the country's rapidly expanding rice economy. First, the flat terrain was highly conducive to wet rice cultivation. Second, the annual inundation of the flood plain regularly replenished soil fertility. Third, there was considerable potential for irrigation, and thus double-cropping – potential which was realised in the early twentieth century with the construction of the Rangsit Scheme to the north-east of Bangkok, and the later completion of the Chai Nat barrage across the head of the Chao Phrya delta. The fact that almost all substantial investment in irrigation took place on the Central Plain further emphasised the area's advantage over other, more peripheral parts of the country. Fourth, the area lay close to Bangkok with its rapidly growing population and port facilities.

Thus farmers on the Central Plain became most heavily involved in the commercial rice economy. As in Indo-China and Burma, rice cultivation was, understandably, heavily concentrated in favour of the prime ecological areas which, because of their association with major river systems, were also close to the region's coasts. Farmers in more peripheral areas were almost completely bypassed. The North-East, for example, suffered the double disadvantage of a poor physical environment and isolation from the rest of the country by virtue of the very poor communications system outside the Central region. However, farmers in peripheral regions were at least spared some of the less desirable effects of the expansion of the commercial rice economy, especially landlessness, tenancy and indebtedness.

The expansion of the rice economy in Thailand was principally the domain of established, small-scale, indigenous farmers. The situation was thus little different from that which prevailed in Burma and Indo-China. As in those cases, there also occurred in Thailand a quite widespread accumulation of land by wealthy landowners, with cultivation being undertaken by tenant farmers (Mougne, 1982, p. 253). However, these developments took place without the support of colonial land policies that were common to the rest of South-East Asia.

Another contrast between Thailand and the other mainland states is that both the state and large-scale private corporations played a very minor role in the development of the country's rice economy. In Indo-China, the French created an environment which was conducive to foreign capital investment in the requisite infrastructure (irrigation, drainage, transportation, finance). In Burma, the colonial administrators used revenues derived from the burgeoning rice industry to finance infrastructural developments in the Irrawaddy delta region. In Thailand, however, the government was not only reluctant, but probably unable, to invest heavily in irrigation and flood control. Only during the latter part of the reign of King Chulalongkorn (1868–1910) was a more concerted effort made to improve irrigation facilities and increase land reclamation (Tanabe, 1977, p. 24; Ingram, 1955, pp. 83–5). As a result of the Thai government's hesitancy, exports of rice increased only one-third to one-half as much as had been the case in neighbouring Burma during the period 1860–90 (Ingram, 1955, p. 80). By the turn of the twentieth century, the Central Plain accounted for virtually all of Thailand's rice exports, so limited was the spatial spread of the industry to other parts of the country. The commercial cultivation of rice in the Central Plain contrasted sharply with the predominantly subsistence cultivation of rice in peripheral areas like the North East (van der Heide, 1906; Grahame, 1924; Smyth, 1898). Increases of rice production in the Central Plain resulted mainly from the extension of the cultivated area rather than from technological improvements, although the replacement of broadcasting with transplanting helped to raise levels of productivity by increasing the intensity of cultivation (Johnson, 1975, p. 210; Takaya, 1987). As with the other mainland states, the development of commercial rice cultivation in Thailand also relied on population in-migration. In the case of the Irrawaddy and Mekong deltas, this principally took the form of colonisation. In Thailand, because the Central Plain was already quite heavily populated, population movement was dominated by seasonal migration of labourers especially from the economically backward and environmentally marginal North-East (Johnson, 1975, pp. 229–34).

As foreign capital flowed into Thailand following the kingdom's greater integration with the international economy, there was steady improvement in transport infrastructure, particularly railways and port facilities. Commodity production became more diversified, with the rapid expansion of teak and tin, and after 1900 the introduction of rubber, and with this came an extension of the spatial pattern of economic activity. In this respect, Thailand's experience was again similar to that of her neighbours. The result was a slight diminution in the extent of regional disparity, although (in common with the rest of the region) much of the development in the peripheral regions took place in economic enclaves.

The Northern region became more closely involved in Thailand's economic transformation through the intensified exploitation of the region's teak and hardwood resources from 1896 onwards. Until the mid-nineteenth century, world demand for tropical hardwoods had largely been met by southern India. Rising demand in Europe, the depletion of forest reserves in southern India, and the falling costs of transportation which followed the opening of the Suez Canal in 1869 and the increased use of steam shipping, combined to make South-East Asia's vast forest resources the subject of increasing European attention. Burma provided the initial focus, and Moulmein developed as a major exporter of teak cut by Burmese foresters, some of whom also operated in northern Thailand (Falkus, 1989, p. 133). The continued expansion of demand, combined with over-rapid forest removal and the imposition of conservation measures in Burma, served to focus the attention of logging concerns on the direct exploitation of the Thai forests. Here the development of the industry was already quite advanced, with the heavy involvement of Chinese enterprise which also extended to the export trade through Bangkok. As in Burma, foreign concerns, such as the Borneo Company, came to dominate the industry, relegating 'indigenous' concerns to an insignificant position. In 1902 four British companies were accounting for around two-thirds of Thailand's teak production (Falkus, 1989, p. 143).

The Southern region of Thailand also benefited from the expansion of world market demand for South-East Asia's agricultural and minerals production, with tin extraction and rubber cultivation becoming particularly important to the regional economy. In contrast to the development of rice, and to a lesser extent teak production, tin mining rapidly became dominated by foreign capital. With the introduction of the steam dredger in the early twentieth century, the British were able to carve for themselves a substantial niche in the Malayan tin industry (van Helton and Jones, 1989, p. 164). Up until then, Chinese miners, employing labour-intensive methods, had monopolised the industry (Wong Lin Ken, 1965, pp. 60–4). The steam dredge made possible the working of low-grade deposits and swampy areas which could not be worked effectively by Chinese methods. Thereafter, foreign corporations dominated the tin industry.

After 1900 Western firms also began to extend their operations into the tin mining areas of southern Thailand, so that the Thai industry increasingly became an annex of that of the Malay states. The Thai-Chinese smelting sector declined rapidly, and by the 1930s all ore was processed in the Malay states. Similarly, from 1907 Western-owned dredging firms began to supplant the Chinese-controlled hydraulic production, although labour-intensive methods retained their importance (Ingram, 1955, p. 100).

Whilst the expansion of tin mining (and also rubber cultivation) in Thailand also extended economic activity into the hitherto underdeveloped Southern region, its effects on the local population were very much restricted by, firstly, its very localised development and, secondly, by the domination of the industry by both foreign corporations and capital-intensive production methods.

It can be seen, therefore, that, although a basic regionalism can be identified in Thailand dating back several centuries before 1855, the pattern of economic activity which followed the opening up of Thailand to world trade and external influence served, initially, to emphasise what was already an established core region and, subsequently, to extend economic activity selectively and superficially to parts of the peripheral regions. As such, Thailand followed very closely the pattern of development and change which took place in the colonial territories of South-East Asia in response to the growing demands of the world market and international capital.

Conclusion

The imperatives of capitalist production, rather than formal European colonialism *per se* (notwithstanding their obvious interrelationship), were responsible for fundamental changes in the spatial pattern of economic activity in

South-East Asia. The expansion of agricultural production for international markets and the intensified exploitation of natural resources involved consolidation of the initial advantage of established core regions and selective opening up of the interiors. Large areas, and significant sections of the population, remained virtually unaffected by these transformations. Even where changes were most in evidence, the impact on, and involvement of, local populations was extremely variable and unequal. Infrastructural improvements, in most cases aided by foreign capital, appear to have played an important role in the unbalanced and uneven process of development.

This pattern of development and change can be identified in Thailand, in spite of the fact that there was no formal political and economic subjugation. The differences are only of degree, timing and detail. In Thailand the retention of political independence provides an additional element of variation in the processes of incorporation and Western domination that operated at the global scale. There is no evidence that the absence of direct Western rule engendered a distinctive 'non-colonial' form of development.

> [When examining the] economic changes experienced by Siam during the decades of late European imperialism, the first impression is not of a distinctive Siamese experience but of a striking similarity between the evolution of the economy of Siam and that of the economies of British Burma and French Indo-China in the period beginning from the middle of the nineteenth century. (Brown, 1988, p. 2)

The same is essentially true of the Dutch East Indies, Spanish Philippines and British Malaya.

While specific elements of Thailand's post-1945 development can only be understood in the context of the kingdom's particular experience of the incorporation process, it is equally true of the other South-East Asian states which experienced direct Western rule. In terms of explaining the contemporary pattern of development, the particular colonial experiences of, for example, the Philippines and Malaysia, may be more significant than Thailand's retention of formal independence.

The patterns of annexation and incorporation which operated in South-East Asia show great variation. Not only did the various Western powers adopt different approaches, but the reactions of the indigenous states were also extremely varied. The colonial powers had very different attitudes towards their respective colonial territories. In many ways these reflected the particular circumstances of the individual metropolitan states. The French and Dutch imposed very direct rule, which was regarded as permanent: the colonial territories were seen as an extension of the home country. Thus, Indo-China was *la France d'outre-mer* and the Netherlands East Indies 'Tropical Holland'. France, and more especially Holland, were more dependent on their Asian colonies than was the case with Britain. The degree of this 'dependency relationship' reflected the relative strength of British, Dutch and French capitalism as well as the extent and variety of their colonial possessions.[7] However, in terms of the exploitation of the respective territories, these were differences in degree rather than kind. While each interaction set an individual stamp on the states concerned, it is important not to become preoccupied by these; the economic and political forms that resulted had considerable similarity.

A preliminary investigation of Thailand in the context of incorporation into the world economy between 1855 and 1940 suggests that the distinction between colonial and non-colonial development is not a meaningful one in explaining contemporary patterns of uneven development.

Notes

1. Depending on the definition of 'colonialism' we might include countries such as Liberia, Ethiopia, Turkey, Bhutan, Nepal, Iran, Afghanistan, Japan and Thailand.
2. Siam was renamed Thailand in 1939, and again in 1947 after reverting to Siam towards the end of the Second World War.
3. See, for example, Knox and Agnew, 1989, pp. 239–72; Kitching, 1982, pp. 152–6; Frank, 1967; Amin, 1976; Wallerstein, 1979.
4. The 'inner islands' are usually taken to comprise Java, Bali and Lombok; and the 'outer islands' Sumatra, Kalimantan, Sulawesi, Nusatenggara, East Timor and Irian Jaya. Christine Drake (1989) has suggested that, with the exploitation of natural resources in several outer provinces, and also considerable deprivation in parts of Java, a more meaningful distinction today is made on economic and welfare grounds rather than locational ones.
5. On Java, population density increased from 96 persons per square kilometre in 1817 to 940 by 1940. The acceleration of the rate of population appears to be closely associated with the imposition of European control and incorporation into the world market. However, the nature of the interrelationship is a matter of considerable debate (Boomgard, 1987; Owen, 1987; Reid, 1987; White, 1973). It is of particular interest that during the second half of the nineteenth century Thailand experienced a similar increase in population despite the absence of direct colonial rule (Dixon, 1991; Mougne, 1982, p. 58).
6. Following the sacking of Ayutthaya in 1767, the capital was re-established nearer the mouth of the Chao Phraya river in Bangkok/Thon Buri.
7. For a fuller discussion see Dixon, 1991.

References and Further Reading

Akira, S. (1989) *Capital Accumulation in Thailand*, Tokyo: Centre for East Asian Cultural Studies.

Amin, S. (1976) *Unequal Development*, New York: Monthly Review Press.

Boomgard, P. (1987) 'Morbidity and mortality in Java, 1820–1880: changing patterns of disease and death', in N.G. Owen (ed.) *Death and Disease in Southeast Asia*, Singapore: Oxford University Press, pp. 48–59.

Booth, A. (1988) *Agricultural Development in Indonesia*, Sydney: Allen & Unwin.

Bradley, W.L. (1981) *Siam Then: The Foreign Colony in Bangkok before and after Anna*, Pasadena: William Carey Library.

Brown, I. (1988) *The Elite and the Economy in Siam, c. 1890–1920*, Singapore: Singapore University Press.

Caldwell, M. (1978) Foreword, in D. Elliott, *Thailand: The Origins of Military Rule*, London: Zed, pp. 8–20.

Canlas, M., Miranda, M., and Putzel, J. (1988) *Land, Poverty and Politics in the Philippines*, London: Catholic Institute for International Relations.

Chin Yoon Fong (1977) 'Dutch policy towards the outer islands', in Khoo Kay Kim (ed.) *The History of Southeast and South Asia*, Kuala Lumpur: Oxford University Press, pp. 129–35.

Constantino, R., and Constantino, L.R. (1978) *The Philippines: The Continuing Past*, Manila: Foundation for National Studies.

Corbridge, S. (1986) *Capitalist World Development: A Critique of Radical Development Geography*, London: Macmillan.

Cushner, N.P. (1971) *Spain in the Philippines: From Conquest to Revolution*, Manila: Institute of Philippine Culture, Ateneo de Manila University.

Dixon, C.J. (1977) 'Development, regional disparity and planning: the experience of northeast Thailand', *Journal of Southeast Asian Studies*, 8 (2), pp. 210–23.

Dixon, C.J. (1991) *Southeast Asia in the World Economy*, Cambridge: Cambridge University Press.

Drakakis-Smith, D. (1991) 'Colonial urbanisation in Africa and Asia: a structural analysis', in R. Lewis (ed.) *Urban Essays for Harold Carter*, Cambria: University of Wales.

Drake, C. (1989) *National Integration in Indonesia: Patterns and Policies*, Honolulu: University of Hawaii Press.

Evers, Hans-Dieter (1987) 'Trade and state formation in the early Bangkok period', *Modern Asian Studies*, 24 (4), pp. 751–71.

Falkus, M. (1989) 'Early British business in Thailand', in R.P.T. Davenport-Hines and G. Jones (eds) *British Business in Asia since 1860*, Cambridge: Cambridge University Press, pp. 96–116.

Feeney, D.C. (1977) 'Paddy prices and productivity: irrigation and Thai agricultural development', *Explorations in Economic History*, 16.

Fisher, C.A. (1974) 'Geographical continuity and political change in Southeast Asia', in M.W. Zacher and R.S. Milne (eds) *Conflict and Stability in Southeast Asia*, Honolulu: Anchor, pp. 3–78.

Forbes, D.K. (1984) *The Geography of Underdevelopment: A Critical Survey*, London: Croom Helm.

Frank, A.G. (1967) *Capitalism and Underdevelopment in Latin America*, New York: Monthly Review Press.

Fryer, D.W. (1979) *Emerging Southeast Asia: A Study in Growth and Stagnation*, London: George Philips.

Furnivall, J.S. (1944) *Netherlands East Indies: A Study of a Plural Society*, Cambridge: Cambridge University Press.

Geertz, C. (1963) *Agricultural Involution in Java: The Processes of Ecological Change in Indonesia*, Berkeley: University of California Press.

Ginsberg, N. (1973) 'From colonialism to national development: geographical perspectives on patterns and policies', *Annals of the Association of American Geographers*, 63 (1), pp. 1–21.

Gore, C. (1984) *Regions in Question: Space, Development Theory and Regional Policy*, London: Methuen.

Gourou, P. (1958) *The Tropical World*, London: Longman.

Grahame, W.A. (1924) *Siam*, vol. 1, London: Alexander Moring.

Hall, D.G.E. (1970) *A History of South-East Asia*, London: Macmillan.

Holm, D.F. (1977) 'The role of the state railways in Thai history', Ph.D. thesis, Yale University.

Hong Lysa (1984) *Thailand in the Nineteenth Century: Evolution of the Economy and Society*, Singapore: Institute of Southeast Asian Studies (ISEAS).

Hoogvelt, A.M.M. (1978) *The Sociology of Developing Societies*, 2nd edn, London: Macmillan.

Ingram, J.C. (1955) *Economic Change in Thailand Since 1850*, Stanford, Calif.: Stanford University Press.

Johnson, D.B. (1975) 'Rural society and rice economy in Thailand', Ph.D. thesis, University of London.

Kirk, W. (1990) 'Southeast Asia in the colonial period: a study of cores and peripheries in the development process', in D.W. Dwyer (ed.) *Southeast Asia*, London: Longman, pp. 15–47.

Kitching, G. (1982) *Development and Underdevelopment in Historical Perspective*, London: Methuen.

Khoo Kay Kim (1977) 'Descriptive account of the eastern Malay states', in Khoo Kay Kim (ed.) *The History of Southeast Asia*, Kuala Lumpur: Oxford University Press, pp. 22–40.

Knox, P., and Agnew, J. (1989) *The Geography of the World Economy*, London: Edward Arnold.

Likhit Dhiravegin (1977) *Siam and Colonialism (1855–1909): An Analysis of Diplomatic Relations*, Bangkok: Thai Watana Panich.

Lim, H.K. (1978) *The Evolution of the Urban System in Malaya*, Kuala Lumpur: Penerbit University Malaya.

Marr, D. (1971) *Vietnamese Anti-Colonialism: 1885–1925*, Berkeley: University of California Press.

Mehmet, O. (1977) 'Colonialism, dualistic growth and the distribution of economic benefits in Malaysia', *Southeast Asian Journal of Social Science*, 5 (1–2), pp. 1–23.

Moffat, A.L. (1961) *Mongkut, King of Siam*, Ithaca, NY: Cornell University Press.

Mougne, C.M. (1982) 'The social and economic correlates of demographic change in a northern Thai community', Ph.D. thesis, University of London.

Murray, M.J. (1980) *The Development of Capitalism in Colonial Indochina, 1870–1940*, Los Angeles: University of California Press.

Myint, H. (1972) *Southeast Asia's Economy: Development Policies in the 1970s*, Harmondsworth: Penguin.

Nartsupha, Chatthip, and Prasartset, Suthy (1978) *The Political Economy of Siam, 1851–1910*, Bangkok: Social Science Association of Thailand.

Nartsupha, Chatthip, Prasartset, Suthy and Chenvidyakarn, Montri (1978) *The Political Economy of Siam, 1910–1932*, Bangkok: Social Science Association of Thailand.

Osborne, M. (1979) *Southeast Asia: An Introductory History*, Sydney: Allen & Unwin.

Owen, N.G. (1987) 'The paradox of nineteenth-century population growth in South East Asia: evidence from Java and the Philippines', *Journal of Southeast Asian Studies*, 18, pp. 45–57.

Parnwell, M.J.G. (1991) 'Colonialism and uneven development in South-East Asia', *Malaysian Journal of Tropical Geography*, in press.

Reid, A.C. (1987) Low population growth and its causes in pre-colonial South East Asia, in N.G. Owen (ed.) *Death and Disease in South East Asia*, Singapore: Oxford University Press, pp. 33–47.

Resnick, S.A. (1970) 'The decline of rural industry under export expansion: a comparison among Burma, Philippines and Thailand, 1870–1938', *Journal of Economic History*, 30 (2), pp. 133–48.

Robison, R. (1986) *Indonesia: The Rise of Capital*, Sydney: Allen & Unwin.

Sar Desai, D.R. (1977) *British Trade and Expansion in South East Asia*, New Delhi: Allied Publishers.

Slater, D. (1975) 'Underdevelopment and spatial inequality: approaches to the problems of region planning in the Third World', *Progress in Planning*, 3 (1), pp. 97–167.

Smyth, H.W. (1898) *Five Years in Siam*, London: Murray.

Sundaram, Jomo Kwame (1988) *A Question of Class: Capital, the State and Uneven Development in Malaya*, Singapore: Oxford University Press.

Takaya, Y. (1987) *Agricultural Development of a Tropical Delta*, Honolulu: University of Hawaii Press.

Tanabe, Shigeharu (1977) 'Historical geography of the canal system in the Chao Phraya river delta (from the Ayutthaya period to the fourth reign of the Ratanakosin dynasty)', *Journal of the Siam Society*, 65 (1), pp. 23–72.

Tate, D.J.M. (1971) *The Making of Modern South-East Asia*, Vol. 1: *The European Conquest*, Kuala Lumpur: Oxford University Press.

Tate, D.J.M. (1979) *The Making of Modern South-East Asia*, Vol. 2: *The Western Impact: Economic and Social Change*, Kuala Lumpur: Oxford University Press.

Taylor, J.G. (1979) *From Modernization to Modes of Production: A Critique of the Sociologies of Development and Underdevelopment*, London: Macmillan.

Taylor, J.G., and A. Turton (eds) (1988) *Sociology of 'Developing Societies': Southeast Asia*, London: Macmillan.

Thailand: NESDB (1977) *Fourth National Economic and Social Development Plan*, Bangkok: Office of the Prime Minister.

Thailand: NESDB (1982) *Fifth National Economic and Social Development Plan*, Bangkok: Office of the Prime Minister.

Thailand: NESDB (1987) *Sixth National Economic and Social Development Plan*, (in Thai), Bangkok: Office of the Prime Minister.

van Helton, J.-J., and Jones, G. (1989) 'British business in Malaysia and Singapore since the 1870s', in R.P.T. Davenport-Hines and G. Jones (eds) *British Business in Asia since 1860*, Cambridge: Cambridge University Press.

van der Heide, J.H. (1906) 'The economical development of Siam during the last half century', *Journal of the Siam Society*, 3, pp. 74–101.

Viraphol, Sarasin (1977) *Tribute and Profit: Sino-Siamese Trade, 1652–1855*, Cambridge, Mass.: Harvard University Press.

Wallerstein, I. (1979) *The Capitalist World Economy*, Cambridge: Cambridge University Press.

White, B. (1973) 'Demand for labour and population growth in colonial Java', *Human Ecology*, 1 (3), pp. 217–36.

Wong Lin Ken (1965) *The Malayan Tin Industry to 1914*, Tucson: University of Arizona Press.

Wyatt, D. K. (1984) *Thailand: A Short History*, New Haven, Conn.: Yale University Press.

Index